Node.js Projects
Building Real-World Web Applications and Backend APIs

Jonathan Wexler

Node.js Projects

by Jonathan Wexler

Copyright © 2025 Jon Wexler. All rights reserved.

Published by O'Reilly Media, Inc., 141 Stony Circle, Suite 195, Santa Rosa, CA 95401.

O'Reilly books may be purchased for educational, business, or sales promotional use. Online editions are also available for most titles (*http://oreilly.com*). For more information, contact our corporate/institutional sales department: 800-998-9938 or *corporate@oreilly.com*.

Acquisitions Editors: Amanda Quinn and Aaron Black	**Indexer:** Ellen Troutman-Zaig
Development Editor: Michele Cronin	**Cover Designer:** Susan Brown
Production Editor: Gregory Hyman	**Interior Designer:** David Futato
Copyeditor: Dwight Ramsey	**Cover Illustrator:** Monica Kamsvaag
Proofreader: Sonia Saruba	**Interior Illustrator:** Kate Dullea

August 2025:   First Edition

Revision History for the First Edition

2025-07-31:   First Release

See *http://oreilly.com/catalog/errata.csp?isbn=9781098173142* for release details.

The O'Reilly logo is a registered trademark of O'Reilly Media, Inc. *Node.js Projects*, the cover image, and related trade dress are trademarks of O'Reilly Media, Inc.

The views expressed in this work are those of the author and do not represent the publisher's views. While the publisher and the author have used good faith efforts to ensure that the information and instructions contained in this work are accurate, the publisher and the author disclaim all responsibility for errors or omissions, including without limitation responsibility for damages resulting from the use of or reliance on this work. Use of the information and instructions contained in this work is at your own risk. If any code samples or other technology this work contains or describes is subject to open source licenses or the intellectual property rights of others, it is your responsibility to ensure that your use thereof complies with such licenses and/or rights.

978-1-098-17314-2

[LSI]

Table of Contents

Preface. vii

1. Introduction and Setup. 1
   Installing VS Code   1
      Mac Installation   2
      Windows Installation   3
      Linux Installation   3
   Understanding Node   4
   Why Node Stands Out   5
   What's Happening Under the Hood?   5
   Installing Node   5
      Mac Installation   7
      Windows Installation   7
      Linux Installation   7
   Becoming a Node Developer   8
   Mastering the Craft   8
   Using Fastify in This Book   10
   Summary   14

2. Practical Application. 15
   Your Prompt   16
   Get Planning   16
   Get Programming   17
   Translating User Input to CSV   21
   Working with External Packages   28
   Summary   32

iii

3. Building a Node Web Server... 35

Your Prompt	36
Get Planning	36
Building the Application Skeleton	39
Working with Fastify	39
Adding Routes and Data	43
Building Your UI	47
Sprucing Up the UI	52
Summary	55

4. Build a Secure Local Password Manager.. 57

Your Prompt	58
Get Planning	58
Building a Local Command-Line Manager	59
Saving Passwords with MongoDB	68
Summary	75

5. Content Aggregation Feed... 77

Your Prompt	78
Get Planning	78
Reading and Parsing a Feed	82
Building an Aggregator	84
Adding Custom Items to Your Aggregator	88
Summary	90

6. Library API... 91

Your Prompt	92
Get Planning	92
Get Programming with an API Layout	96
Adding Routes and Actions to Your App	99
Connecting a Database to Your App	105
Summary	112

7. Natural Language Processor Sentiment Analysis................................ 113

Your Prompt	114
Get Planning	114
Get Programming with String Processing Packages	117
Analyzing Sentiment	123
Connecting a Database and Visualization	126
Summary	138

8. Marketing Mailer 139

Your Prompt	140
Get Planning	140
Get Programming	142
Adding a Framework for Your Mailer Service	148
Connecting a Database	153
Implementing a Marketing Pixel for Email Engagement	158
Integrating a Task Scheduler	160
Summary	163

9. Web Scraper 165

Your Prompt	166
Get Planning	166
Get Programming	167
Parsing with HTML-Friendly Tools	173
Scraping Web Pages with a Headless Browser	175
Summary	180

10. App Authentication 181

Your Prompt	182
Get Planning	182
Get Programming	184
Building a Login Form	188
Saving and Securing User Accounts	196
Using JWTs for API Authentication	213
Summary	218

11. Coffee Order Manager 219

Your Prompt	220
Get Planning	220
Get Programming	223
Adding a Redis Server	229
Integrating a Robust Messaging System	233
Summary	244

12. Music Label Blockchain Market 245

Your Prompt	246
Get Planning	246
Get Programming	249
Coding the Blockchain	257
Running the Real-World Example	270
Summary	272

13. **Building an AI-Powered Learning Assistant with Google's Gemini API**............. 273
    Your Prompt   274
    Get Planning   274
    Get Programming   276
    Customizing the AI Assistant for Learning Assistance   280
    Setting Up the Fastify Server   282
    Setting Up Your Database and User Authentication   285
    Summary   299

A.   **Node Cheat Sheet and Project Initialization.**.................................. 301

B.   **Setting Up Your Development Tools.**.. 311

C.   **Working with Databases in Node Projects.**.................................. 317

D.   **Working with the Code Examples and Containerizing Projects.**.................. 331

E.   **Setting Up Developer Accounts and API Credentials.**.......................... 337

Index.... 345

Preface

When I began writing this book in 2022, I saw just how much the tech community had evolved since *Get Programming with Node.js* (Manning). While many foundational concepts remained, the approach to development had advanced significantly. Node.js had long passed its 10-year mark since Ryan Dahl's initial release, and the internet was flooded with tutorials on building "simple web servers." The truth is, most projects still rely on web servers—but the expectations for how we build and use them have changed. Today, a server isn't just a server; it's the centerpiece of complex, resilient, and scalable applications. Likewise, the way we use JavaScript has deepened, opening up a wide array of tools and techniques to explore.

Node.js Projects is crafted to showcase these new techniques and empower you to grow as a developer by focusing on five key principles: a practical learning approach, modular learning, diverse use cases, incremental skill building, and immediate feedback and gratification. Each project is designed to provide hands-on, real-world experience, enabling you to apply Node.js in modular, digestible steps. This approach not only supports gradual skill development but also ensures that each chapter delivers a satisfying sense of accomplishment, reinforcing your growth as you progress through varied and increasingly challenging applications.

Programming newcomers quickly grasp how to piece together an application, but building an app is more than code—it's about understanding architecture and design. Each chapter places you in the role of an engineer making real-world decisions. I believe practical experience isn't copying and pasting code but developing the mindset, problem-solving skills, and communication required to build products with impact.

The scope of software challenges varies: some projects unfold over months, while others involve quick, focused problem-solving. This book provides a balance, offering both bite-sized coding exercises and larger, more complex projects. This modular structure encourages you to complete sections at your own pace, allowing you to pause, shift focus, or dive into chapters that align with your interests and skill level.

JavaScript, and by extension Node.js, has experienced incredible growth over the past 15 years. This evolution has allowed Node.js to become a go-to tool for creating everything from high-performance web apps to real-time notification systems and video streaming platforms. Learning Node.js today means understanding a wide range of potential applications. Each chapter offers you not only technical skills but a mindset for approaching real-world scenarios you're likely to encounter on the job. This way, you'll develop the versatility to apply Node.js to diverse projects, enhancing both your confidence and your adaptability.

You might wonder, with so many free online resources, why choose a book on Node.js? And in a world where AI tools are taking on more and more development tasks, why should an engineer devote time to deep, structured learning? It's true that learning Node.js has become more accessible than ever, but with that accessibility comes a challenge: finding resources that simulate the thought process and structure of real-world development. *Node.js Projects* builds skills incrementally, guiding you toward tangible accomplishments with each project. This structured path is designed to help you gain confidence and skill with each chapter.

Ultimately, I didn't want to write "just another" Node.js book. This is a collection of the most valuable lessons and techniques I've encountered as the industry has evolved. My goal is to help you achieve long-term growth through incremental, satisfying progress. Each chapter introduces concepts that go beyond Node.js and reflect the standards of today's developer community. Whether it takes a week or a year to complete these projects, I'm confident that this journey will make you a stronger, more versatile engineer.

Conventions Used in This Book

The following typographical conventions are used in this book:

Italic
> Indicates new terms, URLs, email addresses, filenames, and file extensions.

`Constant width`
> Used for program listings, as well as within paragraphs to refer to program elements such as variable or function names, databases, data types, environment variables, statements, and keywords.

`Constant width italic`
> Shows text that should be replaced with user-supplied values or by values determined by context.

This element signifies a tip or suggestion.

This element signifies a general note.

Using Code Examples

Supplemental material (code examples, exercises, etc.) is available for download at *https://oreil.ly/node-projects-code*.

If you have a technical question or a problem using the code examples, please send email to *support@oreilly.com*.

This book is here to help you get your job done. In general, if example code is offered with this book, you may use it in your programs and documentation. You do not need to contact us for permission unless you're reproducing a significant portion of the code. For example, writing a program that uses several chunks of code from this book does not require permission. Selling or distributing examples from O'Reilly books does require permission. Answering a question by citing this book and quoting example code does not require permission. Incorporating a significant amount of example code from this book into your product's documentation does require permission.

We appreciate, but generally do not require, attribution. An attribution usually includes the title, author, publisher, and ISBN. For example: "*Node.js Projects* by Jonathan Wexler (O'Reilly). Copyright 2025 Jon Wexler, 978-1-098-17314-2."

If you feel your use of code examples falls outside fair use or the permission given above, feel free to contact us at *permissions@oreilly.com*.

O'Reilly Online Learning

For more than 40 years, *O'Reilly Media* has provided technology and business training, knowledge, and insight to help companies succeed.

Our unique network of experts and innovators share their knowledge and expertise through books, articles, and our online learning platform. O'Reilly's online learning platform gives you on-demand access to live training courses, in-depth learning paths, interactive coding environments, and a vast collection of text and video from O'Reilly and 200+ other publishers. For more information, visit *https://oreilly.com*.

How to Contact Us

Please address comments and questions concerning this book to the publisher:

> O'Reilly Media, Inc.
> 141 Stony Circle, Suite 195
> Santa Rosa, CA 95401
> 800-889-8969 (in the United States or Canada)
> 707-827-7019 (international or local)
> 707-829-0104 (fax)
> *support@oreilly.com*
> *https://oreilly.com/about/contact.html*

We have a web page for this book, where we list errata, examples, and any additional information. You can access this page at *https://oreil.ly/node-projects*.

For news and information about our books and courses, visit *https://oreilly.com*.

Find us on LinkedIn: *https://linkedin.com/company/oreilly-media*.

Watch us on YouTube: *https://youtube.com/oreillymedia*.

Acknowledgments

Writing *Node.js Projects* has been a journey of late nights, deep debugging sessions, and real-world experiments, and it wouldn't have been possible without the support and insight of many people.

First and foremost, thank you to the team at O'Reilly for championing this book from idea to finished product. Your thoughtful guidance, editorial expertise, and commitment to quality helped shape this into something truly useful for developers at all levels.

To the technical reviewers and early readers: your attention to detail, generous feedback, and willingness to challenge assumptions made this book sharper and more accurate. Thank you for helping me catch bugs, unclear examples, and unnecessary complexity before they reached print.

To the broader Node.js community: your open-source contributions, blog posts, GitHub discussions, and Stack Overflow threads provided inspiration, solutions, and sometimes just the reassurance that I wasn't the only one stuck on a problem. This book is built on the ecosystem you've created.

To the students, colleagues, and fellow developers I've worked with over the years: many of the ideas and patterns in this book were born out of our shared projects and conversations. Thank you for the collaboration and curiosity.

To my family and friends: your encouragement and patience during long writing sprints kept me going. I'm deeply grateful for your support.

Finally, to you, the reader: thank you for choosing this book. I hope it empowers you to build, break, fix, and create confidently with Node.js.

CHAPTER 1
Introduction and Setup

This chapter is your guide to setting up a development environment for Node.js. It covers the core tools needed, such as VS Code, Node.js, and Fastify, along with optional components to enhance your workflow. While tools like Fastify are more specialized, feel free to skip their setup for now and revisit those sections when they are covered in later chapters.

You'll find various installation methods explained, including using a graphical user interface (GUI), third-party tools, or binary packages. Binary installations, while sometimes precompiled, may require extra steps for extraction and configuration, making them particularly useful for servers without a graphical interface. Although the provided instructions are tailored to the tools recommended for this book, you're welcome to use alternatives that meet your development needs. The goal is to equip you with a solid foundation to start coding and running your Node.js applications effectively.

For the sake of economy, throughout the remainder of this book, we'll refer to Node.js simply as Node.

Before writing your first line of code, it's important to choose a text editor that supports modern JavaScript development and integrates well with Node tooling.

Installing VS Code

Visual Studio Code (VS Code) is a popular open source text editor, widely recommended for Node development due to its robust features, flexibility, and extensive customization options. This section will guide you through installing VS Code on macOS, Windows, and Linux.

> AI-powered code editors are becoming increasingly popular, and one such tool is Cursor (*https://cursor.com*), an AI-enhanced editor built on VS Code that can assist with code suggestions and explanations. While helpful, beginners should balance its use with learning core concepts independently.

The easiest way to install VS Code is by visiting the VS Code download page (*https://oreil.ly/BIrFY*). Figure 1-1 displays the installation options for each operating system.

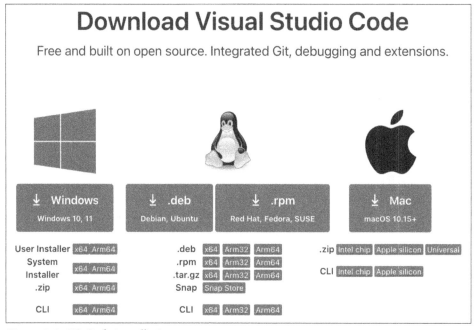

Figure 1-1. VS Code installation page

The image provides options for installing VS Code on Mac, Windows, and Linux systems. The following sections break down how to proceed on each operating system.

Mac Installation

Make sure to identify the type of Mac you have (Intel or Apple Silicon).

1. Download the appropriate installer for your Mac.
2. Open the downloaded file and drag the VS Code icon to the *Applications* folder.

3. Open VS Code from the *Applications* folder.

You may need to allow the application to run in System Preferences under Security & Privacy if you encounter any issues.

Windows Installation

To install VS Code on a Windows machine, follow these steps:

1. Download the installer for Windows.
2. Open the downloaded file and follow the installation wizard steps.
3. Once installed, you can launch VS Code from the Start Menu.

During installation, ensure you select the option to add VS Code to your PATH for easy command-line access.

Linux Installation

The installation for Linux machines is a bit different, as it requires command-line steps. For the standard Debian/Ubuntu machine setup, run the following commands in your command-line window:

```
sudo apt update ❶
sudo apt install software-properties-common apt-transport-https wget ❷
wget -q https://packages.microsoft.com/keys/microsoft.asc -O- | \
  sudo apt-key add - ❸
sudo add-apt-repository \
  "deb [arch=amd64] https://packages.microsoft.com/repos/vscode
stable main" ❹
sudo apt update ❺
sudo apt install code ❻
```

❶ Updates the package lists to ensure you get the latest version and dependencies.

❷ Installs required tools for adding repositories and handling HTTPS.

❸ Downloads and adds the Microsoft GPG key to verify packages.

❹ Adds the official Microsoft VS Code repository.

❺ Updates the package lists again to include the new VS Code repository.

❻ Installs VS Code.

> For other distributions, refer to the official documentation (*https://oreil.ly/MfEaG*).

To improve your development experience, consider installing VS Code extensions such as Prettier for formatting, ESLint for catching bugs early, and npm Intellisense for smart autocomplete when importing packages.

With your editor ready to go, let's take a moment to understand what Node is and why it's the core technology behind everything you'll build in this book.

Understanding Node

Node is an open source tool, which means anyone can view, modify, and share its code for free. It's also cross-platform, so it works on different operating systems like Windows, macOS, and Linux. Node is a runtime, meaning it provides an environment for running JavaScript code outside the browser—normally, JavaScript is only used inside web browsers for things like interactive buttons or animations. With Node, developers can use JavaScript to build server-side applications, like websites or APIs.

Node is built on Chrome's V8 JavaScript engine, a technology that converts JavaScript into machine code, which is the language your computer understands. This process makes JavaScript run faster and more efficiently. Because of this speed, Node is described as lightweight (it doesn't require a lot of resources) and efficient (it gets a lot done with minimal overhead). It's particularly great for creating scalable applications, which means programs that can handle more users or data without slowing down.

One of Node's standout features is its nonblocking, event-driven architecture. In simple terms, it doesn't wait for one task to finish before starting another. Imagine you're folding laundry and boiling water at the same time. Instead of waiting by the stove, you fold clothes until the water boils. Similarly, Node switches between tasks, maximizing productivity. This is why Node is ideal for real-time applications like chat apps, online games, or tools where users collaborate live: everything stays responsive, even with many users.

Why Node Stands Out

Node has become a popular choice for developers due to its unique features and advantages:

Unified development
Uses JavaScript on both the client and server sides, eliminating the need for multiple programming languages across your stack and simplifying development workflows.

Vast ecosystem
Includes npm, a massive package repository with millions of prebuilt tools, making it faster and easier to build applications.

Industry adoption
Trusted by leading companies like Netflix, LinkedIn, and PayPal for its ability to handle high traffic and real-time demands.

Scalability and efficiency
Designed to handle thousands of simultaneous connections without slowing down, thanks to its event-driven, nonblocking architecture.

Smooth operations
Node ensures requests flow efficiently, even under heavy workloads. Imagine a highway with no traffic jams.

What's Happening Under the Hood?

Underneath, Node uses the V8 engine, which makes JavaScript fast by converting it directly into machine code. The magic of handling thousands of simultaneous tasks comes from Node's event loop and Libuv library. The event loop is like a receptionist managing multiple customers at once: while one waits for a response (e.g., fetching data), the receptionist moves on to help others. Libuv is like the behind-the-scenes team that takes care of time-consuming tasks, such as reading files from a disk or resolving domain names (DNS lookups). While Node focuses on quickly switching between tasks, Libuv ensures that these slower operations happen in the background without blocking the main thread. Think of it like a chef in a busy kitchen—while the head chef keeps preparing quick dishes, Libuv is the team working on slow-cooking the stew. This allows Node to keep moving to the next task without getting stuck waiting for one operation to finish.

Installing Node

You're about to install Node, a powerful and versatile platform that allows you to run JavaScript code on your computer, outside of a web browser. With Node, you can build everything from simple websites to complex server-side applications, automate tasks, and much more.

As you get started, keep in mind that installing Node is a straightforward process, but there are a few things to watch out for. Depending on your operating system, you might need to adjust some settings or install additional tools, like version managers or build essentials. Follow each step below, including tips for troubleshooting common issues.

For all installations, visit the Node download page (*https://oreil.ly/Gj_m8*), where you'll be able to choose the Node installation for your machine setup (Figure 1-2).

nvm (Node Version Manager) lets you easily install and switch between multiple versions of Node, which is ideal for testing projects across environments. Learn more by visiting the project's GitHub repo (*https://oreil.ly/1pJQF*).

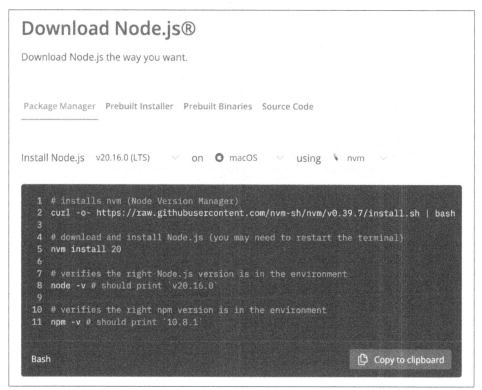

Figure 1-2. Node installation page

Ensure you select the option to install npm (Node Package Manager) during installation.

Mac Installation

Make sure to identify the type of Mac you have (Intel or Apple Silicon). Then:

1. Download the appropriate installer for your Mac. As of the writing of this book, you should choose Node version 22.16.0 or later.
2. Open the downloaded file and follow the on-screen instructions to install Node.

You may also use Homebrew for installation by running `brew install node` in a new terminal window.

Windows Installation

Make sure you are using a Windows system with administrative privileges to install software. Then:

1. Download the installer for Windows. As of the writing of this book, you should choose Node version 22.16.0 or later.
2. Open the downloaded file and follow the on-screen instructions to install Node.

Linux Installation

The installation for Linux machines requires command-line steps. For the standard Debian/Ubuntu machine setup, run the following commands in your command-line window:

```
sudo apt update ❶
sudo apt install nodejs npm ❷
```

❶ Updates the package lists to ensure you get the latest version of the packages.

❷ Installs Node and npm (Node Package Manager).

For other distributions, refer to the official documentation (*https:// oreil.ly/7Qm6M*).

Becoming a Node Developer

To start, you'll need to understand the core modules (`fs` for file handling, `http` for servers, and `events` for custom logic). A foundational skill is asynchronous programming, which lets you perform tasks in the background without freezing the app. Imagine you're ordering pizza while doing homework—promises and async/await are the delivery updates that let you know when the pizza arrives, so you don't have to stop working.

You'll also want to learn how to build APIs using frameworks like Express.js or Fastify, where you define "routes" like paths in a map to determine how your app responds to users. From there, working with databases like MongoDB or PostgreSQL comes next, allowing you to store and retrieve data efficiently.

Mastering the Craft

To become an expert, focus on real-world projects. For example, build a chat app to practice real-time communication or a task manager with data persistence to hone database skills. Dive into performance optimization by profiling your app, like identifying slow database queries or excessive memory usage. Imagine fine-tuning a car engine for peak performance where every little improvement counts.

Stay connected with the Node community through forums, open source contributions, and newsletters like *Node Weekly*. The key to mastery is continuous learning, experimenting, and engaging with others who share your passion for development.

By understanding Node from its fundamentals to its advanced capabilities, you'll not only gain a tool for development but also a versatile skill set that's highly valued in the industry. To inspire your journey, let's explore some advanced concepts that make Node unique and powerful.

Advanced Node Concepts

Before we dive deeper into how Node handles tasks behind the scenes, it's essential to understand Node's core mechanism for managing asynchronous operations.

Event Loop

The *event loop* in Node is like a factory manager who divides tasks into phases to ensure everything runs smoothly and efficiently. Each phase handles a specific type of job:

Timers
> For scheduled tasks (e.g., alarms)

I/O operations
> For input/output tasks (e.g., reading files)

Callbacks
> For responses that need immediate attention

The event loop processes these phases in order, ensuring tasks are completed without one blocking another.

Imagine you're running a restaurant:

- The chef prepares food (timers).
- The server delivers it (I/O operations).
- The cashier processes payments (callbacks).

All this happens seamlessly, keeping the workflow smooth.

Streams and Buffers

Streams and buffers in Node manage data efficiently in chunks, making it easier to handle large files or continuous data flows:

Streams
> Like water pipes, delivering small, manageable amounts of data over time

Buffers
> Temporarily store data until it's ready to be used

Watching a movie online uses streams. The video plays as it's being downloaded. If you had to download the entire video before watching, it would take much longer. Streams enable faster and more efficient handling of tasks like video streaming or real-time file uploads.

Scalability with Clustering

Node can handle larger workloads by using *clustering*, which spawns multiple instances of the application to share the load:

- Each instance runs independently but shares the same application logic.
- A *load balancer* distributes incoming requests among these instances.

Think of clustering like opening multiple checkout counters in a busy supermarket:

- Each counter (Node instance) serves customers (requests) independently.
- The manager (load balancer) directs each customer to the next available counter.

This setup ensures more users can be served simultaneously, optimizing performance.

For a deeper look at Node.js setup, project initialization, and modern syntax patterns, refer to Appendix A. For additional tools and practices that enrich your development environment—like formatters, debuggers, and using Git, refer to Appendix B. Appendix C provides context and step-by-step guidance for working with databases and queue systems, which are used in later chapters. Appendix D covers how to set up and run your projects using Docker for a consistent development environment. Appendix E explains how to create and configure third-party accounts, such as cloud providers and API platforms, required for some of the projects in this book.

What follows is a high-level overview to help you understand what Node is and why it matters. Node has become a core part of modern web development thanks to its speed, scalability, and thriving ecosystem. This makes Node a natural foundation for exploring powerful web frameworks like Fastify.

Using Fastify in This Book

Fastify is a high-performance, low-overhead Node web framework designed to be extremely fast and lightweight. That means it can do a lot of work without slowing down or using too many of your computer's resources.

It is optimized for creating APIs and web services that require rapid response times, making it ideal for both small projects and large-scale applications. Fastify excels at processing HTTP requests and delivering responses with minimal latency, which is crucial for web applications where fast response times enhance user experience and system efficiency. Additionally, Fastify can handle a large number of requests per second (RPS), making it an excellent choice for applications that need to serve many users simultaneously, such as APIs or microservices.

Under the Hood

Fastify achieves its high performance through a combination of efficient design principles and smart architectural decisions (Figure 1-3). It uses Node's low-level HTTP module, a built-in feature written in C++ that handles incoming requests and outgoing responses efficiently, without the need for extra libraries. This keeps the core of Fastify lightweight and fast. Fastify also employs schema-based validation and serialization using AJV, a powerful JSON schema validator.

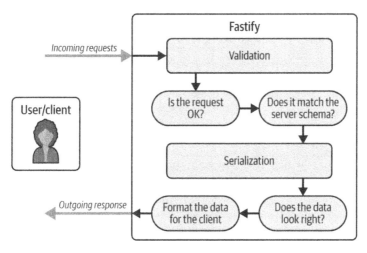

Figure 1-3. Diagram of Fastify's low-overhead architecture

This means that when data is sent to your application, Fastify ensures it matches the expected format (validation), and when data is sent back to the user, it formats the output efficiently (serialization). Precompiling these processes ahead of time further reduces the workload during each request.

Fastify's asynchronous, nonblocking architecture is another key to its scalability. Node operates using an event loop, which allows multiple tasks (like handling HTTP requests, querying a database, or reading files) to happen concurrently without creating multiple threads. This means that even if one operation is slow, such as waiting for a database to respond, other requests can continue being processed without delay. Fastify builds on this core behavior of Node to handle many simultaneous requests with ease.

Another strength of Fastify is its modular plug-in system. Plug-ins are reusable pieces of functionality (like authentication or logging) that can be added to your application. Fastify's plug-in system ensures these features are isolated and don't interfere with one another. For example, if you're adding a new feature to one route, it won't unintentionally affect another. This makes Fastify not only scalable but also easier to maintain as your application grows.

Fastify also includes Pino, a high-performance logging library, which records important application events without adding unnecessary load. Logs are essential for debugging and monitoring, and Pino's optimized design ensures that logging doesn't slow down your application. For more information on Pino, see the Pino website (*https://getpino.io*).

This book uses Fastify over Express.js because of these performance benefits and its developer-friendly features. While Express is versatile and widely used, Fastify offers built-in support for JSON-based APIs, a focus on high-speed request handling, and optimizations that make it particularly well suited for building modern web services. With Fastify, you'll gain hands-on experience with efficient design patterns that are ideal for high-performance applications, especially those that need to scale effectively as they grow.

Table 1-1 compares Fastify with three other popular Node frameworks: Express, Koa, and Hapi. Each column gives a quick overview of the core strengths and differences of each framework, which you can use to help decide which is best suited for your project.

Table 1-1. Node frameworks

Framework	Performance	Schema-based validation	Built-in plug-ins	Ideal use case	HTTP/2 support
Fastify	High	Yes (JSON Schema)	Limited; lightweight	High-performance APIs and microservices	Yes
Express	Medium	No (requires additional libraries)	Extensive middleware ecosystem	General-purpose web applications	Yes (with middleware)
Koa	Medium	No (requires middleware)	Minimal, modular	Flexible, customizable applications	Yes (with middleware)
Hapi	Medium-High	Yes (Joi)	Rich plug-in ecosystem	Enterprise-level applications, APIs with complex needs	Yes

In a nutshell, Fastify excels in performance and is ideal for high-speed APIs and microservices due to its schema-based validation and minimal overhead. Express remains a versatile choice with a large plug-in ecosystem, suitable for general-purpose web applications.

Throughout this book, Fastify will serve as the foundational framework for your Node applications, helping you build scalable, responsive, and high-performance services. As you work through the chapters, you'll learn how to harness Fastify's strengths while gaining a deeper understanding of how to create efficient, modern web applications.

Chapter Exercises

1. Verify your Node and VS Code setup:

   a. After completing the installations, confirm everything is working properly by opening your command line and running `node -v` and `npm -v`. You should see the version numbers for both Node and npm, indicating they are installed correctly.

   b. Launch VS Code and open a new folder named `hello-node`.

   c. Inside the folder, create a file named *index.js* with the following code: `console.log("Node is working!");`

   d. Navigate to your project's root directory in your command line and run the file by running `node index.js`.

   e. You should see the message `Node is working!` printed to your console.

   If anything doesn't work, revisit the installation steps in this chapter and double-check the instructions specific to your operating system.

2. Explore Fastify's starter template:

   a. Get your hands dirty with Fastify by generating a basic project. In your command line, run `npm init fastify@latest fastify-test-app` and follow the prompts to create a new project. This command uses the Fastify CLI to set up a new project with all the necessary files and dependencies.

   b. Navigate into the new project directory in your command line and run `npm install` to install dependencies.

   c. Run `npm run dev` to start the development server, open your browser, and go to *http://localhost:3000*. You should see a JSON message like `{ "root": true }`. This indicates your Fastify server is running properly.

These exercises ensure your development environment is ready and introduce you to running code with Node and launching a Fastify-based web server.

Summary

In this chapter, you:

- Set up your Node development environment by installing essential tools like VS Code and Node on macOS, Windows, and Linux
- Learned the role of Node as a fast event-driven JavaScript runtime built on the V8 engine
- Explored the fundamentals of Fastify's architecture for building APIs and web services

CHAPTER 2

Practical Application

This chapter covers the following:

- Getting started with a Node app
- Reading user input on the command line
- Writing data to a CSV

Whether you are new to programming or a seasoned engineer, you probably opened this chapter to get started with Node. Many Node projects span thousands of lines of code, but some of the most useful and practical applications can be written in only a handful of lines. Let's skip the part where you get overwhelmed and jump into the *practical application*.

In this chapter, you'll get a first glance at what Node can offer out of the box and off the grid. You will learn to build a simple program that can run on anyone's computer and save real people real time and money. By the end of the chapter, you'll have Node locked and loaded on your computer with a development environment ready to build *practically* anything.

Tools and Applications Used in This Chapter

Before you get started, make sure to install and configure the tools and applications required for this project. Installation instructions for Node, Fastify, and VS Code are provided in Chapter 1, while project initialization steps, such as setting up your directory structure, configuring *package.json*, and using modern syntax, are covered in Appendix A. Once completed, return here to continue. Building a project from scratch helps deepen your understanding of each component, giving you greater control and flexibility as you progress.

Your Prompt

A travel agent wants to hire you to convert their Rolodex (*https://oreil.ly/3kNLV*) (physical information cards) into some digital format. They just bought a few new computers and want to start importing data. They don't need anything fancy like a website or mobile application, just a computer prompt to create a tabular format, or comma-separated values (CSV), of data.

Get Planning

Luckily, you just started building Node applications and you see this as a great opportunity to use some of Node's default, out-of-the-box libraries. This business only wants to manually enter data that can be written to a *.csv* file. So you start diagramming the requirements of the project, and your result is shown in Figure 2-1. The diagram details the following steps:

1. Physical information cards are collected by the user.
2. Open the command line and start the application by running `node index`.
3. Enter the name, phone number, and email address in the command-line prompt.
4. After each entry, contact data is saved through your application to a CSV file on your computer.

Each contact has a full name, phone number, and email address listed on their card. You decide to build a simple Node command-line application so users can manually enter these three data values for each contact card.

When you're finished, the user should be able to open their command line, run `node index.js`, and follow the prompts to enter contact information. After each contact is entered, it will be saved to a CSV file as a comma-delimited string.

.csv is a precursor to many of the mainstream database tables used today. While not ideal for storing long-term data, it's a great way to visualize rows of data for viewing and processing without a database.

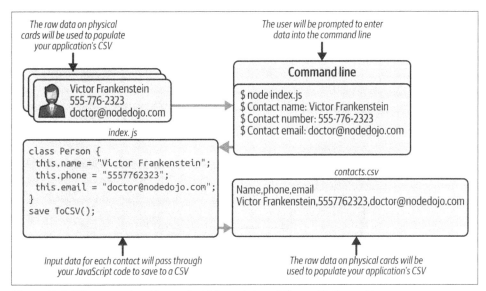

Figure 2-1. Diagramming the project blueprint and flow of information

Get Programming

With Node set up, you begin setting up your project. Choose a location where you'd like to store your project code for this chapter and run `mkdir csv_app` in your command line to create the project folder.

To keep your coding projects separate from other work on your computer, you can dedicate a directory for coding. Creating a directory called *src* at the root level of your computer's user directory is a good place. That location is */Users/<USERNAME>/src* for Macs (*~/src*), and *C:\Users\<USERNAME>\src* for Windows computers.

Next, you'll follow steps to initialize your Node app. When complete, your project directory structure should look like Figure 2-2.

These steps are also described in Appendix B.

Within the csv_app folder, run npm init to start the process of creating a new Node application configuration file. You will see a prompt and can fill out your responses as in Example 2-1.

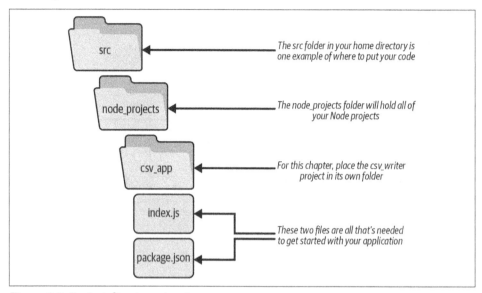

Figure 2-2. Project directory structure

Example 2-1. Prompt for npm init

```
package name: (csv_app)  ❶
version: (1.0.0)
description: An app to write contact information to a csv file.
entry point: (index.js)  ❷
test command:
git repository:
keywords:
author: Jon Wexler
license: (ISC)
```

❶ This is the name of your project.

❷ *index.js* is where your application will start.

This process has created a new file for you: *package.json* (Example 2-2). This is your application's configuration file, where you'll instruct your computer on how to run your Node app.

What's package.json?

Every Node project has a special file called *package.json*. Think of it as your app's instruction manual and toolkit. It explains what your app needs to work, what tasks it can do, and even details about the project itself. If you're new to Node, understanding this file is crucial, so let's break it down.

Why is *package.json* important? Imagine you're baking a cake. You need ingredients, tools, and step-by-step instructions. Similarly, a Node app needs specific libraries (ingredients), configurations (tools), and scripts (steps) to work. The *package.json* file organizes all of this in one place, making it easy to share your project with others or set it up on a new computer.

Key parts of *package.json* include the following:

Dependencies
> These are the "ingredients" your app needs: third-party libraries or packages it relies on. For example, if your app uses Google Maps, you'd include the @google/maps package here. This tells others (and their computers) what to install to make the app work.

Scripts
> These are commands that automate tasks for your app, like starting it, testing it, or building it. For example, the most common script is `npm start`, which starts your app. You can also add custom scripts like `npm run build` to prepare files for deployment.

Version
> This tracks the app's version, which is helpful as you make updates. Versions follow a format like 1.0.0, where the numbers represent major changes, minor updates, or small fixes (called "patches").

Name and description
> These fields describe your project. The name field gives your app a unique identifier, and the description explains what it does.

License
> This tells others the terms for using, sharing, or modifying your app. For example, you might allow open use with an MIT license or set stricter terms.

If you're working on a team or sharing your code, *package.json* ensures everyone is on the same page. It automates setup, lists required libraries, and saves you from manually explaining how to run your app.

For more information, visit the Node documentation (*https://oreil.ly/AdqHu*).

Your first step is to add `"type"`: `"module"` to your *package.json*. This enables ES6 module syntax (`import/export`) in your Node project. Starting from Node v13.2.0, stable support for ES6 modules was introduced, making them increasingly popular in Node projects. Many developers now prefer ES6 modules over the older CommonJS syntax (`require/module.exports`) for cleaner and more modern code.

Example 2-2. Contents of package.json

```
{
  "name": "csv_app",
  "version": "1.0.0",
  "type": "module", ❶
  "description": "An app to write contact information to a csv file.",
  "main": "index.js",
  "scripts": {
    "test": "echo \"Error: no test specified\" && exit 1"
  },
  "author": "Jon Wexler",
  "license": "ISC"
}
```

❶ This addition allows for module import syntax in your application.

Next, you create the entry point to your application, a file titled *index.js*. This is where the guts of your application will go.

For this project, you realize that Node comes prepackaged with everything you need already. You can make use of the `fs` module—a library that helps your application interact with your computer's filesystem—to create the CSV file. Within *index.js* you add the `writeFileSync` function from the `fs` module by writing `import { write FileSync } from "fs"`.

You now have access to functions that can create files on your computer. Now you can make use of the `writeFileSync` function to test that your Node app can successfully create (or overwrite) files and add text to them. Add the code in Example 2-3 to *index.js*. Here you are creating a variable called `content` with some placeholder text. Then, within a `try/catch` block, you run `writeFileSync`, a synchronous, blocking function, to create a new file called *test.txt* within your project's directory. If the file is created with your added content, you will see a message logged to your command-line window with the text `Success!` Otherwise, if an error occurs, you'll see the stack-trace and contents of that error logged to your command-line window.

With ES6 module import syntax you may make use of destructuring assignment. Instead of importing an entire library, you may import the functions or modules you need only through destructuring. For more information, read Mozilla's JavaScript reference pages (https://oreil.ly/c5oaZ).

Example 2-3. Contents of index.js

```
import { writeFileSync } from "fs"; ❶

const content = "Test content!"; ❷

try { ❸
  writeFileSync("./test.txt", content); ❹
  console.log("Success!"); ❺
} catch (err) {
  console.error(err); ❻
}
```

❶ Destructure the fs module to import its writeFileSync function.

❷ Assign the content variable to a string.

❸ Add a try/catch block to wrap your call.

❹ Write to a new file called *test.txt*.

❺ Log success upon file write.

❻ Log an error if writeFileSync fails.

You're ready to test this by navigating to your *csv_app* project folder within your terminal window and running node index.js. Now, check to see if a new file called *test.txt* was created. If so, open it up to see Test content! within. Now you're ready to move to the next step and cater this app to handle user input and write to a CSV file.

Translating User Input to CSV

Now that your app is set up to save content to a file, you begin writing the logic to accept user input in the command line. Node comes with a module called readline that does just that. By importing the createInterface function, you can map the application's standard input and output to the readline functionality, as seen in Example 2-4. Like the fs module, no additional installations are required other than the default out-of-the-box Node installation on your computer.

In this code, `process.stdin` and `process.stdout` are ways that your Node app's `process` streams data to and from the command line, enabling interaction with the user directly through the terminal.

Example 2-4. Mapping input and output to readline in index.js

```
import { createInterface } from "readline";  ❶

const readline = createInterface({  ❷
  input: process.stdin,
  output: process.stdout
});
```

❶ Destructure the `readline` module to import `createInterface`.

❷ Call `createInterface()` with `stdin` and `stdout` to configure terminal-based user input and output for your Node app.

Next, you make use of this mapping by using the `question` function in your `readline` interface. This function takes a `message`, or prompt you'll display to the user on the command line, and will return the user's input as a return value.

Because this function is asynchronous, you can wrap its return value in a `Promise` to make use of the async/await syntax from ES6. If you need a refresher on JavaScript `Promises`, visit Mozilla's JavaScript reference pages (*https://oreil.ly/DRTvA*).

Create a function called `readLineAsync` that waits for the user to reply and press Enter before the string value is resolved (Example 2-5). In this way, your custom `readLineAsync` function will eventually resolve with a response containing the user's input without holding up the Node app.

Example 2-5. Promise wrapped readLineAsync function in index.js

```
const readLineAsync = (message) =>  ❶
  new Promise((resolve) => readline.question(message, resolve));  ❷
```

❶ Declares an asynchronous function `readLineAsync` that takes a `message` as input.

❷ Wraps `readline.question` in a `Promise` to enable async/await usage, resolving with the user's input.

Using promisify to Wrap Your Synchronous Functions

Using `promisify` from Node's built-in `util` module is a powerful technique to convert traditional callback-based functions into promise-based ones, allowing for easier and cleaner asynchronous code using `async/await`. In many Node APIs, especially older ones, asynchronous functions rely on a callback where the first argument is an error (if any), and the second is the result. This approach can lead to "callback hell" and less readable code. By using `promisify`, you can transform these callback functions into promises, simplifying your asynchronous flow and reducing the complexity of error handling.

For example, using `promisify` to convert a function like `fs.readFile` or `readline.question` into a promise allows you to seamlessly integrate these functions into modern JavaScript code. This makes the code more maintainable, as you can use `async/await` instead of deeply nested callbacks, resulting in a cleaner, more synchronous-like structure. `promisify` is particularly useful when you are working with legacy Node modules or want to upgrade your codebase incrementally to use more modern patterns without significant refactoring. See Example 2-6 for how to use `promisify` with `readline.question`.

This code sets up a CLI using Node's `readline` module, allowing for asynchronous input from the user with the help of `promisify`. The key parts include converting the callback-based question method into a promise (using `promisify`), enabling the use of `async/await` to prompt the user for their name, and then closing the interface once the interaction is complete.

Example 2-6. Promise wrapped `readLineAsync` function in index.js

```
import { promisify } from 'util';  ❶
...
const readLineAsync = promisify(readline.question).bind(rl);  ❷
(async () => {
  try {
    const name = await readLineAsync('What is your name? ');  ❸
    console.log(`Hello, ${name}!`);
  } catch (err) {
    console.error('Error:', err.message);  ❹
  } finally {
    readline.close();  ❺
  }
})();
...
```

❶ Import the `promisify` function from the `util` module.

Translating User Input to CSV | 23

❷ The readLineAsync method is wrapped with promisify to convert it into a promise-based function.

❸ Prompt for user input using async/await.

❹ Add a try/catch block to handle any potential errors that occur.

❺ Adding a finally block ensures that the readline interface is closed.

With these functions in place, all you need is to call readLineAsync for your application to start retrieving user input. Because your prompt has three specific data values to save, you can create a class to encapsulate that data for each contact. As seen in Example 2-7, within *index.js* you import appendFileSync from the fs module, which will create and append to a given filename. Then you define a Person class which takes name, number, and email as arguments in its constructor. Finally, you add a save ToCSV method to the Person class to save each contact's information in a comma-delimited format suitable for CSV to a file called *contacts.csv*.

Example 2-7. Defining the Person class in index.js

```
import { appendFileSync } from "fs"; ❶

class Person { ❷
  constructor(name = "", number = "", email = "") {  ❸
    this.name = name;
    this.number = number;
    this.email = email;
  }
  saveToCSV() { ❹
    const content = `${this.name},${this.number},${this.email}\n`; ❺
    try {
      appendFileSync("./contacts.csv", content); ❻
      console.log(`${this.name} Saved!`);
    } catch (err) {
      console.error(err);
    }
  }
}
```

❶ Destructure the fs module to import appendFileSync.

❷ Define the Person class.

❸ Define a constructor with name, number, and email.

❹ Add a `saveToCSV` method for saving contact information to CSV.

❺ Use string interpolation to separate each contact's information with commas.

❻ Save and append the `content` string into a file called *contacts.csv* in your project's directory.

> If you want to ensure that the *contacts.csv* file exists before you try to append to it, you may also import the `existsSync` function from the `fs` module and check if the file exists before appending to it using `existsSync("./contacts.csv")`. This way, you can avoid errors if the file does not exist.

The last step is to instantiate a new `Person` object for each new contact you're manually entering into your application. To do this, you create an async `startApp` function that uses a `while` loop controlled by a `shouldContinue` variable. Initially set to `true`, this variable determines whether the loop continues.

Within the loop, the function collects the user's input for `name`, `number`, and `email` using the `readLineAsync` function. Each input is gathered in sequence, ensuring that the function waits for the user to provide each value before proceeding.

Once all the required values are collected, a new `Person` object is instantiated with the input values, and the `saveToCSV()` method is called on the `person` instance to save the data to a file. After saving, the user is prompted to decide whether to continue entering more data by typing y. If the user enters y, the loop continues; otherwise, `shouldContinue` is set to `false`, and the `readline` interface is closed, ending the application (Example 2-8).

Example 2-8. Collecting user input within `startApp` in index.js

```
const startApp = async () => {   ❶
  let shouldContinue = true;
  while (shouldContinue) {   ❷
    const name = await readLineAsync("Contact Name: ");
    const number = await readLineAsync("Contact Number: ");
    const email = await readLineAsync("Contact Email: ");

    const person = new Person(name, number, email);   ❸
    person.saveToCSV();

    const response = await readLineAsync("Continue? [y to continue]: ");   ❹
    shouldContinue = response.toLowerCase() === "y";   ❺
  }
}
```

```
  readline.close();  ❻
};
```

❶ Declares an asynchronous `startApp` function to manage the app's flow.

❷ Uses a `while` loop controlled by the `shouldContinue` variable for repeated prompts.

❸ Creates a `Person` instance with the collected `name`, `number`, and `email` inputs.

❹ Asks the user if they want to continue entering data.

❺ Updates `shouldContinue` based on the user's response (y to continue).

❻ Closes the `readline` interface, ending the application.

Then add `startApp()` at the bottom of *index.js* to start the app when the file is run. Your final *index.js* file should look like Example 2-9.

Example 2-9. Complete index.js

```
import { appendFileSync } from "fs";
import { createInterface } from "readline";

const readline = createInterface({
  input: process.stdin,
  output: process.stdout,
});

const readLineAsync = (message) =>
  new Promise((resolve) => readline.question(message, resolve));

class Person {
  constructor(name = "", number = "", email = "") {
    this.name = name;
    this.number = number;
    this.email = email;
  }
  saveToCSV() {
    const content = `${this.name},${this.number},${this.email}\n`;
    try {
      appendFileSync("./contacts.csv", content);
      console.log(`${this.name} Saved!`);
    } catch (err) {
      console.error(err);
    }
  }
}
```

```
const startApp = async () => {
  let shouldContinue = true;
  while (shouldContinue) {
    const name = await readLineAsync("Contact Name: ");
    const number = await readLineAsync("Contact Number: ");
    const email = await readLineAsync("Contact Email: ");

    const person = new Person(name, number, email);
    person.saveToCSV();

    const response = await readLineAsync("Continue? [y to continue]: ");
    shouldContinue = response.toLowerCase() === "y";
  }
  readline.close();
};

startApp();
```

In the project folder on your command line, run node index to start seeing text prompts, as seen in Figure 2-3.

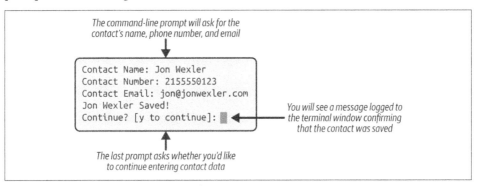

Figure 2-3. Command-line prompts for user input

When you are done entering all the contact's details, you can then see that the information has been saved to a file called *contacts.csv* in the same folder. Each line of that file should be comma-delimited, looking like Jon Wexler,2155550123,Jon@jonwexler.com.

This should be just what the travel agency needs to convert their physical contact cards into a CSV file they can use in many other ways. In the next section, you'll explore how third-party libraries can simplify your code even further.

Working with External Packages

It didn't take much code to build an application that is as functional and effective as `csv_app`. The good news is your work is done. There's even better news! While Node offers built-in modules for a variety of tasks, there are plenty of external libraries (npm packages) you can install to reduce your written code even further.

To improve the readability of your written code so far, you can install the `prompt` and `csv-writer` packages by running `npm install "csv-writer@^1.6.0" "prompt@^1.3.0"` in your project folder on your command line. This command will also list these two packages in your *package.json* file.

Refer to the npm website for more information about `prompt` (*https://oreil.ly/xEcxI*) and `csv-writer` (*https://oreil.ly/D6Fby*).

In your *index.js* file, import `prompt` and use it to replace your `readLineAsync` calls, as shown in Example 2-10. Start by initializing `prompt` with `prompt.start()` and setting the `prompt.message` to an empty string to remove unnecessary prefixes in the terminal. You can now remove the `readLineAsync` function, `readline` interface mappings, and `readline` module imports from your code.

`prompt.get` is used to collect the user's input for multiple prompts at once, returning an object where each prompt's name corresponds to its response. These responses are directly passed to a new `Person` constructor.

After saving the `person`'s values to a CSV file using the `saveToCSV` method, the program prompts the user to decide if they want to continue. The user's response is destructured and assigned to the `again` variable, which determines whether the program recursively calls itself to collect additional inputs or exits.

Example 2-10. Replacing `readLineAsync` with `prompt` in index.js

```
import prompt from "prompt";
prompt.start();
prompt.message = "";
...
const startApp = async () => {  ❶
  const questions = [  ❷
    { name: "name", description: "Contact Name" },
    { name: "number", description: "Contact Number" },
    { name: "email", description: "Contact Email" },
  ];
```

```
  const responses = await prompt.get(questions);   ❸
  const person = new Person(responses.name, responses.number, responses.email);   ❹
  await person.saveToCSV();

  const { again } = await prompt.get([
    { name: "again", description: "Continue? [y to continue]" },
  ]);   ❺

  if (again.toLowerCase() === "y") await startApp();   ❻
};
```

❶ Defines the `startApp` function as asynchronous to allow for `await` usage.

❷ Creates an array of questions for collecting `name`, `number`, and `email` inputs.

❸ Prompts the user for the questions and collects the responses.

❹ Instantiates a `Person` object with the collected responses.

❺ Asks the user if they want to continue adding contacts.

❻ Recursively calls `startApp` if the user opts to continue; otherwise, the program ends.

Similar to how the external `prompt` package displaced the `readline` module, `csv-writer` replaces the need of your `fs` module imports and defines a more structured approach for writing to your CSV by including a header, as shown in Example 2-11. Place this code at the top of your *index.js* file, just below the `prompt` import and initialization.

Example 2-11. Importing and setting up `csv-writer` in index.js

```
import { createObjectCsvWriter } from "csv-writer";   ❶
...
const csvWriter = createObjectCsvWriter({   ❷
  path: "./contacts.csv",
  append: true,
  header: [
    { id: "name", title: "NAME" },
    { id: "number", title: "NUMBER" },
    { id: "email", title: "EMAIL" },
  ],
});
```

❶ Use a named import to bring in `createObjectCsvWriter` from `csv-writer`.

❷ Configure `csvWriter` to write to *contacts.csv*, append to the file, and include headers.

Finally, you modify your `saveToCSV` method on the `Person` class to use `csvWriter.writeRecords` instead (Example 2-12).

Example 2-12. Update `saveToCSV` in `Person` class to use `csvWriter.writeRecords` in index.js

```
...
async saveToCSV() {
  try {
    const { name, number, email } = this; ❶
    await csvWriter.writeRecords([{ name, number, email }]); ❷
    console.log(`${name} Saved!`);
  } catch (err) {
    console.error(err);
  }
}
...
```

❶ Destructure your `Person` instance variables.

❷ Use `csvWriter.writeRecords` to write a row of values to your CSV file.

With these two changes in place, your new *index.js* file should look like Example 2-13.

Example 2-13. Using external packages in index.js

```
import { createObjectCsvWriter } from "csv-writer";
import prompt from "prompt";

prompt.start();
prompt.message = "";

const csvWriter = createObjectCsvWriter({
  path: "./contacts.csv",
  append: true,
  header: [
    { id: "name", title: "NAME" },
    { id: "number", title: "NUMBER" },
    { id: "email", title: "EMAIL" },
  ],
});
```

```
class Person {
  constructor(name = "", number = "", email = "") {
    this.name = name;
    this.number = number;
    this.email = email;
  }

  async saveToCSV() {
    try {
      const { name, number, email } = this;
      await csvWriter.writeRecords([{ name, number, email }]);
      console.log(`${name} Saved!`);
    } catch (err) {
      console.error("Error saving contact:", err);
    }
  }
}

const startApp = async () => {
  const questions = [
    { name: "name", description: "Contact Name" },
    { name: "number", description: "Contact Number" },
    { name: "email", description: "Contact Email" },
  ];

  const responses = await prompt.get(questions);
  const person = new Person(responses.name, responses.number, responses.email);
  await person.saveToCSV();

  const { again } = await prompt.get([
    { name: "again", description: "Continue? [y to continue]" },
  ]);

  if (again.toLowerCase() === "y") await startApp();
};

startApp();
```

Now when you run node index, the application's behavior should be exactly the same as in the previous section. This time your *contacts.csv* file should list headers at the top of the file. This is a great example of how you can use Node out of the box to solve a real-world problem, then refactor and improve your code by using external packages built by the thriving online Node community!

Chapter Exercises

1. Add input validation for email and phone number:

   a. Update your CLI application so that it only accepts valid email addresses and phone numbers.

   b. Use a regular expression to check that the email contains a valid format like example@domain.com, and that the phone number contains only digits.

   c. If the input is invalid, show an error message and prompt the user to enter the value again.

   d. After implementing this, try running the app and attempt to enter incorrect data (e.g., abc@, 123abc456) to make sure it correctly asks again.

For a basic email check, you can use /\\S+@\\S+\\.\\S+/, but feel free to improve it!

2. Include a timestamp for each contact entry:

   a. Modify the Person class or your CSV writer code to include a createdAt field.

   b. When the user submits a contact, automatically add the current date and time in ISO format using new Date().toISOString().

   c. Update your CSV logic to include a CREATED_AT header and write this new field alongside the contact's name, number, and email.

   d. Run your application, enter a few contacts, and confirm that each row now includes the timestamp in the final column.

These exercises will help solidify your understanding of input validation, formatting, and data enrichment—all common tasks in real-world Node applications.

Summary

In this chapter, you:

- Developed a Node application to automate the conversion of contact data from physical cards into a CSV format.
- Learned how to read user input from the command line using both built-in Node libraries and external packages.

- Efficiently stored contact information in a CSV file with structured headers using the `csv-writer` package.

- Enhanced your project by integrating external libraries, improving both code readability and functionality.

- Established a foundational workflow for building command-line tools that solve real-world problems with minimal code.

CHAPTER 3

Building a Node Web Server

This chapter covers the following:

- Using Node as a web interface
- Building a Node web app with Fastify
- Serving static pages with dynamic content

Node is about using JavaScript on the server. JavaScript itself is already an asynchronous language by nature, but not until 2009 was it used outside your standard web browser. As dependence on the internet grew worldwide, businesses demanded new innovative development strategies that also took into account hirable skill sets already in the market. Thereafter, JavaScript took off for frontend and backend development, setting up new application design patterns with Node's single-threaded event loop.

In this chapter, you'll explore the most common use case for Node, a web application, and how the event loop plays a role. By the end of this chapter, you'll be able to use Node's most popular project framework, Fastify, to build both simple web servers and more extensive applications.

Tools and Applications Used in This Chapter

Before you get started, make sure to install and configure the tools and applications required for this project. Installation instructions for Node.js, Fastify, and VS Code are provided in Chapter 1, while project initialization steps, such as setting up your directory structure, configuring *package.json*, and using modern syntax, are covered in Appendix A. Once completed, return here to continue. Building a project from scratch helps deepen your understanding of each component, giving you greater control and flexibility as you progress.

Your Prompt

The owners of a local restaurant, What's Fare is Fair, have decided to invest some money into a homegrown web application to better serve their customers. They've reached out to you, an eager software engineer, to help craft a lightweight application that can display their landing page, static menu, and operating hours.

Get Planning

After careful consideration, you realize this business needs only a simple web server to serve static content to its customers. In this case you only need to support three web pages of content. Being an experienced Node engineer, you know that you may use the built-in http module, but find it more flexible to work with a popular external library called Fastify. Before you get programming, you diagram the requirements of the project and your result, as shown in Figure 3-1.

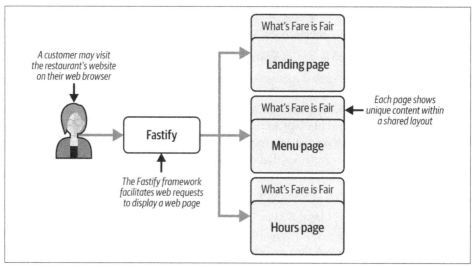

Figure 3-1. Project blueprint

A Word on Web Servers

Node's runtime environment is versatile enough to create applications that communicate over the internet using standard protocols, with HTTP being the most common. While Node's built-in http module allows you to build web servers, setting up even a basic website can require significant code and configuration.

To streamline this process, frameworks like fastify provide a more comprehensive solution. Fastify not only simplifies the implementation of http for handling web requests and responses, but also introduces a structured approach to organizing your application's files, integrating third-party packages, and building web applications more efficiently. In fact, many other Node frameworks build upon Fastify as a foundation for their additional tools and features. For more details on Fastify and its capabilities, visit the Fastify website (*https://fastify.dev*).

As customers visit the restaurant's site, your Fastify app will efficiently route them to the requested pages. Leveraging Node's single-threaded event loop, Fastify handles incoming requests asynchronously. Each request represents a customer's attempt to access a specific page via a URL. Despite running on a single thread, Node's nonblocking architecture allows it to handle multiple requests concurrently by offloading tasks (like database queries or file reads) to the background. This means your app can quickly process each customer's request without being held up by others, as long as no heavy, CPU-bound operations (like calculating the 50th Fibonacci number) are blocking the event loop. Thanks to this approach, Fastify ensures fast, scalable performance even under load. You visualize how Node's event loop manages and prioritizes incoming requests.

Blocking the Event Loop

The Node event loop is the heart of how every Node application runs. Since JavaScript in Node operates on a single thread, it's crucial to allow this thread to handle as many tasks as possible without delays. Figure 3-2 illustrates some common ways the event loop can be blocked.

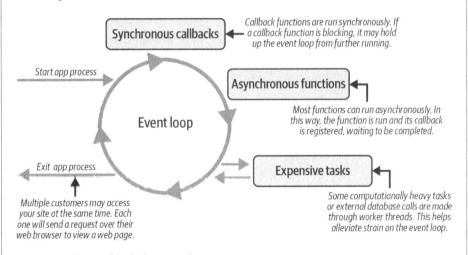

Figure 3-2. How to block the event loop

Although Node uses a single thread, it can create additional threads from a "thread pool," often referred to as "worker threads." These worker threads are typically assigned more resource-intensive tasks, such as filesystem operations, database queries (I/O), or cryptographic functions. The purpose of these worker threads is to offload heavy tasks from the main event loop, allowing it to stay responsive. However, if the event loop itself is busy handling complex or slow-running tasks, your app's performance can suffer.

The main thread is responsible for coordinating asynchronous tasks and processing their callbacks when they're ready. However, if those callbacks include operations like nested loops, processing large datasets, or other CPU-heavy computations, the event loop gets "blocked." This means it can't handle other incoming tasks until it finishes the current one, leading to slower responses.

In the context of a web server, each event loop cycle corresponds to handling requests from clients. If the event loop is blocked by one client's request—like generating a web page with complex processing—other clients will have to wait until that task is complete. As you build your web servers, it's important to differentiate between tasks that run in constant time (quick operations) versus tasks that run in exponential time (like nested loops or CPU-intensive algorithms) and could block the event loop.

For more information, visit the Node website (*https://oreil.ly/MbnEj*).

Figure 3-3 illustrates how web requests are processed within your Fastify-powered web application. Similar to Figure 3-1, customers access the restaurant's website without any predictability regarding the number of visitors or the rate at which requests arrive. Each request, however, is processed individually as it enters your application. Node's event loop efficiently queues incoming requests, assigning responses while simultaneously managing new ones. Thanks to the queue system, the event loop handles each request as soon as resources are available. For example, when a customer requests the restaurant's menu, Fastify routes them to a static web page displaying the business hours, ensuring that all requests are handled smoothly, even under varying load conditions.

For more information about Node's event loop, see the official documentation page (*https://oreil.ly/_6ork*) or Mozilla's JavaScript reference pages (*https://oreil.ly/NZdpc*).

With the big picture captured, it's time to get programming.

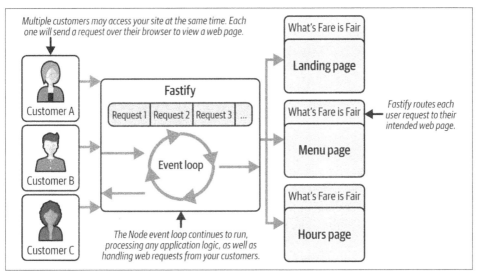

Figure 3-3. Development workflow

Building the Application Skeleton

While this project can be relatively straightforward, it's often helpful to break tasks down into more manageable segments. To start, you create an application skeleton that contains the Fastify framework and some of your application logic.

Working with Fastify

Initialize a new Node application by creating a new folder called `restaurant_web_server`, entering the folder on your command line, and running `npm init` (Example 3-1).

Example 3-1. Prompt for `npm init`

```
package name: (restaurant_web_server) ❶
version: (1.0.0)
description: An web application for a local restaurant.
entry point: (index.js) ❷
test command:
git repository:
keywords:
author: Jon Wexler
license: (ISC)
```

❶ This is the name of your project.

❷ *index.js* is where your application will start from.

After running through the prompt, your *package.json* file will appear in the project's folder. This file contains both the application's general configurations and the dependent modules.

Next, run `npm install fastify@^4.28.1` to install the `fastify` package. You'll need an internet connection, as running this command will fetch the contents of the `fastify` package from the npm registry (*https://www.npmjs.com*) and add them to your `node_modules` folder at the root level of your project. Unlike the `fs` and `http` modules that are prepackaged with Node, the `fastify` module is not offered with your initial installation. Instead, Fastify is bundled into a package called `fastify` that can be downloaded and installed separately through Node's package management registry tool, npm.

Both Node and Fastify are projects supported by the OpenJS Foundation. For more information about open source JavaScript projects from OpenJS, visit the OpenJS Foundation website (*https://openjsf.org*).

After installing `fastify` you notice that `fastify` is added to your *package.json* file under a section called `dependencies`, as seen in Example 3-2.

There are a variety of ways to write npm commands, some shorter and others more explicit in their phrasing. To learn more about npm command-line shorthands and flags, refer to the npm documentation (*https://oreil.ly/T34wJ*).

Example 3-2. Package dependencies in package.json

```
"dependencies": {
  "fastify": "^4.28.1" ❶
},
```

❶ `fastify` v^4.28.1 is listed as the sole dependency.

The use of ^ in npm package versioning means your application will ensure that this version, or any compatible versions of the package with minor or patch updates, will be installed to your application. The ~ before the version number means only patch updates will be installed, but not minor version changes. For more about *package.json* and how versioning works, see the npm documentation (*https://oreil.ly/bKCz7*).

With `fastify` installed, you create a file called *index.js* at the root level of your project folder. Next you import `fastify` into your application on the first line by adding `import Fastify from 'fastify'`.

As of Node v12, ES6 module imports are supported natively, but they are not enabled by default. You need to add `"type": "module"` to your *package.json* file to use the `import` syntax. Alternatively, if you do not want to modify *package.json*, you can use the *.mjs* file extension for individual files.

As shown in Example 3-3, you then type `const app = Fastify()` to instantiate a new instance of a Fastify application and assign it to a variable called `app`. You also assign another variable called `port` a development port number of 3000.

In development, you can use almost any port number to test your code. Ports like 80, 443, and 22 are usually reserved for specific purposes—80 for regular web traffic, 443 for secure (SSL) web traffic, and 22 for SSH connections. Port 3000, however, has become a popular default choice among software engineers for development.

Your `app` object has functions to handle incoming web requests. You add `app.get` on `"/"`, which listens for HTTP GET requests to your web app's home page. The `app.get` callback function processes the request and directly returns a plain-text response using `"Welcome to What's Fare is Fair!"`. This response is sent back to the customer's web browser when they visit your app's home page. The code is streamlined by using a `return` statement.

Fastify's `app.get` is named according to the HTTP request type. The most common requests are GET, POST, PUT, and DELETE. To get more familiar with these request methods, refer to Mozilla's JavaScript reference pages (*https://oreil.ly/bMdS9*).

After defining your routes, you call `await app.listen({ port })` to start the server. Once it's running, a confirmation message is logged using `console.log(...)`.

Example 3-3. Setting up your Fastify app in index.js

```
import Fastify from "fastify"; ❶
const app = Fastify(); ❷
const port = 3000; ❸

app.get("/", async (request, reply) => { ❹
  return "Welcome to What's Fare is Fair!"; ❺
});

await app.listen({ port }); ❻
console.log(`Web Server is listening at http://localhost:${port}`); ❼
```

❶ Import the Fastify module to create a server.

❷ Create an instance of Fastify, which acts as your web server.

❸ Define the port on which the application will run (defaults to 3000).

❹ Register a route that listens for HTTP GET requests at the root URL ("/").

❺ Respond with a plain-text message using the `return` statement.

❻ Start the server and bind it to the defined port using `await app.listen({ port })`.

❼ Log a confirmation message to the console, including the server's address, once it is successfully running.

> If you do not use `process.exit(1)` when an error occurs during startup, your application might continue running in a broken state, which could cause unpredictable behavior. Exiting the process ensures the error is caught early and handled appropriately.

Once your application has started successfully, Fastify takes over handling incoming requests and sending responses. Understanding how Fastify structures its request-response cycle is key to building efficient and reliable routes.

> In Fastify, you handle requests using `request` and send responses using `reply`. The function is marked as `async` to work with Fastify's promise-based routing. Fastify automatically serializes the returned value as the response body. With the `reply` object you can set headers, status codes, and even stream responses.

Now, you can start your application by running `node index` in your project's command-line window. You should then see a logged statement that reads: `Web Server is listening at http://localhost:3000`.

> `localhost` is a special hostname that refers to your own computer, used for testing and development without sending data over the internet. It's mapped to reserved IP addresses like 127.0.0.1 (IPv4) and ::1 (IPv6) via the system's hosts file, bypassing DNS lookups. When you use `localhost`, your computer loops the request back to itself through a virtual network adapter called the loopback.

This means you can open your favorite web browser and visit *http://localhost:3000* to see the text in Figure 3-4.

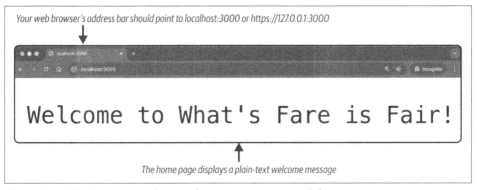

Figure 3-4. Viewing your web server's response in your web browser

With your application's foundation out of the way, it's time to add some flair to the What's Fare is Fair site.

Adding Routes and Data

With your application running, you move on to add more routes and context to your restaurant's site. You already added one route: a GET request to the home page (/). Now you can add two more routes for the menu page and operating hours page, as depicted in Example 3-4. Each `app.get` provides a new route at which your web pages are reachable.

Example 3-4. Adding two more routes in index.js

```
app.get("/menu", async (request, reply) => {  ❶
  return "TODO: Menu Page";
});

app.get("/hours", async (request, reply) => {  ❷
  return "TODO: Hours Page";
});
```

❶ A Fastify route for GET requests to the /menu path

❷ A Fastify route for GET requests to the /hours path

You can stop your Node server by pressing Ctrl+C in the command line of your running project. With your new changes in place, you can start your project again by running node index. Now when you navigate to *http://localhost:3000/menu* and *http://localhost:3000/hours*, you'll see the text change to your TODO messages.

This is a good start, but you'll need to fill in some meaningful data here. Your contact at What's Fare is Fair provides you with pictures of their menu (Figure 3-5). This image provides insight into the structure of the data in the restaurant's menu. For example, each item has a title, price, and description.

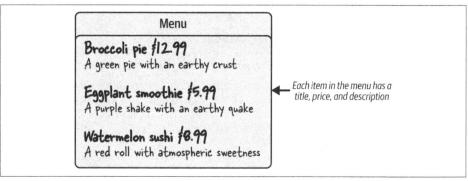

Figure 3-5. Menu items

Similarly, the restaurant provides a visual of their operating hours, as shown in Figure 3-6. Here, you notice that certain days share the same hours of operation, while one day has different hours, and one day the restaurant is closed. Being able to examine this information ahead of building your web pages can help you design your project in an efficient way.

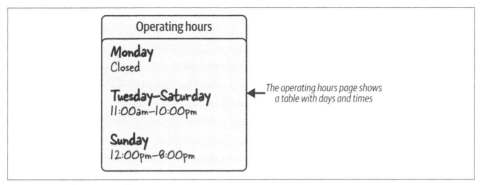

Figure 3-6. Operating hours

With these two references for data, you can convert the menu and hours list into JavaScript-friendly data modules. First, you create a folder called data in your project directory, where you'll add a *menuItem.js* and an *operatingHours.js* file. From these files you use the ES6 export default syntax to export all of the files' contents for use in other modules, as shown in Examples 3-5 and 3-6.

Example 3-5. Menu data in menuItems.js

```
export default [ ❶
  {
    name: "Broccoli Pie",
    description: "A green pie with an earthy crust",
    cost: 12.99,
  },
  {
    name: "Eggplant Smoothie",
    description: "A purple shake with an earthy quake",
    cost: 5.99,
  },
  {
    name: "Watermelon Sushi",
    description: "A red roll with atmospheric sweetness",
    cost: 8.99,
  },
];
```

❶ Export an array of menu items for use in other parts of the project.

Transforming the data from a physical menu to this digital JSON-like structure will make it easier for you to systematically display relevant menu items to the restaurant's customers. Because operating hours are the same every day except for Monday and Sunday, the normal hours can be listed as defaultHours values in *operatingHours.js*.

Example 3-6. Hours data in operatingHours.js

```
export default { ❶
  defaultHours: {
    open: 11,
    closed: 22,
  },
  monday: {
    open: null,
    closed: null,
  },
  sunday: {
    open: 12,
    closed: 20,
  },
};
```

❶ Export an object with default operating hours and values for special cases.

To make use of this data, you import the two relative modules at the top of *index.js* (Example 3-7).

Example 3-7. Importing data modules into index.js

```
import operatingHours from "./data/operatingHours.js"; ❶
import menuItems from "./data/menuItems.js";
```

❶ Import custom modules from their relative data directory.

To test that these values are being loaded properly, you replace the return statements in the /menu and /hours routes with reply.send(menuItems) and reply.send(opera tingHours), respectively. Doing so should replace the static text you previously saw when loading your web page with more meaningful data provided by the restaurant. This step in the process helps you validate that the data you're expecting is properly flowing to the web pages you intend it to reach.

Restart your Node server and visit *http://localhost:3000/menu* and *http://localhost:3000/hours*. Your result for the menu page on your web browser should look like Figure 3-7.

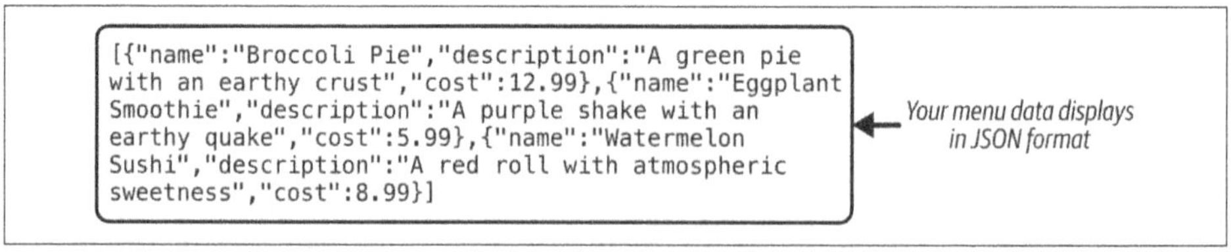

```
[{"name":"Broccoli Pie","description":"A green pie
with an earthy crust","cost":12.99},{"name":"Eggplant
Smoothie","description":"A purple shake with an
earthy quake","cost":5.99},{"name":"Watermelon
Sushi","description":"A red roll with atmospheric
sweetness","cost":8.99}]
```

Your menu data displays in JSON format

Figure 3-7. Menu data

46 | Chapter 3: Building a Node Web Server

With this data displayed on the browser, the next step is to format it to be more visually appealing.

Building Your UI

You could build a user interface using a frontend framework like React.js, Vue.js, or Angular.js. However, to keep this app simple, you'll set up server-side rendering (SSR) using Embedded JavaScript (EJS) templates with Fastify.

There are a variety of templating engines, such as EJS and Pug, that work well with Node and Fastify. Check out the EJS website (*https://ejs.co*) and the Pug website (*https://oreil.ly/EQ6xL*) to learn more about these tools.

On the command line, navigate to your project folder and run `npm install @fastify/view@^9.1.0 ejs@3.1.6`. This installs the `ejs` package, which facilitates converting HTML content with dynamic data into static HTML pages, and the `@fastify/view` Fastify plug-in, which allows you to use EJS as a templating engine in your Fastify project.

The `@fastify/view` plug-in is a Fastify plug-in that allows you to use a variety of templating engines with Fastify. This package is a separate plug-in in Fastify to maintain the framework's core philosophy of being lightweight, modular, and highly performant. For more information on how to use this plug-in, visit the Fastify website (*https://oreil.ly/3RRsh*).

Next, you configure Fastify to use the `ejs` templating engine (Example 3-8). Once configured, you can use Fastify's `reply.view` method to render pages with HTML and EJS templates.

Example 3-8. Updating Fastify routes to render EJS files in index.js

```
import ejs from 'ejs'; ❶
import fastifyView from '@fastify/view';
...
app.register(fastifyView, { ❷
  engine: {
    ejs: ejs,
  },
});

app.get("/", (req, reply) => {
  reply.view("views/index.ejs", { name: "What's Fare is Fair" }); ❸
```

Building Your UI | 47

```
});

app.get("/menu", (req, reply) => { ❹
  reply.view("views/menu.ejs", { menuItems });
});

app.get('/hours', (req, reply) => { ❺
  const days = [
    "monday",
    "tuesday",
    "wednesday",
    "thursday",
    "friday",
    "saturday",
    "sunday",
  ];
  reply.view("views/hours.ejs", { operatingHours, days });
});

app.listen({ port: 3000 }, (err, address) => {
  if (err) throw err;
  console.log(`Server running at ${address}`);
});
```

❶ Import the EJS templating engine and the Fastify view plug-in.

❷ Set EJS as your templating engine.

❸ Use `reply.view` to display the *index.ejs* page in your pages folder.

❹ Use `reply.view` to display the *menu.ejs* page in your pages folder, passing `menu
Items` data.

❺ Use `reply.view` to display the *hours.ejs* page in your pages folder, passing `opera
tingHours` and `days` data.

To properly render these pages, you need to create a folder called `views` at the root
level of your project and add three new files: *index.ejs*, *menu.ejs*, and *hours.ejs*. These
files will be located by the EJS templating engine in Fastify when a request is made to
the corresponding route. To complete the process, you can fill these files with a mix
of HTML and EJS. Example 3-9 shows an example of your landing page, *index.ejs*.

Example 3-9. Landing page content in index.ejs

```
<!DOCTYPE html> ❶
<html lang="en">

<head>
```

48 | Chapter 3: Building a Node Web Server

```
  <meta charset="UTF-8">
  <title>Restaurant</title>
</head>

<body>
  <h1>Welcome to <%= name %></h1> ❷
</body>

</html>
```

❶ Basic HTML5 structure with your main content in the body tag

❷ Text to display the dynamic `name` data from your *index.js* file

> EJS uses <%= %> to display content within the HTML. In Example 3-10 you use this syntax to display the business name. If you want to run JavaScript on the page without printing anything, leave out the =.

When you restart your project and visit *http://localhost:3000*, your browser should look like Figure 3-8.

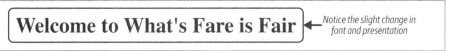

Figure 3-8. Browser rendering of index.ejs

You go on to add the same HTML structure to *menu.ejs* and *hours.ejs*. Modifying only the body tags of each, your *menu.ejs* will contain a `for` loop iterating over each menu item. From there you display the name, description, and cost of each item (Example 3-10).

Example 3-10. Menu page content in menu.ejs

```
<h1>Our Menu</h1>
<ol>
  <% for (let item of menuItems) { %> ❶
    <li>
      <strong><%= item.name %></strong> ❷
      <span><%= item.description %></span> ❸
      <span><%= item.cost %></span>
    </li>
  <% }%>
</ol>
```

❶ Loop through the `menuItems` values, assigning each object as `item` with each iteration.

❷ Display the menu item in bold.

❸ Display the description and cost alongside the name.

With this code in place, restart your node server and navigate to *http://localhost:3000/menu* in your web browser to see a page that looks like Figure 3-9.

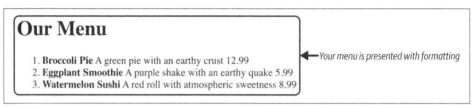

Figure 3-9. Browser rendering of menu.ejs

Similarly, in *hours.ejs*, you iterate over each day in your `days` array. From there, you determine whether you have data for that day to display, or simply use the default values previously defined. You use an `if-else` condition here in EJS to separate the UI for days that have hours to display and Monday, when the restaurant is closed (Example 3-11).

Example 3-11. Hours page content in hours.ejs

```
<h1>Our Hours</h1> ❶
<% for(let day of days) { %> ❷
 <% const hoursObj = operatingHours[day] || operatingHours['defaultHours'] %> ❸
 <section style="display: inline-flex; flex-direction: column; padding: 5px;">
    <h2><%= day.toUpperCase() %></h2> ❹
    <div>
      <% if (hoursObj.open) {%> ❺
        <p>Open: <%= hoursObj.open %></p> ❻
        <p>Closed: <%= hoursObj.closed %></p>
      <% } else {%>
        <p>CLOSED</p> ❼
      <% } %>
    </div>
 </section>
<% }%>
```

❶ Display the page name.

❷ Loop over `days`, assigning each value to `day` on each iteration.

❸ Define an hoursObj variable to contain the opening and closing hours data.

❹ Display the fully capitalized day name.

❺ Check whether the day has opening hours data.

❻ Display the opening and closing hours.

❼ Display the message when closed.

With this last page complete, you restart your node server and navigate to *http://local host:3000/hours* in your web browser to see a page that looks like Figure 3-10.

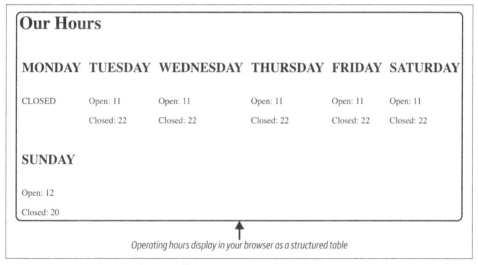

Figure 3-10. Browser rendering of hours.ejs

Admittedly, these pages aren't visually appealing, even though they display the required information for the restaurant. This is the stage where you might consider enhancing the UI with HTML, CSS, and client-side JavaScript. While these additions are out of scope for a server-side Fastify project, you can easily integrate them. To learn more about serving static assets like stylesheets and images in Fastify, visit the fastify-static GitHub repo (*https://oreil.ly/6wZLF*). Next, you'll explore how adding some basic styling can improve the look and feel of your web application.

Sprucing Up the UI

Building a full stack application typically involves work on both the frontend and backend. As a Node engineer, your primary focus will often be on the backend. As such, there's no hard requirement to be fluent in HTML or CSS, or their relative libraries and frameworks. It's best to commit time to building out the UI, or to allocate the work for someone with frontend experience.

To quickly add a CSS library to Fastify, start by creating a `public` folder at the root level of your project. Then, you need to install the `@fastify/static` by running `npm install @fastify/static@^7.0.4` at the root level of your project in the command line.

Next, register the `@fastify/static` plug-in in your *index.js* file to serve static assets from the public directory (Example 3-12). Once set up, you can add any *.css* files, images, or other static content to your public folder and access those resources directly in your EJS files. Then you'll need to reference your CSS files in the <head> tag of your EJS files. For example, `<link rel="stylesheet" href="public/style sheets/style.css" />` would link to a *style.css* in the *public/stylesheets/* folder.

Example 3-12. Adding static assets to your Fastify app in index.js

```
...
import fastifyStatic from '@fastify/static'; ❶
import { join } from "path"; ❷
const publicPath = join(process.cwd(), "public"); ❸
...

app.register(fastifyStatic, { ❹
  root: publicPath, ❺
  prefix: '/public/', ❻
});
...
```

❶ Import the `@fastify/static` plug-in, used to serve static files such as CSS, images, and other assets in Fastify.

❷ Import `join` from `path`, used to construct a cross-platform compatible file path to the `public` folder.

❸ Create an absolute path to the `public` directory at the root of your project.

❹ Register the `fastifyStatic` plug-in to enable serving static files.

❺ Set the directory `publicPath` from which static files will be served.

❻ Set the URL prefix for static files to `/public/`.

Look at Figures 3-11, 3-12, and 3-13 to see how the addition of stylesheets can improve the aesthetics of the pages you built.

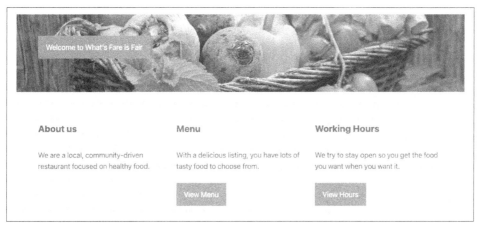

Figure 3-11. Browser rendering of styled index.ejs

The landing page can be designed with any layout you prefer. Fastify supports a wide range of templating engines, allowing for flexible and customizable layouts. Popular engines like EJS, Pug, and Handlebars can be easily integrated with Fastify using plug-ins. For more information on using templating engines with Fastify, visit the point-of-view GitHub repo (*https://oreil.ly/cruSV*).

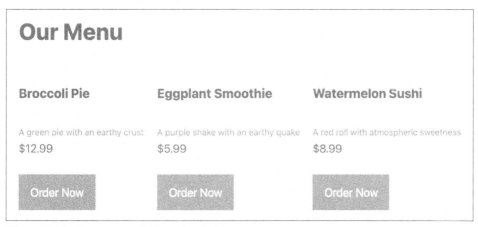

Figure 3-12. Browser rendering of styled menu.ejs

Sprucing Up the UI | 53

The menu UI immediately feels more familiar with a visual that indicates the customer may place an online order. Online purchasing can be added to a Node app like this. For now, it's simply a visual that may encourage the restaurant to invest more time to build a more robust application.

Our Hours						
MONDAY	TUESDAY	WEDNESDAY	THURSDAY	FRIDAY	SATURDAY	SUNDAY
CLOSED	Open: 11	Open: 11	Open: 11	Open: 11	Open: 11	Open: 12
	Closed: 22	Closed: 22	Closed: 22	Closed: 22	Closed: 22	Closed: 20

Figure 3-13. Browser rendering of styled hours.ejs

The hours of operation may be displayed in a variety of ways. In Figure 3-13, a flexbox style is added to ensure all days and times are spaced out without overlap.

If you have the time to dedicate to improving the UI of a Node web app, or if you can work alongside a frontend developer, you may find the end result more pleasing to your customer.

Chapter Exercises

1. Add a new page to your site:

    a. Create a new EJS template file called *about.ejs* inside your *views* folder.

    b. Add a heading and a short paragraph describing the restaurant's history or mission.

    c. In your *index.js* file, define a new GET route (/about) that renders the *about.ejs* view.

    d. Restart your Node server and navigate to *http://localhost:3000/about* to confirm it works.

Reuse the HTML structure from your other *.ejs* files for consistency.

2. Enhance the hours page with today's status:

   a. Update the /hours route handler to determine the current day using new Date().getDay() and map it to your days array.

   b. Pass an additional variable called today to your EJS template.

   c. In *hours.ejs*, highlight the current day using an if statement and apply a special CSS class or style to make it stand out visually.

These exercises reinforce how to pass and render dynamic data from your server to EJS templates—key skills in server-side web development.

Summary

In this chapter, you:

- Built a Fastify web server, learning how Node's event loop handles asynchronous requests and avoids blocking.

- Configured routes to serve dynamic content and organized your project using separate data modules.

- Implemented server-side rendering with EJS and improved the visual design of web pages using static assets.

- Integrated key Fastify plug-ins to enhance functionality and streamline your application.

CHAPTER 4
Build a Secure Local Password Manager

This chapter covers the following:

- Data hashing concepts
- Working with Bcrypt
- Saving data to a MongoDB collection

Building applications on the server provides immediate benefits over building on the client. One of those benefits is enhanced control over data security.

The server engineer is typically responsible for protecting data in the database, determining what data the client can view, and who can see it. For this reason, there are a multitude of hashing packages on the npm registry to use with Node to hide sensitive data from everyone other than the data's original owner.

Although it is commonly expanded as "Node Package Manager," npm is not officially an acronym. The creators of npm have stated that it originally stood for "npm is not an acronym."

In this chapter, you will build a password manager using the bcrypt hashing package and mongodb for persistent storage. You'll start by understanding what happens under the hood with hashing and how you can use this mechanism to build an effective productivity tool. Later, you'll introduce document storage with MongoDB to keep your hashed data for future access.

Tools and Applications Used in This Chapter

Before you get started, make sure to install and configure the tools and applications required for this project. Installation instructions for Node.js, Fastify, and VS Code are provided in Chapter 1, while project initialization steps, such as setting up your directory structure, configuring *package.json*, and using modern syntax, are covered in Appendix A. Installation instructions for MongoDB are available in Appendix C. Once completed, return here to continue. Building a project from scratch helps deepen your understanding of each component, giving you greater control and flexibility as you progress.

Your Prompt

Your blockchain startup, Crypto Spies, is growing. With each new service your company uses, you're finding it harder to keep track of your passwords, and you don't yet trust external companies to manage them for you. You decide to set a few hours aside and build your own password manager. This way, you can quickly access passwords from your homemade manager running on your computer.

Get Planning

You've decided that you want this Node application to run on your own machine, only allow access via a hashed password, and save your personal passwords in a database. To get this application working in only a short time, you choose an existing hashing library to hash your passwords, and MongoDB to store those passwords. Before you start programming, you diagram the requirements of the project and your result.

Figure 4-1 shows the flow of information for your completed application. Your application will store both a hashed master password and plain-text passwords. The following steps detail how the application should work:

1. To start, a master password is typed into your command line and sent to your Node application.

2. Your application logic hashes that password and saves it to your database.

3. The next time you access your application, you type your master password, which will be validated against your hashed password.

4. If the typed password matches your master password, you may choose to save personal passwords or view a list of saved passwords.

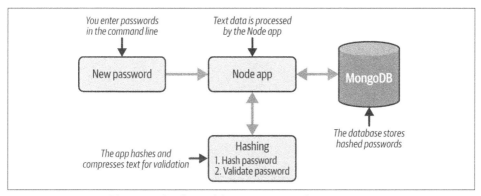

Figure 4-1. Project blueprint for flow of data in password manager app

As you type new passwords to save to your database, the password text enters into your Node app. From there, application logic hashes your password and saves it to your database. To retrieve that list of passwords, you must retype a master password that only you know.

Now, it's time to start coding.

Building a Local Command-Line Manager

It's best to build a simple version of your application and incrementally add capabilities. For your first version, you plan to build a Node application with the logic to hash your main password and store your list of other passwords in memory (this means the list gets deleted whenever you close your application process).

> Before you incorporate a database to save your data long-term, your computer has the ability to temporarily save the data in memory. This means that the data in your application is only preserved for as long as the application is running and the computer is turned on.

Start by creating a new project folder called *password_manager*. This folder may be created where you plan to save Node projects on your computer. Navigate to this folder on your command line and run `npm init` to initialize the Node project. Your initialization prompt should resemble Example 4-1.

Example 4-1. Prompt for `npm init`

```
package name: (password_manager)  ❶
version: (1.0.0)
description: A Node app for storing passwords
```

```
entry point: (index.js) ❷
test command:
git repository:
keywords:
author: Jon Wexler
license: (ISC)
```

❶ This is the name of your project.

❷ *index.js* is where your application will start.

Next, run `npm install bcrypt@^5.0.1` to install the `bcrypt` package. The `bcrypt.hashSync` function is one of many you can use to hash your password. The process of hashing your password involves two steps: hashing your password and validating a plain-text password against your hashed password. Figure 4-2 shows how the hashing function is a one-way procedure. In this way, it is very difficult to reverse engineer the original password from the hashed value.

First, you type the main password that you'll use to access your other passwords. Bcrypt's `hash` function uses a salt (randomly generated text) to jumble your password text a number of times equal to your salt rounds value. The resulting hashed password is then stored in your database. Later, when you type your password again to access your manager, your input text is again hashed and compared to the stored password hash. `bcrypt`'s `compare` function will evaluate your plain text against the hashed password. If your password matches the hashed password in your database, you are authorized. In this way, `bcrypt` does not reverse a hashed password, but instead rehashes a retyped password and compares the result with the password hash in the database.

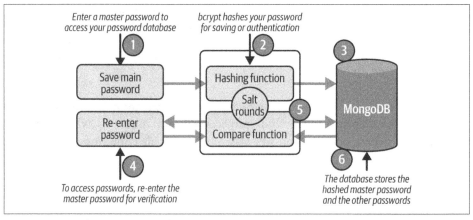

Figure 4-2. Hashing process with `bcrypt`

Now, create your *index.js* file at the root level of your project directory. This is where most of your application logic will live. You can test some of bcrypt's functions by adding the code in Example 4-2 to *index.js*.

Example 4-2. Testing bcrypt in index.js

```
import bcrypt from "bcrypt"; ❶
const password = "test1234"; ❷
const hash = bcrypt.hashSync(password, 10); ❸
console.log(`My hashed password is: ${hash}`); ❹
```

❶ Import the bcrypt package.

❷ Define a test password.

❸ Use the hashSync function to hash your password, with 10 salt rounds (a cost factor of 2^10 = 1024 iterations).

❹ Output your hashed password to your console.

With this code in place you can run `node index` at the root level of your project in your command-line window. Your resulting output should look like `My hashed password is: $2b$10$/mL0.3etH.eG1.tsFY` (with a different hash value, of course).

> If you don't see a logged statement in your command-line window, check to make sure your *index.js* file was saved in the same directory from which you're running the application.

With your test case working, you build out the functions needed to facilitate saving a new hashed password. Figure 4-3 demonstrates the flow of logic according to the function names you'll use. To start, your application runs a prompt function to enable user interaction on the command line. Then, you check whether there is already a stored master password hash. If a master password hash exists, you run promptOld Password to prompt the user to retype their password. Otherwise, you run prompt NewPassword to prompt the user to type a new master password for the first time. When the user types their new password, the saveNewPassword function will save the resulting hash to the database.

If the user types their existing master password, you compare their input to the stored password hash through compareHashedPassword. If their password is validated you display a menu of items to choose from through the showMenu function. Within this menu, the user may choose to view their list of passwords (viewPasswords), add a

Building a Local Command-Line Manager | 61

new password to your list (`promptManageNewPassword`), reverify your hashed password, or exit the app.

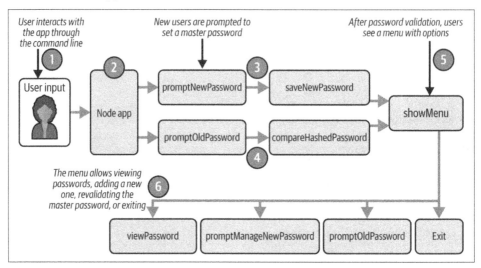

Figure 4-3. Code logic-flow diagram

The code for this logic can be written one function at a time. First, install the `prompt-sync` package by running `npm install prompt-sync@^4.2.0` at the root level of your project in your command line. Then, add the `bcrypt` and `prompt-sync` imports to your *index.js* file. Also, add a JavaScript object with a `passwords` key mapped to an empty object to represent your database. As you add new passwords to save, this object will get populated (Example 4-3).

 In other chapters the `prompt` package is used, which provides a different syntax for prompting the user in async functions than `prompt-sync`. Here, you are blocking further interactions with your app until prompts are responded to, due to their synchronous nature.

Example 4-3. Add module imports and mock db to the top of index.js

```
import bcrypt from "bcrypt"; ❶
import promptModule from "prompt-sync";
const prompt = promptModule(); ❷
const mockDB = { passwords: {} }; ❸
...
```

❶ Import `bcrypt` and `prompt-sync` packages.

❷ Instantiate `prompt` to use its async-await functionality.

❸ Define an object to represent the local database.

With your imports in place you can create your first function, `saveNewPassword`, which takes a plain-text password, `password`, as an argument and makes use of the Bcrypt `hashSync` function to convert the text to a hashed value. That resulting value is then set in the mock database, `mockDB`. You let the user know the password is saved with a log message, and then call the `showMenu` function, which you'll soon write (Example 4-4).

Example 4-4. Add the `saveNewPassword` function in index.js

```
...
const saveNewPassword = (password) => {
  mockDB.hash = bcrypt.hashSync(password, 10); ❶
  console.log("Password has been saved!"); ❷
  showMenu(); ❸
};
...
```

❶ Hash the plain-text password and save the password hash to the `hash` key in your local database.

❷ Print a message to the console.

❸ Call the `showMenu` function.

After the `saveNewPassword` is added, you'll create a function called `compareHashedPassword`, as shown in Example 4-5. In this function, you accept a plain-text `password` argument, which is compared to the stored password hash in `mockDB`. The resulting value is either `true` or `false`.

Example 4-5. Add the `compareHashedPassword` function in index.js

```
...
const compareHashedPassword = async (password) => ❶
  await bcrypt.compare(password, mockDB.hash); ❷
...
```

❶ Define a custom function to compare a plain-text password to a hashed password.

❷ Compare the input password to the value in your local database.

Building a Local Command-Line Manager | 63

The next two functions will prompt the user to type a new password or retype an old password (Example 4-6). promptNewPassword logs a message to the command-line console for the user to type their main master password. The typed password is subsequently saved in your saveNewPassword function. Meanwhile, promptOldPassword prompts the user to retype their old master password. The input text is validated, determining whether the user can view the menu by running showMenu, or if the password is incorrect, the user is prompted again until the correct password is entered.

Example 4-6. Prompting the user to type passwords in index.js

```
...
const promptNewPassword = () => {
  const response = prompt("Enter a main password: ");   ❶
  return saveNewPassword(response);   ❷
};

const promptOldPassword = async () => {
  let verified = false;   ❸
  while (!verified) {
    const response = prompt("Enter your password: ");   ❹
    const result = await compareHashedPassword(response);   ❺
    if (result) {
      console.log("Password verified.");
      verified = true;   ❻
      showMenu();   ❼
    } else {
      console.log("Password incorrect. Try again.");   ❽
    }
  }
};
...
```

❶ Prompt the user to type in a new master password.

❷ Save the user's input using saveNewPassword.

❸ Define a flag to track whether the password has been verified.

❹ Prompt the user to retype their existing master password.

❺ Compare the input against the stored hashed password.

❻ Set verification flag to true once the password is validated.

❼ Show the menu if the password is correct.

❽ Display an error and retry if the password is incorrect.

So far, you've added functions to facilitate the user's initial interactions and authentication. Example 4-7 adds code to show a menu of options to choose from once authenticated. showMenu logs four options for the user to select. The first option runs viewPasswords to show them all their saved passwords. Option 2 runs promptManage NewPassword to allow the user to save a new password to their database. The third option reruns promptOldPassword, allowing the user to revalidate their master password. Finally, the user may quit the application, exit, by selecting option 4. If none of the four options are chosen, the user will be notified and prompted to select again.

Example 4-7. Building the showMenu function in index.js

```
...
const showMenu = async () => {
  console.log(`
    1. View passwords
    2. Manage new password
    3. Verify password
    4. Exit`); ❶
  const response = prompt(">");

  if (response === "1") viewPasswords(); ❷
  else if (response === "2") promptManageNewPassword();
  else if (response === "3") promptOldPassword();
  else if (response === "4") process.exit();
  else { ❸
    console.log(`That's an invalid response.`);
    showMenu();
  }
};
...
```

❶ Prompt the user with four options to select.

❷ After selecting a value from 1 to 4, the user may view their passwords, add a new one, verify their main password, or exit the app.

❸ If no valid option is selected, the user is prompted again.

With the menu ready to display, you only need to add the functions to view stored passwords and add the functions to view and save passwords in memory. Add the code in Example 4-8, where viewPasswords destructures your passwords from the mockDB. With your passwords as a key/value pair, you log both to your console for each stored password. Then you show the menu again, which prompts the user to make another selection. promptManageNewPassword is the function that prompts the user to type the source for their password—effectively an application or website name for which they are storing their password. Then the user is prompted for a password

Building a Local Command-Line Manager | 65

they want to save. The source and password pair are saved to your mockDB and, again, you run showMenu to prompt the menu items.

Example 4-8. Adding the viewPasswords and promptManageNewPassword functions in index.js

```
...
const viewPasswords = () => {
  const { passwords } = mockDB; ❶
  Object.entries(passwords).forEach(([key, value], index) => {
    console.log(`${index + 1}. ${key} => ${value}`);
  }); ❷
  showMenu(); ❸
};

const promptManageNewPassword = () => {
  const source = prompt("Enter name for password: "); ❹
  const password = prompt("Enter password to save: ");

  mockDB.passwords[source] = password; ❺
  console.log(`Password for ${source} has been saved!`);
  showMenu(); ❻
};
...
```

❶ Destructure passwords from your mockDB.

❷ Iterate through passwords in your local database and log them to your console.

❸ Call showMenu to display the menu options.

❹ Prompt the user to add a new password and source name to manage.

❺ Save the source and password pair in mockDB.

❻ Call showMenu to display the menu options.

Your application is ready to run. The last piece to add is the code in Example 4-9. Here, mockDB is checked for an existing hash value. If one does not exist the user is prompted to create one through promptNewPassword. Otherwise, the user is prompted to retype their master password through promptOldPassword.

66 | Chapter 4: Build a Secure Local Password Manager

Example 4-9. Determine the entry point for your application in index.js

```
...
if (!mockDB.hash) promptNewPassword(); ❶
else promptOldPassword();
```

❶ Check whether you have a local password saved or if you need to type a new main password.

With this code in place you have most of the logic you need to run the password manager. The only downside is the local database temporarily stores your managed passwords while the application is running. Because the local database is only an in-memory object, it will get deleted each time you start your app.

To test this, go to the root level of your project folder in your command line and run node index. You should be prompted to type a new password like in Figure 4-4. After typing your password, it will be hashed by bcrypt and you'll see a menu of items to choose from.

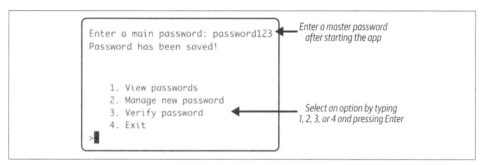

Figure 4-4. Typing your main password to access your application menu

From here you can select 2 and press Enter to add a new password to manage. Try typing a source like jonwexler.com and a password, as seen in Figure 4-5.

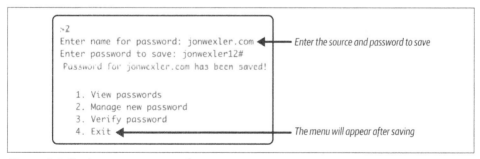

Figure 4-5. Saving a new password to manage

After pressing Enter, this password is saved to your in-memory object. You should then see the original menu items appear. Select 1 and press Enter to see the list of passwords now containing your `jonwexler.com` password (Figure 4-6).

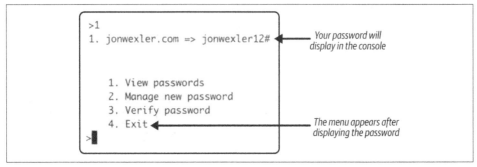

Figure 4-6. Selecting to view all managed passwords

You can also test your main password (the first password you typed when you started the app) by selecting 3 and pressing Enter. If you type in the wrong original password, you'll see a log statement letting you know the password is incorrect. Otherwise, you'll be prompted that the password matches the hashed password and returned to the menu.

Now you can safely exit the application by typing 4 and pressing Enter. This step safely kills the Node process and exits your command-line app. The next step is to add a persistent database so you don't have your passwords deleted every time you run your app.

Saving Passwords with MongoDB

After completing most of the logic of your Node app, the next step is to introduce a way to save application data when the application is no longer running. MongoDB is one database you can use to store this information. MongoDB is a document-oriented database manager, meaning it manages NoSQL nonrelational databases. Because your application is intended to store your own collection of passwords, using MongoDB collections is appropriate for this project.

In Figure 4-7 you see a diagram with an example of how your data could be stored. This structure is similar to JavaScript Object Notation (JSON), making it easier to continue to work with JavaScript on the backend. Notice that in this figure you store the `password_hash` as a hashed value for your main password. Then you have a list of `passwords` that map a `source` name to a plain-text `password`. Additionally, MongoDB will assign an `ObjectId` to new data items within a collection.

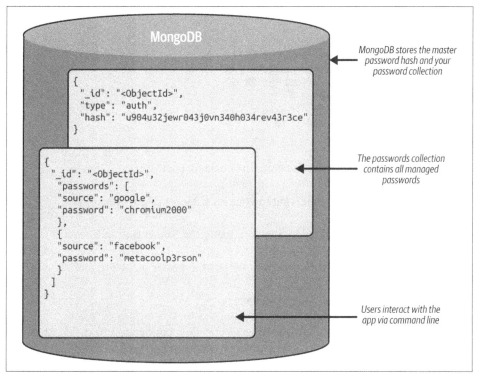

Figure 4-7. Diagram of saving passwords to MongoDB

For this section, you'll need to ensure MongoDB is properly installed. Visit Appendix C for installation steps.

Go to your project's root level at the command prompt and run `npm install mongodb@^6.8.0`.

Once installed, the `mongodb` package will provide your Node application the tools it needs to connect to your database and start adding data. For this reason, you no longer need your temporary in-memory storage, `mockDB`, from earlier in this chapter. Instead, you use the `MongoClient` to set up a new connection to your local MongoDB server. Your development server should be running at `mongodb://localhost:27017` on your computer. Last, you set up a database name, `passwordManager`, to connect.

In *index.js*, add the code in Example 4-10.

Example 4-10. Import mongodb and define database connection variables

```
...
import { MongoClient } from "mongodb"; ❶
const dbUrl = "mongodb://localhost:27017"; ❷
const client = new MongoClient(dbUrl); ❸
let hasPasswords = false; ❹
let passwordsCollection, authCollection;
const dbName = "passwordManager"; ❺
...
```

❶ Import the `MongoClient` class from the `mongodb` package.

❷ Define the `dbUrl` for connecting to your local MongoDB server.

❸ Create a new MongoDB client instance using the connection URL.

❹ Declare a `hasPasswords` flag to track whether a master password already exists.

❺ Set the database name to `passwordManager`.

Next, create an `async` function to establish your app's connection to the database. In Example 4-11 you'll find the code you need to add to connect to the database. The `client.connect` function will attempt to initiate a connection with your local MongoDB server. Then, `client.db(dbName)` will connect to a database by the name assigned to `dbName`. In your case, you'll have two MongoDB collections in the database: `authCollection` to handle storing your password hash, and `passwordsCollection` to store the list of passwords. Declare these variables at the top of *index.js*. Once connected, this function will search for an existing password hash by running `authCollection.findOne({ "type": "auth"})`. `hasPasswords = !!hashedPassword` converts the result from your search into a boolean value. In the end, you set `passwordsCollection` and `authCollection`.

> The reason you need an async function is that connecting to the MongoDB database is an asynchronous I/O operation. When you connect to a database and run a command, the time it takes to complete can vary. Using async-await lets us write this code in a way that looks synchronous, pausing execution at each `await` until we receive a response from the database, without blocking the rest of the application.

Example 4-11. main function to initialize the database

```
...
const main = async () => {  ❶
  try {
    await client.connect();  ❷
    console.log("Connected successfully to server");
    const db = client.db(dbName);  ❸
    authCollection = db.collection("auth");  ❹
    passwordsCollection = db.collection("passwords");
    const hashedPassword = await authCollection.findOne({ type: "auth" });  ❺
    hasPasswords = !!hashedPassword;  ❻
  } catch (error) {
    console.error("Error connecting to the database:", error);  ❼
    process.exit(1);
  }
};
```

❶ Define a function main to initialize your database.

❷ Call client.connect to establish a connection to your database server.

❸ Create or connect to a database with the name passwordManager.

❹ Find or create a database collection called authCollection and one called pass wordsCollection.

❺ Check if a hashed password with type of auth existed in your authCollection collection.

❻ Assign hasPasswords to the boolean value of your resulting search in the database.

❼ Catch any errors and exit the process if there is an issue connecting to the database.

At the bottom of *index.js* add the code in Example 4-12 to call the main function and begin processing your app. This code first runs the main function, which sets up the database connection and checks if a main password already exists. Based on the result, it either prompts the user to create a new main password if none exists (prompt NewPassword), or asks for the existing password to verify access (promptOldPass word).

Saving Passwords with MongoDB | 71

Example 4-12. Call main to set up MongoDB collections

```
...
await main(); ❶
if (!hasPasswords) promptNewPassword(); ❷
else promptOldPassword();
```

❶ Call `main`, used to assign the `passwordsCollection` and `authCollection` collections.

❷ Prompt the user to either create or verify a master password based on whether one exists in the database.

Now you can restart your Node application by exiting any running application and typing `node index`. If your application successfully connected to the database, you should see `"Connected successfully to server"` logged to your command line.

After saving passwords, if you want to delete the database of passwords and start from scratch, you can always add `await pass wordsCollection.deleteMany({})` or `await authCollection .deleteMany({})` to delete your passwords or main hashed password, respectively.

With your database connected, you need to modify some of your application logic to handle reading and writing to your MongoDB collections. Change `saveNewPassword` to become an `async` function. Within that function, assign a new variable `hash` to the result of `bcrypt.hashSync` and then save it to the database with `await auth Col lection.insertOne({ "type": "auth", hash })`. This will save the hashed password `hash` to the `authCollection` in your database.

Next, change the `compareHashedPassword` to `async`, and so the first line is `const { hash } = await authCollection.findOne({ "type": "auth"})`. This line will search your `authCollection` for a hashed password and send that to the `bcrypt` compare function.

You may want to check whether a password hash exists before running the `compare` function. If no password hash exists, you can return `false` to indicate that the password is not valid.

The last three functions to change are in Example 4-13. Here, `viewPasswords` is modified to pull all passwords (by source and password value) from your `passwords Collection`. `showMenu` will remain the same, but like the other functions will become async and, for readability, uses a `switch`/`case` statement. In this function you add `await` before each function call, as they are now performing I/O operations. Last, `promptManageNewPassword` uses the `findOneAndUpdate` MongoDB function to add a new password entry if it doesn't exist, or override and update a password entry if an old value exists. The options `returnDocument` and `upsert` tell the function to override the changed value and return a copy of the modified value when the save operation is complete.

Example 4-13. Adding database calls to functions in index.js

```
...
const viewPasswords = async () => {
  const passwords = await passwordsCollection.find({}).toArray(); ❶
  passwords.forEach(({ source, password }, index) => { ❷
    console.log(`${index + 1}. ${source} => ${password}`);
  });
  showMenu();
};

const showMenu = async () => {
  console.log(`
    1. View passwords
    2. Manage new password
    3. Verify password
    4. Exit`);
  const response = prompt(">");

  switch (response) {
    case "1":
      await viewPasswords(); ❸
      break;
    case "2":
      await promptManageNewPassword();
      break;
    case "3":
      await promptOldPassword();
      break;
    case "4":
      process.exit();
    default:
      console.log("That's an invalid response.");
      await showMenu();
  }
};

const promptManageNewPassword = async () => {
  const source = prompt("Enter name for password: ");
  const password = prompt("Enter password to save: ");
  await passwordsCollection.findOneAndUpdate(
    { source },
```

Saving Passwords with MongoDB | 73

```
    { $set: { password } },
    {
      returnDocument: "after",
      upsert: true,
    }
  ); ❹
  console.log(`Password for ${source} has been saved!`);
  showMenu();
};
```

❶ Query all passwords from the `passwordCollection`.

❷ Iterate through the passwords and log them to the console.

❸ When the user input is "1", run the `viewPasswords` function.

❹ Use `findOneAndUpdate` to look for an existing password that matches your `source` and then set the new `password`.

With this code in place, you have a fully functional database to support your password manager application. Quit any previously running Node application and restart the application by running `node index`. Nothing should change about the prompts you see in the command line. Only this time, the values you type will persist even when you quit the application.

With this application complete, you can always run the application locally and add or retrieve passwords secured behind your hashed main password. Some next steps you could take would be to add a client with a UI to help with visualizing your password data or setting up your database in the cloud so that your passwords are persistent from computer to computer.

Chapter Exercises

1. Make the hashing process configurable:

    a. Update your `saveNewPassword` function to use a configurable number of salt rounds instead of a hardcoded value (e.g., `10`).

    b. Prompt the user to enter the number of salt rounds when they create their master password. This value controls how computationally expensive the hash operation is.

    c. Store the chosen salt rounds alongside the hashed password in your `authCollection`, for example: `{ type: "auth", hash, saltRounds }`.

74　|　Chapter 4: Build a Secure Local Password Manager

d. When verifying the password later, retrieve the stored salt rounds and reuse them when comparing the typed password with the stored hash.

Increasing salt rounds improves security but slows performance. Try experimenting with different values (e.g., 8, 12, 15) and observe the impact on runtime.

2. Allow password retrieval by source name:

   a. Add a new CLI option to your main menu: `5. Find password by source`.

   b. When selected, prompt the user to enter a source name (e.g., `gmail`).

   c. Query the `passwords` collection for that specific source and print its corresponding username and password.

   d. If no match is found, display a helpful message like `"No password saved for that source."`

These exercises strengthen your understanding of secure hashing configuration and introduce real-world database querying patterns based on user input.

Summary

In this chapter, you:

- Built your own password manager application
- Implemented secure password hashing logic utilizing the `bcrypt` package
- Set up a MongoDB database collection for passwords
- Configured Node to use the `mongodb` package with user input

CHAPTER 5

Content Aggregation Feed

This chapter covers the following:

- Parsing and displaying data from RSS feeds
- Fetching content from multiple sources using modern APIs
- Creating a real-time feed reader using Node
- Allowing user input to extend the aggregated results

Dashboards are the cornerstone of modern data visualization, enabling users to track metrics, monitor trends, and stay informed in real time. While dashboards often rely on APIs to fetch and display data, one of the original tools for content aggregation was the Really Simple Syndication (RSS) feed. RSS organizes content—typically in XML format—into structured feeds that present snippets of text, headlines, and the latest updates from various sources. This allowed users to skip manually visiting multiple websites and instead view curated updates in a single custom reader.

Though RSS feeds have waned in popularity, their underlying architecture remains highly relevant. Combined with modern APIs, they provide a powerful framework for creating versatile content aggregation platforms that can pull data from diverse sources.

In this chapter, you'll go beyond RSS to build a content aggregator that integrates both RSS feeds and APIs. You'll learn how to fetch and process data in XML and JSON formats, normalize and combine it into a unified structure, and serve the aggregated content through a command line or web client. By the end, you'll have a modern aggregator capable of delivering real-time, relevant data from multiple sources—all in one place.

Tools and Applications Used in This Chapter

Before you get started, make sure to install and configure the tools and applications required for this project. Installation instructions for Node.js, Fastify, and VS Code are provided in Chapter 1, while project initialization steps, such as setting up your directory structure, configuring *package.json*, and using modern syntax, are covered in Appendix A. Once completed, return here to continue. Building a project from scratch helps deepen your understanding of each component, giving you greater control and flexibility as you progress.

Your Prompt

Your coworkers at the office are passionate about food and love discussing the latest trends, recipes, and innovations. However, with content scattered across websites, blogs, and social media, it's become a challenge to stay informed. While sharing links in the group chat helps, you know there's a better way to keep everyone in the loop.

You decide to build a unified content aggregator for your company, pulling in the latest food-related articles, social media posts, and industry updates from both RSS feeds and APIs. Whether it's the buzz about plant-based steak or the hottest new food truck in town, your aggregator will ensure everyone gets fresh and relevant updates in one place. With this project, you'll create a centralized hub for all things food, combining the best of RSS and modern API integration into a "Feeding" feed.

Get Planning

The goal of this project is to build an app that aggregates new and relevant content from multiple sources for a large group of people. While popular content aggregation apps exist, you'll design your own Node app to combine data from RSS feeds and modern APIs. You'll start by experimenting with existing RSS and API packages available on npm. From there, you'll follow the design requirements of the project, as shown in Figure 5-1.

In this diagram, you can see the flow of logic and information. Starting from the client (any computer or device with a network connection), a request is made to your Node app to fetch the latest aggregated content. Your app processes data from multiple sources, including RSS feeds and APIs, normalizing and parsing it into a unified format. It then returns a summary list of results that can be displayed on your command-line client or a web interface. This layout ensures a seamless flow of real-time updates from diverse content sources.

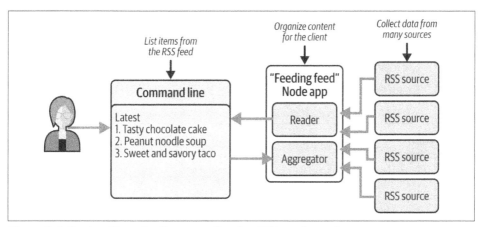

Figure 5-1. Project blueprint for an application RSS reader and aggregator

Before you start coding, it's helpful to review how RSS works and understand the type of data you'll encounter. RSS operates by pulling content from various sources across the web, often from news sites or blogs that want to provide their audience with quick and easy access to top headlines or updates. For example, you could use the *Bon Appétit* recipes RSS feed for your app, which is available at *https://www.bonappetit.com/feed/recipes-rss-feed/rss*. You can view the raw feed content by clicking the link in your web browser, as shown in Figure 5-2.

RSS feeds typically use XML (Extensible Markup Language), a structured data format with tags similar to HTML. The XML structure helps organize the feed's data into sections, making it easier to parse and use. An RSS feed's XML file usually starts with an rss tag to define the document type, followed by a channel tag containing metadata about the feed, such as the name, link, and language of the source. Within the channel tag, you'll find the main content items, each wrapped in an item tag. Each item contains details like a title, description, and publication date. Your task will be to extract these items and reformat them for display in your app.

While XML is the traditional format for RSS feeds, it's only one of many data formats used in modern web applications. APIs often provide data in JSON, which is more compact and widely used. This project will focus on parsing XML for RSS while also exploring JSON-based APIs, allowing you to combine and present data from multiple sources seamlessly.

Get Planning | 79

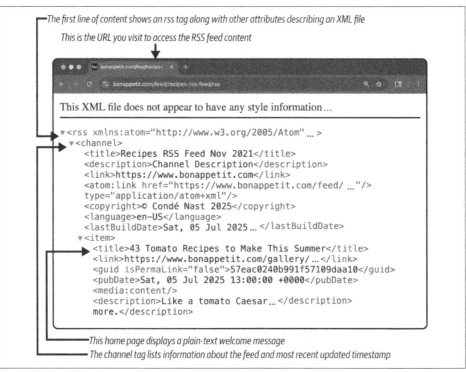

Figure 5-2. RSS feed results for Bon Appétit *recipes in the browser*

The first step in building an application that can use XML data is to call the RSS feed URL directly from within your Node app. Get started by creating a food_feeds_rss_app folder and navigating to the project folder in your command line. From here, run npm init to initialize the Node app with the default configurations, as shown in Example 5-1.

Example 5-1. npm init configurations for your app

```
{
  "name": "food_feeds_rss_app",   ❶
  "version": "1.0.0",
  "description": "",
  "main": "index.js",
  "scripts": {
    "test": "echo \"Error: no test specified\" && exit 1"
  },
  "author": "Jon Wexler",
  "license": "ISC"
}
```

❶ Add your project name to reflect the type of RSS feeds you'll support.

With your app initialized, add "type": "module" to your *package.json* file. This will allow you to use the import syntax for external packages. Next, create an *index.js* file to act as an entry point for your application. Add the code in Example 5-2 to *index.js*. This code uses the Fetch API to make a request to the *Bon Appétit* RSS feed URL and access its XML data. Because you await for a response, you wrap the fetch call in an async function called main. You assign the url variable to the *Bon Appétit* RSS feed endpoint. Then, you assign the response from your fetch call to response. You may now use the response.text() function call to extract the XML data for output to your console.

As of Node v18.0.0, the fetch API is available natively and can be used without installing any external packages. For earlier versions of Node, you'll need to install the node-fetch package by running npm install node-fetch in your project directory.

> ## More on the Fetch API
>
> JavaScript offers multiple ways to access content over HTTP. The foundational XMLHttpRequest interface powers most browser-based AJAX requests, while server-side JavaScript includes the built-in http library, which comes prepackaged with Node. Over time, many external packages have built upon the http module to provide more robust and user-friendly solutions for handling HTTP requests.
>
> The Fetch API was introduced to JavaScript to provide a modern, flexible interface for fetching resources from the web. Its key advantage lies in its Request and Response objects, which encapsulate common functionalities for making and processing HTTP requests asynchronously. Fetch also integrates seamlessly with JavaScript's Promise and async/await syntax, making it more intuitive and efficient for developers to handle asynchronous operations.
>
> Due to its popularity and widespread use, Fetch was added to Node in 2022, starting with version 18.0.0. This addition allows developers to use Fetch natively on the server side without relying on external packages. Fetch's versatility and modern design make it an essential tool for building applications that require HTTP communication.
>
> Learn more about the Fetch API at the official documentation (*https://oreil.ly/M2lPI*).

Example 5-2. Example of fetching an RSS feed using `fetch` in index.js

```
const main = async () => { ❶
  const url = "https://www.bonappetit.com/feed/recipes-rss-feed/rss";
  const response = await fetch(url); ❷
  console.log(await response.text()); ❸
}
main(); ❹
```

❶ Define an async function to encapsulate the HTTP request logic.

❷ Make a GET request for the provided URL.

❸ Use the response `text()` to read the response body as a string and log it to the console.

❹ Call your `main` function.

Save your file, navigate to your project folder in your command line, and run `node index`. You should see the same XML output as you saw by visiting the URL in a web browser, but this time it's printed to your command-line window. With this text output, you could parse each line and extract the information you need. Luckily, there are external packages that help make that process easier for you. In the next section you'll implement the `rss-parser` package.

Reading and Parsing a Feed

Your "Feeding feed" app is designed to both collect data and output it to your users in a meaningful way. Raw XML isn't particularly easy or interesting to read. The tech community recognizes that, and, sure enough, there are a multitude of external libraries to install that can help you. One of those libraries is in the `rss-parser` package. This package encompasses both the fetching of a feed and the parsing of its XML contents. You can install this package by going to your project's root level on your command line and running the command `npm install rss-parser@^3.13.0`.

Once the package is installed, you'll notice that your *package.json* file added a new dependency, and a folder called `node_modules` was created at your project's root level. Next, import the `rss-parser` package into your app by adding `import Parser from 'rss-parser';` to the top of your *index.js* file. On the following line, you instantiate the `Parser` class by adding `const parser = new Parser();`.

Uppercase `Parser` represents the `Parser` class from the `rss-parser` package, while lowercase `parser` is the instance of that class you create to use in your app.

Now you have a `parser` object you can use in place of your Fetch API code. Replace the contents of your `main` function with the code in Example 5-3. This code implements the `parser.parseURL` function by fetching the contents of your RSS feed URL and preparing them in a structured format. You'll then have access to the feed title and items. In the end, you only log what you want to show from that feed. In this case, it's the item title and link.

Example 5-3. Fetching and parsing an RSS feed using `rss-parser` in index.js

```
...
  const url = "https://www.bonappetit.com/feed/recipes-rss-feed/rss";
  const {title, items} = await parser.parseURL(url);  ❶
  console.log(title);  ❷
  const results = items.map(({title, link}) => ({title, link}));  ❸
  console.table(results);  ❹
...
```

❶ Fetch and parse the RSS feed XML, and destructure the response to access the `title` and `items`.

❷ Print the feed's title.

❸ Extract only the `title` and `link` of each item and assign that new array to `results`.

❹ Print the feed contents to your console in a structured table format.

`console.log` is by far the most used logging and debugging function. However, there are other logging types you may use like `console.table`, which prints your content in a format that's easier to read than the former function. Learn more about `console.table` in Mozilla's web APIs reference pages (*https://oreil.ly/qH035*).

After adding the `rss-parser` code, save your file, navigate to your project's root level on your command line, and run the command `node index`. Your output should look similar to that in Figure 5-3.

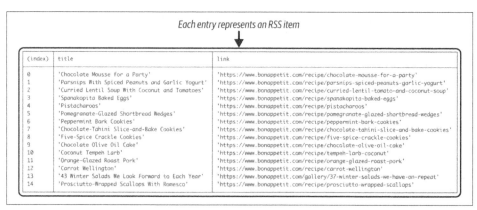

Figure 5-3. Console output for a table of RSS feed items

This output shows you recipe titles and their corresponding URLs. This is a great way to summarize the contents of the *Bon Appétit* recipes RSS feed, though this list is static and processes content only the moment you run your app. Because this feed receives updates, it would be ideal for your Node app to reflect those updates in real time. To fetch new updates every two seconds, change your call to main() at the end of *index.js* to setInterval(main, 2000). setInterval will keep your Node process running indefinitely, processing a new URL request, parsing, and logging every two seconds (two thousand milliseconds). To make this more apparent in your console, add console.clear(); in *index.js* right above the console.table line to clear your console with each interval. Also, add console.log('Last updated ', (new Date()).toUTCString()); right below the table log to print an updated timestamp. Now, when you run your app, while you may not see the feed contents change immediately, you'll notice the updated timestamp changes with each interval.

This command-line RSS reader is a great way to have the latest updates from your favorite RSS feed endpoints running on your computer. In the next section, you'll add more external feeds and build your own aggregator to show only the most relevant content.

Building an Aggregator

With your Node app successfully printing RSS feed content to your console, you may be wondering how you can expand the tool to be more practical. After all, your goal is to collect particular recipes that align with the dietary preferences of your coworkers. The good news is your app is designed to handle more content. With the logic in place to fetch one RSS feed, you can add more feed URLs to call.

RSS feeds can stop working if publishers change or discontinue them. If a feed no longer updates, check for a new URL or an alternate source.

To test fetching from multiple URLs, you can use the Budget Bytes feed and the Reddit /r/Recipes subreddit feed. Both of these feeds offer varying content at different times, making it more of a challenge to parse. To incorporate these additional feeds, you add *https://www.budgetbytes.com/category/recipes/feed/* and *https://www.reddit .com/r/recipes/.rss* to the list of URLs to explore at the top of *index.js* (Example 5-4). The urls constant will later be used to cycle through each URL and collect its corresponding XML response.

Example 5-4. Defining the list of URLs to read from in index.js

```
const urls = [   ❶
  "https://www.bonappetit.com/feed/recipes-rss-feed/rss",
  "https://www.budgetbytes.com/category/recipes/feed/",
  "https://www.reddit.com/r/recipes/.rss"
];
...
```

❶ Assign a list of URL strings to urls.

With this list in place, you may now modify the main function by iterating through each URL to fetch feed content (Example 5-5). First, assign a constant feedItems to an empty array: this is where your eventual feed items will be stored. Next, iterate through the urls array using the map function, which will visit each URL and run the parser.parseURL function to return a Promise in its place. In the following line, you use Promise.all which waits for all the requests to external URLs to return with responses before completing. Each response will be stored in a responses array. Last, you use a custom aggregate and print function to sift through the responses and log your desired output, respectively.

Example 5-5. Defining the list of URLs to read from in index.js

```
const main = async () => {
  const feedItems = [];   ❶
  const awaitableRequests = urls.map(url => parser.parseURL(url));   ❷
  const responses = await Promise.all(awaitableRequests);   ❸
  aggregate(responses, feedItems);   ❹
  print(feedItems);   ❺
}
```

❶ Define a `feedItems` array to store RSS feed items.

❷ Run `parser.parseURL` on each URL, which returns a `Promise` object to eventually return a response from the external RSS endpoint.

❸ Collect responses by awaiting all `Promises` to complete their requests.

❹ Pass the responses and `feedItems` array to a custom `aggregate` function to combine the RSS feed results.

❺ Pass the resulting `feedItems` array to a custom `print` function to log to your console.

Before rerunning your application, you need to define the `aggregate` and `print` functions. Add the code in Example 5-6 below your `main` function. In the `aggregate` function, you collect all the feed data from each external source and, for this project, only retain the items that contain recipes with vegetables. First, loop through the array of responses and examine only the items within each XML response. Then, an inner loop visits each item and destructures the `title` and `link` only, because these are the only pieces of data you care about in this project. With access to each item's title, you check if the title `includes` the string veg. If that condition passes, you add an object with the `title` and `link` to your `feedItems` array.

In your `print` function, you accept `feedItems` as an argument. Next, you clear the console of previous logs using `console.clear`. Print your `feedItems` to your console using `console.table`, and then log your `Last updated` time by generating a new `Date` object and converting it to a human-readable string.

Example 5-6. Defining the `aggregate` and `print` functions in index.js

```
...
const aggregate = (responses, feedItems) => { ❶
  for (let {items} of responses) { ❷
    for (let {title, link} of items) { ❸
      if (title.toLowerCase().includes('veg')) { ❹
        feedItems.push({title, link});
      }
    }
  }
  return feedItems; ❺
}

const print = feedItems => {
  console.clear(); ❻
  console.table(feedItems); ❼
```

86 | Chapter 5: Content Aggregation Feed

```
console.log('Last updated ', (new Date()).toUTCString()); ❽
}
```

❶ Pass your RSS responses and `feedItems` array to the `aggregate` function.

❷ Loop through each feed response and access its `items` array.

❸ Loop through each item, extracting only the `title` and `link`.

❹ If the `title` contains the substring "veg" (case-insensitive), add the item to `feedItems`.

❺ Return the filtered `feedItems` array.

❻ Clear previous logs from the console.

❼ Print the filtered items as a table.

❽ Display the time of the last update in UTC format.

Now, restart your application. You'll notice this time there are fewer results logged to your console (Figure 5-4), but the items shown are from varying sources—all with titles indicating some vegetable or vegetarian recipe. You can modify the aggregate condition to your liking by focusing on other key words, or even examining data other than the `title` and `link` used in this example.

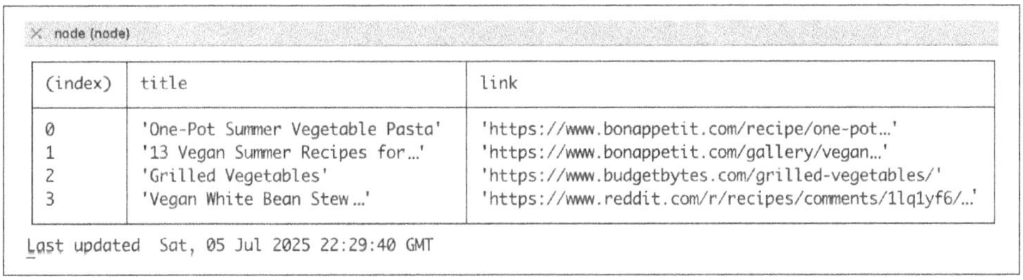

```
✕  node (node)

 (index)   title                            link

 0         'One-Pot Summer Vegetable Pasta'  'https://www.bonappetit.com/recipe/one-pot...'
 1         '13 Vegan Summer Recipes for...'  'https://www.bonappetit.com/gallery/vegan...'
 2         'Grilled Vegetables'              'https://www.budgetbytes.com/grilled-vegetables/'
 3         'Vegan White Bean Stew...'        'https://www.reddit.com/r/recipes/comments/1lq1yf6/...'

Last updated  Sat, 05 Jul 2025 22:29:40 GMT
```

Figure 5-4. Console output for an aggregated table of RSS feed items

Ultimately, when you share this aggregator with your colleagues, they can add any additional RSS source URLs to increase the quantity of meaningful results. Before you wrap this project up, you decide to add one more feature: adding custom items to the feed.

Adding Custom Items to Your Aggregator

Most RSS aggregators collect only the results from external feeds and aggregate the results according to some defined rules. It's not very often you have the opportunity to modify the resulting aggregated list with content not found anywhere else. The client for this project has been your command-line console. However, it's possible to convert this app into a web-accessible tool with the help of a web framework. With a web framework, you can publish the aggregator and allow anyone to read the resulting feed items on their own browser. However, you do not need to rely on the web, or a browser, to design a standalone Node app.

To collect user typed input, install the `prompt-sync` package by running `npm install prompt-sync@^4.2.0` at the root level of your project in your command line. Then, in *index.js* add `import promptModule from 'prompt-sync';` to the top of your file, followed by `const prompt = promptModule({sigint: true});` to instantiate the prompt function with a `sigint` config that allows you to exit your app. Last, add `const customItems = [];` to define an array for your custom feed items. Next, you modify the `print` function by adding the code in Example 5-7 to the top of that function. The `prompt` function will show `Add item:` on your console and wait for a typed response. When the Enter key is pressed, the input is saved to a `res` constant. User input should be in the format: `title + , + link`. Then, the `title` and `link` are extracted by splitting the resulting input string. The new custom item object is added to your `customItems` global constant array.

Example 5-7. Modify the `print` function to accept user input in index.js

```
const res = prompt('Add item: '); ❶
const [title, link] = res.split(','); ❷
if (![title, link].includes(undefined)) customItems.push({title, link}); ❸
...
```

❶ Prompt the user to add a new feed item title and link.

❷ Split the input string with a comma delimiter to destructure a `title` and `link`.

❸ Add the resulting item object to `customItems` if neither the title or link is missing.

Finally, modify your log statement to include your `customItems` array by replacing that line with `console.table(feedItems.concat(customItems));`. Now, when you restart your app, you should see a prompt for a custom feed item. If you have nothing to add, simply press Enter. Otherwise, you may add a custom recipe like `Jon's`

---

88 | Chapter 5: Content Aggregation Feed

famous veggie dish,http://jonwexler.com/recipes and press Enter to add it to
your aggregated items feed. Your result should look like Figure 5-5.

```
X  node (node)
   (index)   title                               link
   0         'One-Pot Summer Vegetable Pasta'    'https://www.bonappetit.com/recipe/one-pot…'
   1         '13 Vegan Summer Recipes for…'      'https://www.bonappetit.com/gallery/vegan…'
   2         'Grilled Vegetables'                'https://www.budgetbytes.com/grilled-vegetables/'
   3         'Vegan White Bean Stew…'            'https://www.reddit.com/r/recipes/comments/1lq1yf6/…'
   4         "Jon's famous veggie dish"          'http://jonwexler.com/recipes'

Last updated  Sat, 05 Jul 2025 22:35:50 GMT
Add item: ▌
```

Figure 5-5. Console output for an aggregated table with custom feed items

Now you have an app you can share with others in your office. You can use the aggregator to collect relevant recipes every two seconds (or at an interval of your choice). You can also add custom links not found in your external sources. When users of your app publicize their results, everyone can benefit from your new aggregated collection of quick-access recipe links. You may continue developing the application to make it accessible across a shared network, or build a web framework with a database into your app to allow web clients to access the feed data.

Chapter Exercises

1. Add a configurable keyword filter to your aggregator:

    a. Modify the aggregator so users can specify a keyword at runtime (e.g., "vegan," "chili," "salad") instead of hardcoding `'veg'`.

    b. Use `prompt-sync` to ask for a keyword before `main()` runs, and store that keyword in a global variable.

    c. Update your `aggregate()` function to filter titles based on whether they include the specified keyword (case-insensitive).

    d. Run your app and test how the feed changes when using different keywords.

> If you want to make it even more dynamic, consider letting users change the keyword live during each update cycle.

Adding Custom Items to Your Aggregator | 89

2. Display how recently each feed item was published:

a. Update the `aggregate()` function to also include the `pubDate` field (if available) from each item.

b. In the `print()` function, compute the age of each item in minutes or hours by comparing `pubDate` to `new Date()`.

c. Display the age of each item in your table under a new column like `Age` or `Published`.

d. If an item is missing a `pubDate`, show `Unknown` or `--`.

These exercises give your aggregator more control and transparency: users can filter results by their interest and see how fresh each item is—just like in a professional news reader.

Summary

In this chapter, you:

- Built an RSS feed aggregator using Node and `rss-parser`
- Retrieved and parsed feed data from external sources using API calls
- Added support for custom user-submitted items via the command line
- Displayed aggregated content in a readable table format
- Enhanced your aggregator with features like keyword filtering and publish-time tracking

CHAPTER 6

Library API

This chapter covers the following:

- Constructing an API with Fastify.js
- Building REST endpoints
- Connecting to a relational database

Although most people are familiar with the internet by way of their web browser, most activity and data transfer happens behind the scenes. Some data, like real-time train schedules, is made available not as just a standalone web app, but as a resource others can use and implement into their own apps. This resource is called an Application Programming Interface (API), and it allows its users to view all or some available data belonging to a restricted environment (like the railroad authority). Some APIs allow the addition, modification, and deletion of data, especially if it's your own data or if you are the authority over that resource itself.

In this chapter, you'll build a RESTful API, meaning it will support access and modification of data through a standard protocol. You'll also connect the API to a database—to which you can add new information and from which you can access older records. In the end, you'll have the translatable skills needed to build an API for just about any type of data.

91

> **Tools and Applications Used in This Chapter**
>
> Before you get started, make sure to install and configure the tools and applications required for this project. Installation instructions for Node.js, Fastify, and VS Code are provided in Chapter 1, while project initialization steps, such as setting up your directory structure, configuring *package.json*, and using modern syntax, are covered in Appendix A. For a deeper explanation of SQLite concepts, see Appendix C. Once completed, return here to continue. Building a project from scratch helps deepen your understanding of each component, giving you greater control and flexibility as you progress.

Your Prompt

Your township is awarding grants to individuals who can modernize the public library. At the top of their list is building a system allowing the public to request books not yet provided or in low supply at the library. Grants have already been handed out to groups designing the mobile and web clients, but there's still a need for someone to build the backend API. You are somewhat familiar with Node and Fastify and decide to take on the challenge.

Get Planning

The goal of this project is to build an API that mobile and web apps can connect to in order to view, add, update, or delete book records. Just like on a website's URLs, you'll create an API that provides endpoints (URIs) accessible by other clients. To start, you'll create a Node app with the Fastify framework and gradually add pieces to support interactions with the library data and persist that data in a database. You follow the design requirements of the project, as shown in Figure 6-1.

Uniform Resource Identifiers (URIs) are a superset of endpoints used to access resources or data. In this case, a URI is used to fetch data from an API. Uniform Resource Locators (URLs) are a subset of URIs, typically associated with accessing a web address.

This diagram shows four behaviors corresponding to HTTP actions (GET, PUT, POST, and DELETE), which you'll need to implement in the API. When a request is made to the API, your app must distinguish among these four request types and perform the relevant app logic on the requested data. In other words, if someone wants to submit a book recommendation, don't accidentally delete a different book from your database. At the end of development, you'll be able to test your API on your web browser, command line, or third-party application like Postman.

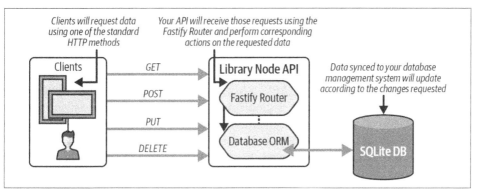

Figure 6-1. Project blueprint for a Node API using four HTTP methods

HTTP Methods

Hypertext Transfer Protocol (HTTP) is an internet protocol used by websites and applications to transmit data across the web. HTTP offers an architecture and semantics for sending packets of data from one IP address to another. Part of this architecture includes defined methods for requesting data.

There are nearly 40 HTTP methods that can be used, though only a handful make up the majority of requests made across the internet. The following HTTP methods are ones that you'll use in this book:

GET
: This request method is used whenever someone visits a landing page or web page with static content. It constitutes the majority of requests on the internet and is the simplest one to implement in your API.

POST
: This request method is used whenever data is sent to a server; for example, if a user logs in to their account. These requests are necessary for most data to eventually enter a database and allow for information to persist across web sessions.

PUT
: This request method is similar to POST in that it sends data in the body of the request. However, this method is used in practice to update or modify existing data on the server. These requests are distinguished from POST data, typically, by an ID that matches a record on the server's database.

DELETE
: This request method effectively sends a primary key to the server, indicating a record that should be deleted. The nature of a DELETE request looks similar to a GET, but unlike the latter, it expects to change the state of data on the server.

> While there are many other request methods used across HTTP, these four are
> enough to get started with developing an API. For more information on HTTP meth‐
> ods, visit Mozilla's HTTP reference pages (*https://oreil.ly/bMdS9*).

Because the library wants your API to bring visibility to popular and sought-after books, the data served by your API should have enough information to identify those books and the level of interest. By the time your database is set up, you'll want to store the title and author of the book, as well as a count of how many requests that book received. In this way, mobile and web clients that use your API can notify the library and its patrons of the most popular requests.

Figure 6-2 shows the flow of data during a POST request for a new book. That request contains the title and author of the book. If the book already exists in the database, its request count increases. Otherwise, that book's record is added to the database for the first time with its own serial ID.

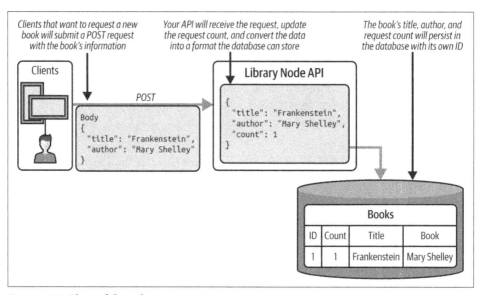

Figure 6-2. Flow of data during a POST request

Once there is some persisted (stored) data, library clients are able to send a GET request using that book's persistent ID (Figure 6-3). The GET request needs to send only an ID parameter, but in turn receives all of the book's data.

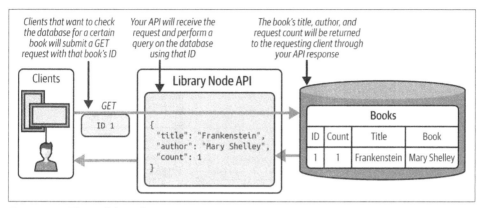

Figure 6-3. Flow of data during a GET request

If a library admin notices a mistake in the book's data, they can modify the title or author and submit a PUT request. In Figure 6-4, a PUT request is sent with updated book information, such as correcting a title or author name. That new data is processed within your API and saved to the database under the same record ID.

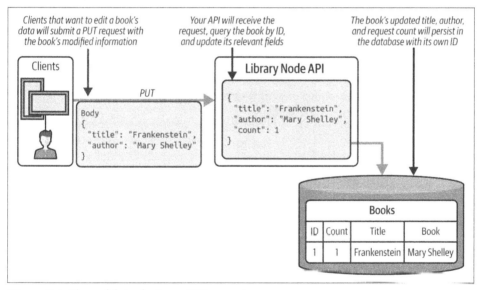

Figure 6-4. Flow of data during a PUT request

Last, if the library obtains enough copies of a certain book to satisfy its patrons, they can submit a DELETE request to remove that book from the database. Figure 6-5 shows that a DELETE request only needs the book's ID as a parameter. From there, the API can perform a delete query on the database.

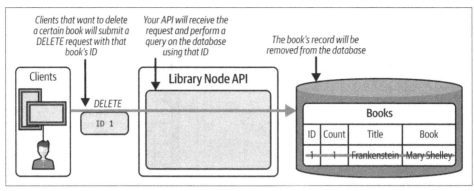

Figure 6-5. Flow of data during a DELETE request

With the architecture and data structures defined, you're ready to start building your API with Node and Fastify. In the next section, you lay out the building blocks for a typical Node app.

Get Programming with an API Layout

To start developing your app, create a new folder named `library_api`. Navigate to your project folder on your command line and run `npm init`. This command initializes your Node app. You can press Enter throughout the initialization steps. The result of these steps is the creation of a file called *package.json*. This file instructs your Node app of any configurations or scripts needed to operate.

Next, create a file called *index.js* within your project folder. This file acts as the entry point for your app.

> ### Additional Steps to Enhance Your App
>
> This book encourages you to build each project from scratch. For that reason, installation steps for Node.js, Git, and VS Code are provided in Chapter 1, while project initialization details—like directory structure, package setup, and modern syntax—are covered in Appendix A. To continue building your app, complete the steps in those sections before proceeding.

To set up your app as an API, you install Fastify by navigating to your project folder on your command line and running the command `npm install fastify@^5.4.0`. This command installs Fastify and adds it as a package dependency in your *package.json* file. With Fastify installed, you import its module and initialize a new Fastify app instance (*instantiate*), called `app`, as shown in Example 6-1. While developing the app, you define the API PORT as 3000 and use the `app.listen` function to set your API to listen for requests on that port number.

Example 6-1. Instantiating your Fastify app and starting to listen for requests in index.js

```
import Fastify from 'fastify'; ❶
const app = Fastify(); ❷
const PORT = 3000; ❸

try {
  await app.listen({ port: PORT }); ❹
  console.log(`Listening at http://localhost:${PORT}`);
} catch (err) {
  console.error(err);
  process.exit(1);
}
```

❶ Import the Fastify module.

❷ Instantiate Fastify to create your API app instance.

❸ Assign the PORT constant to 3000.

❹ Use top-level `await` to start the Fastify server without needing a wrapper function.

Your app is now ready to accept any HTTP requests. For now, you can test this by running `npm start`. You'll notice the command-line console prints a statement, `Listening at http://localhost:3000`, to indicate that your app is running.

With the nodemon package installed, you need to run `npm start` only once while developing your app. Every change you make to the project thereafter automatically restarts your Node process and reflects the changes immediately. See Appendix B for more information on installing nodemon.

Your app is ready to process requests. However, to support an API, you need to instruct Fastify on the type of data your app anticipates receiving. Fastify allows you to register plugins or rely on built-in parsing, which processes incoming requests before you get to see what's inside.

Middleware functions, as the name implies, sit between the request being received by your app, and the request being processed by custom app logic. Here, you rely on Fastify's built-in JSON body parsing, which handles incoming requests with JSON data.

Because this API expects to receive and serve JSON data, it's necessary to ensure this parsing capability is enabled.

Similarly, registering the `@fastify/formbody` plugin allows the Fastify API to parse and understand URL-encoded requests. This helps with deciphering strings that were modified and encoded for better efficiency over the web. Fastify automatically parses standard nested data structures when this plugin is used.

Run the command `npm install @fastify/formbody@^8.0.2` on your command line and add the code in Example 6-2 below your `PORT` definition in *index.js*.

Example 6-2. Adding JSON and URL-encoded parsing support to your Fastify app in index.js

```
...
import formbody from '@fastify/formbody'; ❶
await app.register(formbody); ❷
...
```

❶ Import the Fastify plugin that enables URL-encoded form parsing.

❷ Register the plugin to add support for parsing `application/x-www-form-urlencoded` requests.

To complete the first stage of building your API, add the code in Example 6-3 right below your middleware functions. In this block, `app.get` defines a route which listens for GET requests only. The "/" indicates that your app is listening for requests made to the default URI endpoint: *http://localhost:3000/*. That means if the HTTP request uses the GET method and targets the default URI, the provided callback function is executed. Fastify provides your callback function with a request (`request`) and response (`reply`) object as parameters.(request objects The `request` object is used to examine the contents of the request, while the `reply` object lets you assign values and package data in the response to the client.

 By some conventions, variables that are not used in a function, but still defined, have an underscore applied to their name. This helps the next engineer know not to expect that variable to have any behavior in the function. For that reason, the request argument in this example is called `_request`.

Once a request is processed, you use the `reply.send` function to reply to the client with structured JSON containing a key called `message` and value of "ok". This response indicates to the client that the API server is functioning correctly.

In Example 6-3, `app.setNotFoundHandler` sets up a function to handle all other requests that are not handled by your `GET` route. This is called a *catch-all* error-handling middleware. In this function, the error object, `e`, is the first argument passed in. In this way, if an error occurs, your app won't just crash, but it will return a status code of 500 (internal server error) instead.

Example 6-3. Adding a GET route in index.js

```
...
app.get("/", async (_request, reply) => {  ❶
  reply.send({ message: "ok" });  ❷
});

app.setNotFoundHandler((request, reply) => {  ❸
  const { message, statusCode } = request.error || {};  ❹
  reply.status(statusCode || 500).send({ message });  ❺
});
...
```

❶ Add a `GET` request for the main URI endpoint.

❷ Respond with a JSON message.

❸ Define error-handling middleware with an error argument.

❹ Destructure the `message`, `stacktrace`, and `statusCode` from the error.

❺ Respond with the error JSON message and relevant status code.

Save your changes and navigate to *http://localhost:3000* in your web browser. You should see `{ message: "ok" }` printed on the screen.

If you don't see a message appear in your browser, it's possible that the URL or port number was entered incorrectly. Also, make sure that your server is running. In case of a server error, it's possible that the server will exit its process and wait for your fix before restarting.

In the next section you'll add the other necessary routes to support your library API.

Adding Routes and Actions to Your App

Your app is running, but lacks the ability to differentiate between request types. Moreover, you'll eventually need the ability to create, read, update, and delete

(CRUD) your data. These four actions map to the four main HTTP methods you'll support with Fastify routes. From this point forward, you'll refer to the callback functions within your Fastify routes as your CRUD actions.

Before you add more code to *index.js*, it's important that your project structure is maintained and organized. So far, you have one JavaScript file in your project. By the end of this section, your project directory structure should look like Example 6-4. Now you'll introduce a new folder to separate your routing logic from the rest of your app logic.

The node_modules folder is automatically generated and appears within your project folder whenever you install a new external package.

Example 6-4. Routing directory structure layout

```
library-api ❶
  |
  - index.js
  - routes ❷
    |
    - index.js
    - booksRouter.js
  - package.json
  - node_modules
```

❶ The root level of your project directory tree contains four children.

❷ The routes folder stores the routes for handling book-related transactions.

Navigate to your project folder in your command line and create a new folder called routes. Within that folder create two new files, *index.js* and *booksRouter.js*. Within the *booksRouter.js* file add the code from Example 6-5.

This code introduces a Fastify plugin function. The function contains Fastify's framework logic for handling all types of internet requests. You've already used the Fastify app instance to create a GET route in *index.js*. Now, you're going to more explicitly define your routes inside a reusable plugin you call booksRouter.

This custom router is named booksRouter because it is used only to define routes that have to do with creating, reading, updating, or deleting book records. The first of those routes is the GET route, which is registered using fastify.get(). Within this function, "/:id" indicates that a value can be passed into the endpoint, and Fastify should translate that parameter as a variable by the name id. This way, when a client asks for the book record by ID 42, you can use the integer 42 to query your database for a book with a matching primary key. Next, you destructure the id value from the request's params object.

Because there is no database set up yet, you return the ID to the client in a JSON structure. You wrap the response in a try/catch block; in case anything goes wrong, you'll be able to log your errors to the API server. If something doesn't work as expected, you call reply.send(err) to return the error to the client using Fastify's built-in error handling.

Example 6-5. Adding a GET route for books in booksRouter.js

```
async function booksRouter(fastify, _opts) { ❶
  fastify.get("/:id", async (request, reply) => { ❷
    const { id } = request.params; ❸
    try {
      const book = { id }; ❹
      reply.send(book); ❺
    } catch (e) {
      console.error("Error occurred:", e.message); ❻
      reply.send(e); ❼
    }
  });
}
```

❶ Define a Fastify plugin function that takes in the Fastify instance and optional parameters.

❷ Register a GET route with a dynamic :id parameter.

❸ Destructure the id value from the request's route parameters.

❹ Create a book object with the given ID.

❺ Send the book object as a JSON response to the client.

❻ Log any caught errors to the server console.

❼ Respond with the error using Fastify's error handling mechanism.

To test this, add export default booksRouter to the bottom of your *booksRouter.js* file to allow this module to be accessed elsewhere in your application. Next, open the *index.js* file within your project's routes folder and add the code in Example 6-6. Similar to the code in *booksRouter.js*, this *index.js* registers the booksRouter plugin with the Fastify instance. However, this file does not define new routes, but simply

Adding Routes and Actions to Your App | 101

organizes the existing routes under a namespace. `fastify.register(booksRouter, { prefix: '/books' })` instructs the server to handle all requests with a /books URI path using the `booksRouter` routes. After this change, you'd expect a GET request to be sent to *http://localhost:3000/books/42* for a book with ID 42.

Example 6-6. Registering your app routes in routes/index.js

```
import booksRouter from "./booksRouter.js"; ❶

async function routes(fastify, _opts) { ❷
  fastify.register(booksRouter, { prefix: "/books" }); ❸
}

export default routes; ❹
```

❶ Import the `booksRouter` plugin from *booksRouter.js*.

❷ Define a Fastify plugin function to group and register all your routes.

❸ Register `booksRouter` under the /books namespace.

❹ Export the plugin so it can be used in your main app file.

With the `routes` plugin set up, you import this plugin into *index.js* at your project's root level by adding `import routes from './routes/index.js';`. Then, you register this plugin with your Fastify instance by adding `app.register(routes, { prefix: "/api" });` right above the error handling block in *index.js*. This new code defines an additional namespace called /api. This will be the final namespace change and will allow you to make GET requests to the /api/books/:id route path.

RESTful Routes

This project uses routing to navigate incoming requests through your app. A *route* is simply a way to get from a specified URI endpoint to your app logic. You can create any types of routes you choose, with whatever names you'd like, and as many dynamic parameters. However, the way you design your routing structure has side effects and consequences for those using your API.

For that reason, this project uses Representational State Transfer (REST) as a convention for structuring your routes. REST provides a standard URI endpoint arrangement that lets its users know what type of resource they should expect to get in return. For example, if you are looking for a particular book in the database, your endpoint could be: /Frankenstein/database_books/return_a_book/. While this route path includes most of the information needed to get the book's details, it does not follow RESTful conventions and would likely differ in structure from other routes in your API—making it harder to use consistently.

A RESTful API empowers its users to quickly and easily understand which part of the route path refers to the resource name and which parts include the necessary data for a database query. In this way, a route like /books can be used for both a GET and POST request, with the server understanding that different logic handles each request for the same resource: books. Furthermore, a route like /books/:id adds to the resource name, but provides a dynamic parameter: id. This standard structure makes using and designing an API straightforward and convenient for everyone involved. For more information on RESTful routing, visit Mozilla's REST glossary page (*https:// oreil.ly/WQ8bJ*).

Now, restart your app if it's not already running and navigate to *http://localhost: 3000/api/books/42* in your web browser. You should see { "id": "42" } printed in your window. With your GET route working, it's time to add the routes for POST, PUT, and DELETE. Conveniently, your PUT and DELETE routes look identical to your GET route. All three require an id param. Duplicate the GET route twice, but change one of the duplicates' route method to fastify.put and the other to fastify.delete. This addition should be enough to test those routes.

For the POST route, add the code in Example 6-7 right above your export default booksRouter line at the bottom of *booksRouter.js*.

In this route, fastify.post is used to have Fastify listen for POST requests specifically. Within the action, you destructure the title and author from the request body and return them to the client in JSON format. The body of a request is typically where you'll find request data when posting to create or change information on the server.

Example 6-7. Adding a POST route for books in booksRouter.js

```
...
fastify.post("/", async (request, reply) => { ❶
  const { title, author } = request.body; ❷
  try {
    const book = { title, author }; ❸
    reply.send(book);
  } catch (e) {
    console.error("Error occurred:", e.message);
    reply.send(e);
  }
});
...
```

❶ Register the POST route for books.

Adding Routes and Actions to Your App | 103

❷ Destructure the `title` and `author` from the request body.

❸ Assign the `title` and `author` to a const, book, and return the JSON value to the client.

With these last changes, it's time to test your other non-GET routes. To test these routes, you open a new command-line window and run a cURL command against your API server.

 Client URL (cURL) is a command-line tool for transferring data across the network. Because you are no longer only requesting to see data, you can use this approach to send data to your server directly from your command line.

1. Test the GET route again by running:

   `curl http://localhost:3000/api/books/42`

   The resulting text on your command-line console should read `{"id":"42"}`.

2. Submit a POST request by entering:

   `curl -X POST -d \`
   `'title=Frankenstein&author=Mary Shelley' http://localhost:3000/api/books/`

   This command uses `-X` to specify a POST method and `-d` to send request body data. The result of this command should look like `{"title":"Frankenstein","author":"Mary Shelley"}`.

3. Next, try a PUT request by running:

   `curl -X PUT -d \`
   `'title=Frankenstein&author=Mary Shelley' http://localhost:3000/api/books/42`

   This request contains both an ID and data in the body. Your response should show `{"id":"42"}`.

4. Last, run:

   `curl -X DELETE http://localhost:3000/api/books/42`

   to see the same `{"id":"42"}` response for a DELETE request.

Now that all four routes are accessible, it's time for the final piece of the puzzle: persistent storage in a database.

Connecting a Database to Your App

Data storage can work simply or balloon into a complex problem, depending on how you architect your app. Due to Node's popularity, just about any type of data store and database management system can be used with JavaScript. For this project, you can choose whether to use a NoSQL database like MongoDB, or a SQL (relational) database.

Despite not yet introducing other types of data other than book titles and authors, you choose to save your data in relational database tables. You figure that eventually this project might incorporate the massive amounts of information elsewhere in the library system, and so a relational database may be appropriate.

> There is no wrong choice when it comes to database selection. At this stage in the project's development, all popular database options will work fine.

Although you've narrowed your decision to a SQL database, there are many different database management systems to choose from. You decide to compare using a SQLite DB and a PostgreSQL DB.

> ## Comparing SQLite and PostgreSQL
>
> SQLite and PostgreSQL are two of the most widely used Relational Database Management Systems (RDBMS). While SQLite is capable of handling data in most cases, as its name implies, this RDBMS is lightweight and requires significantly less setup than other systems. SQLite is considered an *embedded* database because it requires no additional server to connect to the database. In this way, SQLite is the preferred choice for quickly developing an app for demonstration, or even for long-term use in an app with minimal traffic.
>
> PostgreSQL, like SQLite, is open source and supports a relational structure between data elements. PostgreSQL adds another layer by supporting object-relational mapping, which supports persistent storage of more data types in application code. PostgreSQL runs on a separate server, which adds more overhead to the overall development process.
>
> To learn more, read the article "SQLite vs PostgreSQL: 8 Critical Differences" (*https://oreil.ly/Hj9Mz*).

Overall, although both databases are sufficient for this project, you find that SQLite will get your app up and running the fastest.

You start to incorporate SQLite by installing its most recent npm package and running the command `npm install sqlite3@^5.1.7`. Now that you have an RDBMS installed, you could just connect to the database and start running SQL queries to search, save, modify, and destroy data. But what's the fun in developing a Node API if you couldn't do it all purely in JavaScript?

Install another package called `sequelize` by running `npm install sequelize@^6.37.7` in your command line. `sequelize` is an object relational mapper (ORM) between JavaScript objects and SQL databases. With this package installed, you can define JavaScript classes with `sequelize` and have them automatically map functions to their corresponding SQL queries. So no SQL knowledge is needed for this project (or, really, any in this book).

Before you continue, take a look at your project directory. In this last section you'll add two more subfolders, as shown in Example 6-8. Create the first folder, `models`, and within it create a file called *book.js*. This file contains the code needed by Sequelize to map your book data to the database. Next, create the `db` folder. Within this folder create a file called *config.js*, which will contain all the configurations needed to set up your database. After adding all the required changes, your database will live within the application folder in a file called *database.sqlite*.

Example 6-8. Project directory structure with a database

```
library-api ❶
  |
  - index.js
  - routes
    |
    - index.js
    - booksRouter.js
  - models ❷
    |
    - book.js
  -db ❸
    |
    - config.js
    - database.sqlite
  - package.json
  - node_modules
```

❶ The root of your project contains your main app file, folders for routes, models, and database configuration, plus your *package.json* and dependencies.

❷ The `models` folder stores all the data classes mapped between your app and the database.

❸ The db folder contains your database connection logic and the SQLite database file.

Open your *config.js* file and add the code in Example 6-9. In this code, you import Sequelize and instantiate a new database connection using SQLite, defining the storage location within the db folder of your project. You then authenticate the connection to the database through db.authenticate(). If the connection is successful, you'll get a logged statement indicating so. Otherwise, you'll log the error that occurred while trying to connect. Luckily, there is no additional server to run with SQLite, so there should not be many issues to troubleshoot at this step. At the end of the file you export both the Sequelize class and db instance.

Example 6-9. Setting up the database configuration in config.js

```
import { Sequelize } from "sequelize"; ❶

const db = new Sequelize({ ❷
  dialect: "sqlite",
  storage: "./db/database.sqlite",
});

try {
  await db.authenticate(); ❸
  console.log("Connection has been established successfully.");
} catch (error) {
  console.error("Unable to connect to the database:", error); ❹
}

export default { ❺
  Sequelize,
  db,
};
```

❶ Import the Sequelize class from the sequelize package.

❷ Instantiate a new Sequelize database connection, db, using SQLite.

❸ Await a connection to the database with db.authenticate().

❹ Log an error message if the database fails to connect.

❺ Export both the Sequelize class and the database instance.

The database is almost ready to get fired up, but first it needs some data to map in your app. Add the code from Example 6-10 to *book.js*. In this file you import the database configs and destructure the Sequelize and db values. Then you use the `db.define` function to create a Sequelize model called `Book`. This model name later maps in the SQLite database to create a corresponding table of the same name. The fields of this model reflect the data your library wants you to store:

- A title as a string (`title`)
- Author name as a string (`author`)
- Number of requests made for the book as an integer (`count`)

These fields are all that's needed to save countless book records in your database (though you will be counting). `Book.sync` will initiate a sync with the database and set up a table called `Books`. At the end of the file, you export the model for use back in your *booksRouter.js* file.

Passing the option `{force: true}` to `Book.sync` ensures that with each startup of the app, the sync function attempts to create a fresh table if any changes occurred since the last run. This is helpful in development if you don't want to fill your database with too many test records.

Example 6-10. Defining a Book model in book.js

```
import config from '../db/config.js'; ❶
const {Sequelize, db} = config; ❷

const Book = db.define('Book', { ❸
  title: { ❹
    type: Sequelize.STRING,
    unique: true
  },
  author: { ❺
    type: Sequelize.STRING
  },
  count: { ❻
    type: Sequelize.INTEGER,
    defaultValue: 0
  },
}, {});

Book.sync(); ❼

export default Book; ❽
```

❶ Import all configs from *config.js*.

❷ Destructure `Sequelize` and db from your config module.

❸ Define the Book model with `Sequelize`.

❹ Define a `title` field as a string that may not have a duplicate value in the database.

❺ Define an `author` field as a string.

❻ Define a `count` field as an integer that will increment with each `POST` request.

❼ Sync the Book model with the SQLite database.

❽ Export the Book model.

With your Sequelize model set up, you'll need to revisit the CRUD actions you previously built in *booksRouter.js*. These actions currently return the data they receive. Now that you have access to a database, you can add the logic needed to support actual data processing in your API.

First, import your Book model into *booksRouter.js* by adding `import Book from '../models/book.js';` to the top of the file. This gives access to the Book ORM object and allows you to create, read, update, and delete Book data. Change the values assigned to the `book` and `books` variables in each route to use the result of your database queries (Example 6-11).

The first change makes a call to `Book.findByPk`, where the `id` from your request params is passed in as a primary key to search within the database for a matching book record. You use the `await` keyword as you're making an asynchronous call to the database and need to wait for the result before continuing. The next change is to the `POST` request, `app.post`, where you use the `Book.create` function and pass in the `title` and `author` you retrieved earlier from the request body. You wait for the `create` function to complete and return the resulting created record to the client. Similarly, the `Book.update` also takes in the `title` and `author` as parameters, but this time they reflect the changed `title` and `author` values. A second parameter in this `PUT` request uses a `where` key to identify the record to update by its primary key: `id`. Last, `Book.destroy` uses the `where` key to search for a record by the specified `id` in the `DELETE` request and removes that matching record from the database.

For more information about model query types and the sequelize API, visit the Sequelize API references (*https://oreil.ly/VwOSc*).

Connecting a Database to Your App | 109

Example 6-11. Updating routes with the Book model in booksRouter.js

```
...
// GET /books/:id
const book = await Book.findByPk(id);  ❶
...
// POST /books/
const book = await Book.create({title, author});  ❷
...
// PUT /books/:id
 const book = await Book.update({title, author}, {  ❸
    where: { id },
  });
...
// DELETE /books/:id
const book = await Book.destroy({  ❹
  where: { id }
});
...
```

❶ Runs a query to find a Book by its primary key

❷ Runs a query to create a new Book record with a title and author field

❸ Runs a query to find a Book by its primary key and update the author and title fields

❹ Runs a query to find a Book by its primary key and delete it from the database

> The response from the PUT and DELETE routes is not the updated or deleted record, but rather the number of records affected by the query. This is because these actions do not return the updated or deleted record by default.

Now test your changes, only this time there are different outcomes because each command results in a database action. Notice the id field that is returned in some of the responses. Also notice the updatedAt and createdAt fields that Sequelize adds automatically to keep track of when data has entered the database or changed. Return to your command line, open a new window, and run the following cURL commands:

1. Submit a POST request by entering curl -X POST -d 'title=Frankenstein&author=Mary Shelly' http://localhost:3000/api/books/. This command uses -X to specify a POST method and -d to send request body data. The result of this command should look like {"count":0,"id":1,"title":"Frankenstein",

"author":"Mary Shelly","updatedAt":"2025-07-13T21:37:53.372Z","creat
   edAt":"2025-07-13T21:37:53.372Z"}.

2. Test the GET route again by running curl http://localhost:3000/api/books/1. The resulting text on your command-line console should read {"id":1,"title":"Frankenstein","author":"Mary Shelly","requests":null,"createdAt":"2025-07-13T21:37:53.372Z","updatedAt":"2025-07-13T21:37:53.372Z"}. This record was saved to the database in the last request. Now it is retrievable by ID.

3. Next, try a PUT request by running curl -X PUT -d 'title=Frankenstein&author=Mary Shelley' http://localhost:3000/api/books/1. This request contains both an ID and data in the body. Your response should show [1] to indicate that 1 record was changed. You may run the GET request again to see the updated value.

4. Last, run curl -X DELETE http://localhost:3000/api/books/1 to see 1 as your response for a DELETE request to indicate that one record was deleted. Running the GET request again should return null, as the record no longer exists.

If you run the POST request a second time with the same data, you get a Validation error in your server's console. This is expected by design, because your Book model has a validation criteria that new books should have unique titles.

Your API is now set up to handle new incoming requests to create, read, update, and delete Book records. If you choose to expand your API, you can add new models or modify the logic in your existing actions.

Chapter Exercises

1. Count requests for existing books before creating a new entry:
   a. Update your POST /api/books route to check if a book with the same title already exists in the database.
   b. If the book exists, increment its count field by 1 and save the update instead of creating a new record.
   c. If the book does not exist, create a new book entry with count initialized to 1.
   d. Test your changes using multiple POST requests for the same title and ensure the count increases correctly.

Connecting a Database to Your App | 111

Use Book.findOne({ where: { title } }) to check for duplicates, then call .save() after modifying the count.

2. Support listing all books in the database:
   a. Add a new GET /api/books route that returns all books in the database.
   b. Use Book.findAll() to fetch the complete list of records.
   c. Respond to the client with a JSON array of all stored books.
   d. Test your endpoint in a browser or with curl http://localhost:3000/api/books.

This allows the library to view all requests in a single place, and optionally sort or filter them on the client side.

Summary

In this chapter, you built a fully functional API with Node and Fastify. Moreover, you added a SQL database and used the Sequelize library to persist data processed in your API logic. With the skills you've learned from this chapter, you may now:

- Design and organize custom RESTful APIs
- Build an API that connects to any SQL database using Sequelize
- Extend your API with new endpoints and resource models

CHAPTER 7

Natural Language Processor Sentiment Analysis

This chapter covers the following:

- Processing text using machine learning–powered libraries
- Wrapping a machine learning model in a Node service
- Building an interactive command-line app

In this chapter, you'll build a sentiment analysis app using Node and natural language processing (NLP) techniques to interpret emotional tone from everyday text and gain practical experience working with machine learning (ML) in JavaScript.

Through these techniques you'll learn the ways of an ML engineer and build your own ML-driven Node app. ML has been growing in importance through its use in technology in just about every industry. As a subset of artificial intelligence (AI), ML teams from startups to enterprise companies are racing to deliver an experience that most closely mimics what you'd expect from a human expert. If you're new to ML, then all you need to know is that a lot of math and statistics are performed on data from the real world to provide you with a JavaScript function that can take an input and offer a result, such as a sentiment score, based on patterns learned during training on labeled datasets. If you are familiar with how ML works, then it's likely you've learned about the various models in use today. An ML model is what data scientists will train in order to build a function that generalizes well to new, unseen inputs.

From helping predict your next purchase, to movie recommendations and facial recognition, there is nearly no limit to what ML models could be used for. Historically, technology has depended on manual conditions (pretty much if statements), or rules, for drawing concluding results. Gradually, languages like Python, which now dominates the ML space, began to offer new tooling and development support for building new models. Fast-forward a couple decades, and now JavaScript engineers can use Node to build comparable models. This means you can also build ML models to recognize objects in an image, build dynamic pricing or stock market forecasting apps, or use NLP to analyze a string of text in a number of ways.

Tools and Applications Used in This Chapter

Before you get started, make sure to install and configure the tools and applications required for this project. Installation instructions for Node.js, Fastify, and VS Code are provided in Chapter 1, while project initialization steps, such as setting up your directory structure, configuring *package.json*, and using modern syntax, are covered in Appendix A. For a deeper explanation of SQLite concepts, see Appendix C. Once completed, return here to continue. Building a project from scratch helps deepen your understanding of each component, giving you greater control and flexibility as you progress.

Your Prompt

A local therapy clinic, Woes Disposed, has been encouraging its clients to write a sentence in their personal journals every hour. The therapists find that self-reflection throughout the day can help enrich one's perspective on life. They also believe that if the client can get immediate feedback on whether their journal entry was positive or negative, it would help track their mood throughout the day and further their development. Ultimately, this practice would like you to build an app to analyze journal text and visualize its sentiment analysis.

Get Planning

The goal of this project is to build an app that can output whether a given input string is a positive or negative statement. The app might ultimately be used through a web client, but can exist with a CLI to start. As strings—say one to three sentences—are typed into the command line, your app should break down the elements of the sentence, analyze the word arrangements, and return a numeric score representing the sentiment of the text. You know that there are npm packages that can help you do just that, and your experience with server-side JavaScript makes it easy to implement this logic in a Node app. You draw up a diagram detailing how your app will handle the flow of data from the client and back in Figure 7-1.

---

114 | Chapter 7: Natural Language Processor Sentiment Analysis

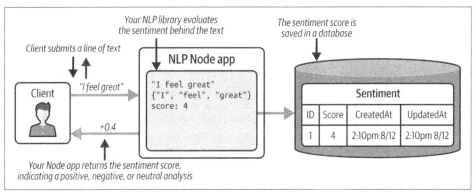

Figure 7-1. Project blueprint for a Node app analyzing text sentiment

Because traditional programming languages aren't well-suited to interpreting natural language text, you'll need the help of ML models. You could train your own NLP ML model, though that would entail getting hundreds of thousands, if not hundreds of millions, of samples of text labeled by humans as either positive or negative, and continuously adjusting various parameters until it properly analyzes new sentences. Fortunately, this work has already been done by the open source community, offering you already trained and proven models you can use on ordinary English text.

NLP aims to improve a computer's ability to understand human text. Sometimes that can be useful for correcting syntax and grammar, identifying similar sentences, and in your case, measuring the sentiment behind the text. However, human language is complicated. English, in particular, has many irregularities, verb conjugations, and multiple meanings for a given word—not to mention that punctuation and misspelled words can impact the results of an NLP model. For that reason, NLP models offer additional tooling to clean your text before analyzing it.

Cleaning Your Input Text for NLP Analysis

Written English can have multiple interpretations to the reader. For example, "I've not been happy to date" could imply that you are not happy to go on a date, or that you've never been happy in general. This is often confusing for human interpreters, and therefore a challenge for computers to solve. Although confusing sentences may continue to pose an obstacle for NLP models, there are some methods that help reduce a complicated sentence to its linguistically fundamental structure. These preprocessing steps are commonly applied before passing input into many traditional NLP pipelines, especially for tasks like sentiment analysis:

1. *Spelling correction*

    As expected, *spelling correction* is used to ensure that any typos or misspelled words are corrected ahead of analysis. After all, there's no use in trying to analyze the sentiment of text that even a human cannot comprehend. Correcting "I havve

Get Planning | 115

a qestion" to "I have a question" makes it a lot easier. For more information on spelling correction, refer to the online edition of *Introduction to Information Retrieval* (Manning et al., Cambridge University Press) (*https://oreil.ly/58Bue*).

2. *Stop word removal*

Stop word removal is the process of stripping out words that don't contribute to the overall understanding of the text. Words like "not" or "never" may carry significant meaning and should not be removed blindly. For more information on stop words, refer to the online edition of *Introduction to Information Retrieval* (*https://oreil.ly/fHBvR*).

3. *Stemming and lemmatization*

Stemming reduces certain words to their roots. For example, "goes" and "going" will be stemmed to "go." *Lemmatization* takes that a step further by mapping words in specific contexts to their lemma. For example, "am," "are," and "is" would be mapped to their lemma, "be." In this way, the input text is further reduced to only the most important fragments needed for analysis. This step is normally built into the model. For more information on stemming and lemmatization, refer to the online edition of *Introduction to Information Retrieval* (*https://oreil.ly/p_wXy*).

Tokenization is one of the first preprocessing steps performed on input text. It involves splitting a sentence into smaller parts, typically words or subwords, called tokens. The choice of tokens can vary depending on the model—some use full words, while others rely on word stems or subword units to better handle grammar and vocabulary. Once tokenized, the text can be passed into a trained NLP model for further analysis. Figure 7-2 shows an example input, `"I am feling grat!"`, which undergoes three preprocessing steps—spelling correction, tokenization, and stop-word removal—before sentiment analysis is performed.

First, the text's spelling is corrected to "I am feeling great." Next, the sentence is split into tokens. A tokenizer could be as simple as calling `.split(" ")` on a string, but is more effective with a tokenization library that takes punctuation into consideration. Last, the tokens are run through stop-word removal to eliminate stop words. In the end, you're left with the words "feeling" and "great." These two words can then be run through an NLP sentiment analysis model to receive a score. In this example, "feeling" is fairly neutral, receiving a score of 1. Whereas "great" is a positive word and gets a score of 3. Combined, the sentiment analysis for this string is 4.

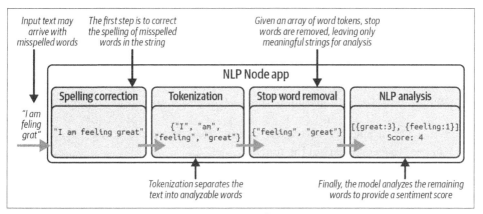

Figure 7-2. NLP preprocessing steps on a string of text

Your app needs to follow the same general structure when handling journal entries. To begin, you decide to test each preprocessing step in code to ensure your third-party npm modules are working as expected.

Get Programming with String Processing Packages

To start developing your app, create a new folder named sentiment_journal. Navigate to your project folder on your command line and run npm init. This command initializes your Node app. You can press Enter throughout the initialization steps. The result of these steps is the creation of a file called *package.json*. This file will instruct your Node app of any configurations or scripts needed to operate.

Next, create a file called *index.js* within your project folder. This file will act as the entry point for your app.

Before you jump into sentiment analysis, you need to make sure the input text is spelled correctly. To test this you use the sample text "I am feling grat!" Your goal is to build a function that takes this text as a parameter and outputs the same sentence with all words spelled correctly. For this, you'll need an npm package to help with identifying misspelled words and correcting them. Navigate to your project folder's root level in your command line and run npm install spellchecker@^3.7.1. spell checker is a popular package that offers functions like isMisspelled, to check if a word has any typos, and getCorrectionsForMisspelling, to offer correctly spelled alternatives.

Add the code in Example 7-1 to *index.js* to start testing this package. In this code snippet, you import the SpellChecker class from spellchecker and use its getCorrectionsForMisspelling function on the sample text grat to get an array of possible spelling corrections.

Example 7-1. Testing spelling correction in index.js

```
import SpellChecker from 'spellchecker'; ❶
const options = SpellChecker.getCorrectionsForMisspelling('grat'); ❷
console.log(options); ❸
```

❶ Import `spellchecker` module.

❷ Get a list of spelling correction options for the sample string using the `get CorrectionsForMisspelling` function.

❸ Output the list of suggested spellings.

You can navigate to the project folder in your command line and start your app to get a log of all the alternative spellings for `grat`. Conveniently, `SpellChecker` returns the corrected spellings in the order of highest probability. This is particularly helpful in this example, because you're looking to correct the string `grat` with the word `great`, which is the first option in the corrected words array. Example 7-2 shows the output after running your app.

Example 7-2. Command-line output for spelling correction options

```
[ ❶
  'great', 'grab', 'grant', 'goat',
  'gray', 'brat', 'grad', 'gran',
  'grate', 'frat', 'rat', 'grit',
  'gram', 'graft', 'ghat', 'gat',
  'drat', 'gnat', 'grata', 'prat',
  'groat', 'gras', 'grot', 'erat',
  'gmat'
]
```

❶ Logged corrected words in your command-line window.

Because you can trust the results of this library, you can generally choose the first result in the array. This is a good start for testing a single word.

Now, replace the last two lines in *index.js* with the code in Example 7-3. This code effectively builds on the spelling correction logic you wrote previously. This time, your code starts with your sample input string and wraps the spelling correction logic in a function called `correctSpelling`. In this function, the input, `inputString`, is split into separate words and an array is defined ahead of time to store all correctly spelled words. A `for` loop iterates over each word and uses the `isMisspelled` function to check whether the word is spelled correctly.

If the word is misspelled, it is passed to the getCorrectionsForMisspelling function, which returns an array of correctly spelled alternatives for the input word. Because you know that the first item in that array is your best replacement option, you choose that word, the 0th index, and add it to the corrections array. If the word was not misspelled, then it is added to the corrections array as is. At the end of the loop, the corrections array combines the words back into a sentence and returns the result. In this way, when the function, correctSpelling, is called with your input String, the resulting text will immediately log to your command-line console.

Example 7-3. Add a spelling correction function to index.js

```
const inputString = 'I am feling grat!'; ❶

const correctSpelling = inputString => { ❷
  const words = inputString.split(' '); ❸
  const corrections = []; ❹
  for (let word of words) {
    if (SpellChecker.isMisspelled(word)) { ❺
      const options = SpellChecker.getCorrectionsForMisspelling(word); ❻
      corrections.push(options[0]); ❼
    } else {
      corrections.push(word);
    }
  }
  return corrections.join(' '); ❽
}
console.log(correctSpelling(inputString)); ❾
```

❶ Define your initial sample input string.

❷ Define a correctSpelling function that takes an input string as a parameter.

❸ Separate the words in your input string and assign them to a variable called words.

❹ Define a variable, corrections, to store all correctly spelled words.

❺ Check whether each word is spelled correctly using SpellChecker.is Mis spelled.

❻ Find all spelling alternatives for the misspelled word using SpellChecker.get CorrectionsForMisspelling.

❼ Add the first option in the corrected words list to your corrections array. Alternatively, add the original word if it is not misspelled.

Get Programming with String Processing Packages | 119

❽ Combine the words in `corrections` to reform the correctly spelled input text.

❾ Log the returned string from `correctSpelling` to your command-line console.

Test this by rerunning your app. Your console output should show I am feeling great. This is a good start, ensuring any input text will be checked for spelling ahead of reaching your analysis model. The next step is to tokenize your corrected string. To handle this example and all other strings to follow, you use a library that supports tokenization.

Install the natural package by running the command `npm install natural@^8.1.0`. This package includes many supporting NLP functions, like tokenization, stemming, and even sentiment analysis. You can import `natural` by adding `import natural from "natural"` to the top of your *index.js* file. Then you instantiate a new `natural.WordTokenizer` tokenizer by adding `const tokenizer = new natural.WordTokenizer()` below the import line. You create a new function called `tokenizeInput` to wrap your new tokenizer instance and split your input string into tokens, as shown in Example 7-4, which passes your corrected input string to the tokenizer. You start by applying `natural`'s tokenization to break the sentence into individual words, making it easier for downstream sentiment analysis to process the text accurately.

Example 7-4. Add a tokenization function to index.js

```
const tokenizeInput = inputString => { ❶
  return tokenizer.tokenize(inputString); ❷
}
```

❶ Define a new `tokenizeInput` function that takes your input string as a parameter.

❷ Return the tokens representing your input string, using the `natural` tokenize function.

Update your log statement to separate each of the function calls, `tokenizeInput` and `correctSpelling`, individually, logging only the final result (Example 7-5). Now the returned value from `correctSpelling` will pass into the `tokenizeInput` function. Rerun your app and you'll see the output change to an array of tokens: ['I', 'am', 'feeling', 'great'].

Example 7-5. Separate the preprocessing step function calls in index.js

```
const correctedSpelling = correctSpelling(inputString); ❶
const tokens = tokenizeInput(correctedSpelling); ❷
console.log(tokens); ❸
```

❶ Assign the result of `correctSpelling` to the variable `correctedSpelling`.

❷ Pass the `correctedSpelling` value to `tokenizeInput` and assign the returned value to `tokens`.

❸ Log the `tokens` array to your console.

With an array of tokens, you can now perform the last two preprocessing steps before sentiment analysis: stemming and stop-word removal. The `natural` package comes with a stemming function, so there's no need to import an additional library for that.

The stemming function can be applied to one word at a time, so you'll need to create a new function, `stemWords`, that takes your tokens as a parameter and loops through them to return their stems, as seen in Example 7-6. In this function, you define a new empty array, `stems`, where you'll add each new stemmed word you process. You loop through your tokens and pass each token into the `natural.PorterStemmer.stem` function, where the word is broken down to its stem using a special algorithm. With each stem produced, they are pushed onto the `stems` array, and eventually returned to the function caller.

Each NLP algorithm *stems* from a proven algorithm, researched and developed by computer-linguistics engineers. The Porter stemming algorithm is one of the popular algorithms you can use to stem your English words. Because there are many supported languages, which each carry their unique grammar and syntax, you may find a different algorithm is more suitable for your use case. You can learn more about the Porter stemming algorithm online (*https://oreil.ly/yXcIIu*).

Example 7-6. Add a stemming function to index.js

```
const stemWords = tokens => { ❶
  const stems = []; ❷
  for (let token of tokens) { ❸
    const stem = natural.PorterStemmer.stem(token); ❹
    stems.push(stem); ❺
  }
  return stems; ❻
}
```

❶ Define the stemWords function that takes tokens as an input parameter.

❷ Define an empty stems array.

❸ Loop through each token to be processed for its stem.

❹ Process the stem of the word using the Porter stemming algorithm within the natural package.

❺ Add the stem to your stems array.

❻ Return the stems array.

You can now update your log statement by first defining a new variable, stemmedWords, which will equal the returned array after passing your tokens into stemWords: const stems = stemWords(tokens). Then log stems. Your output should show ['I', 'am', 'feel', 'great'], indicating that feeling was stemmed to feel.

The last step is to remove stop words, like "I" or "am." For this, you'll install a new package, stopword, by running the command npm install stopword@^3.1.5 at the root level of your project folder in your command line. Next, add stopword to your project by adding import { removeStopwords } from 'stopword' to the top of *index.js*. This will specifically import the removeStopwords function you'll need for this project.

Now you can go to your log statement at the end of *index.js* and add a new variable, const removedStopWords = removeStopwords(stems), which passes your stems array to the removeStopwords function, returning only the words needed for analysis. Rerun your app to see ['feel', 'great'] logged to your console.

That might seem like a lot of steps to build, only to reduce your sentence to two words, but it's a necessary process to get the most out of your sentiment analysis model. In the next section, you'll apply these results to your sentiment analyzer.

Analyzing Sentiment

In the previous section, you ensured that any input text will follow the proper requirements for sentiment analysis. You've already installed the `natural` package, which comes with a sentiment analysis class called `SentimentAnalyzer`. What's more, this can be instantiated with a stemming algorithm. That means you don't need to perform the stemming, or even stop-word removal, steps at all in this case. To test the analyzer function, remove the code you had after defining your `tokens` variable, and add the code in Example 7-7.

The addition of this code destructures the `SentimentAnalyzer`, your analyzer class, and `PorterStemmer`, your stemming class, from the `natural` package. Then, you instantiate a new `SentimentAnalyzer` object configured to do the following:

- Analyze English
- Stem words using the Porter stemming algorithm
- Use a specific vocabulary set identified as `afinn`

With this new `analyzer` set up, you call the provided `getSentiment` function by passing in your array, `tokens`. The result is a sentiment analysis score you can log to your console.

Example 7-7. Analyzing sentiment with tokens in index.js

```
...
const { SentimentAnalyzer, PorterStemmer } = natural; ❶
const analyzer = new SentimentAnalyzer("English", PorterStemmer, "afinn"); ❷
const sentimentResults = analyzer.getSentiment(tokens); ❸
console.log(sentimentResults); ❹
```

❶ Import the `SentimentAnalyzer` and `PorterStemmer` modules from `natural`.

❷ Instantiate a new `analyzer` that includes a stemming configuration.

❸ Analyze your input string's sentiment by running `getSentiment` on your `tokens`.

❹ Log the resulting sentiment score to your console.

Try rerunning your app to get an output score printed to your console. Your score should read 1. This score indicates an overall positive sentiment.

You can test this some more by changing the string `grat` in your input to `bad`. Your resulting score should be `-0.5`, indicating a negative sentiment. In this way, the higher the positive number, the more positive the statement, and the more negative the score, the more negative the statement.

Now that you have a working sentiment analyzer, it will be more helpful if you can analyze more than just static sample text. To capture user input on the command line, you install `prompt`, a package for prompting the user for text input and saving the response. Run `npm install prompt@^1.3.0` at the root level of your project directory in your command line. Next, add the lines in Example 7-8 to the top of *index.js*. In these lines of code, you import the `prompt` package and create a prompt instance. You also configure the prompt by starting it with default settings and removing the default message prefix, so the user sees a clean input prompt when entering their journal text.

When you start the app, you'll get a prompt to type your input. To exit the prompt and app altogether, press Command+C.

Example 7-8. Adding prompt to index.js

```
...
import prompt from 'prompt';   ❶
prompt.start({});   ❷
prompt.message = '';   ❸
...
```

❶ Import `prompt` into your project.

❷ Configure `prompt` to enable manually exiting your app during a prompt.

❸ Clear the prompt message.

To test using a prompt, you'll want to delete the line defining your sample `input String` variable. Then, you add code to wait for a user's input. Because there's no way to tell how long it takes for the user to respond, you'll need to use `await`, which returns a JavaScript `Promise` that eventually is filled with the user's response data.

`prompt.get` takes an array argument containing the items for which you want to prompt the user. In this example, you ask "How do you feel?" and assign the response to `inputString`. The rest of the existing logic for sentiment analysis can remain the same. The last change is to wrap your code in a `try-catch` block. This ensures that if anything goes wrong while awaiting a prompt reply, you can catch the error and log it to your console. Last, this whole block of code must be wrapped in an `async` function to use the `await` logic. Here you use an immediately invoked anonymous function so that your code runs as soon as your app starts. Example 7-9 contains all the code needed in the wrapped async function in *index.js*.

Immediately invoked function expressions (IIFE) are functions that are executed as soon as they are defined in your app. The expression is effectively a function wrapped in parentheses, followed by another set of parentheses to call the function. IIFEs are convenient to use to start an app or run important configuration code as soon as possible.

Example 7-9. Adding a function to prompt the user for input in index.js

```
...
(async () => { ❶
  try { ❷
    const {inputString} = await prompt.get([{ ❸
      name: 'inputString',
      description: 'How do you feel?',
    }]);
    const correctedSpelling = correctSpelling(inputString);
    const tokens = tokenizeInput(correctedSpelling);
    const { SentimentAnalyzer, PorterStemmer } = natural;
    const analyzer = new SentimentAnalyzer("English", PorterStemmer, "afinn");
    const sentimentResults = analyzer.getSentiment(tokens);
    console.log(sentimentResults);
  } catch (e) { ❹
    console.log(`An error occurred: ${e.message}`);
  }
})();
```

❶ Define an IIFE to wrap your app logic.

❷ Wrap your code in a try/catch block to handle potential errors.

❸ Wait for the user response to a prompt using a description and assigning the response value to inputString.

❹ Catch any errors that occur while executing your code and log them to your console.

Now your code should function like before. Only this time, you'll be prompted to answer How do you feel? on your command-line before any sentiment analysis code runs. Try to restart your app and reply to the prompt with "My day is terrific and I feel amazing!" Your command line console should log a score of 1. Your more positive statement got a slightly higher score than your previous sample input. In the next section, you'll put this all together by connecting the app to a database and a command-line-friendly visualization of your data.

Connecting a Database and Visualization

By this point you've built an app that can compute a single journal entry's sentiment each time you run the app. Ideally, a user would receive not only a score for a single entry, but be able to compare it to past entries to track the overall progression of their mood.

Now that you have most of the logic needed to analyze text, you can focus on organizing your code and adding support for saving data and displaying results. Instead of simply showing the sentiment score on the console, you'll create a graph to display the sentiment trends across a series of posts, as shown in Figure 7-3.

By the end of this section, your app will allow users to continually type journal entries, save their sentiment scores to a database, and display the graph in green during a positive change in the score, or red during a negative change.

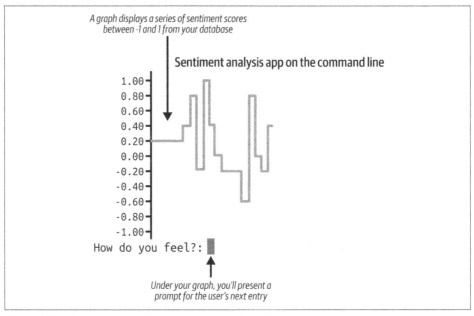

Figure 7-3. Console graph showing a series of sentiment scores

You can begin by setting up the database and database schema for saving sentiment scores. At the root level of your project folder, run the command `npm install sqlite3@^5.1.7 sequelize@^6.37.7` to install the SQLite database management package, along with the database object-relational mapper (ORM), Sequelize. These two packages will allow you to define the structure you want to save and connect to your database.

 Although there are many database options to choose from, you'll implement a simple SQLite database management system. For more information on choosing between database types, revisit "Comparing SQLite and PostgreSQL" on page 105.

Create a new file called *db.js* and add the code in Example 7-10. This code will import the `Sequelize` and `DataTypes` classes from your `sequelize` module. You use the `Sequelize` class to instantiate a new database connection called db. This database is configured to use SQLite and save persisted data in a file called *journal.sqlite* in your project folder. Then you define a new Sequelize model called `SentimentScore` to persist the sentiment scores in a field called `score`. (The model is also exported for use in other modules.) Last, you `await` for the database to establish a connection and register your model when the app starts.

Example 7-10. Setting up your model and database connection in db.js

```
import { Sequelize, DataTypes } from 'sequelize'; ❶

const db = new Sequelize({ ❷
  dialect: 'sqlite',
  storage: './journal.sqlite'
});
export const SentimentScore = db.define('SentimentScore', { ❸
  score: DataTypes.DECIMAL,
});
await SentimentScore.sync(); ❹
```

❶ Import the `Sequelize` and `DataTypes` classes from `sequelize`.

❷ Instantiate a new database configuration with Sequelize, using a SQLite database stored as *journal.sqlite* in your project folder.

❸ Define a `SentimentScore` Sequelize model that saves a `score` field as a decimal value.

❹ Register your `SentimentScore` model with the SQLite database.

You won't see the *journal.sqlite* file appear in your folder until you make use of this *db.js* file in your main *index.js* app logic.

With this model set up, you can now save sentiment scores through the `Sentiment Score` model. Before you create the *index.js* file, you create a new class for all of your preprocessing and sentiment analysis logic. In your project folder, create a new file called *sentimentJournal.js*. This file will act as a separate module from your *index.js* file and contain most of the logic added in previous sections.

When Sequelize models are defined, they are built with special functions to allow interactions with the database. For example, `SentimentScore.create` will allow you to add a new `SentimentScore` record to the database, and `SentimentScore.findAll` queries the database for all existing records. For more information on Sequelize model functions, refer to the Sequelize API references (*https://oreil.ly/XgqGq*).

Earlier in this chapter you used the `natural` package to build out each step of NLP preprocessing. Because you aren't too concerned about customizing the preprocessing steps, you can use a library that performs all the steps for you. At the root level of your project, install the `sentiment` package by running the command `npm install sentiment@^5.0.2`. This package will provide all of the analysis tools and even return the breakdown of tokens along with the resulting sentiment score. You will continue to use the `spellchecker` package. Add the code from Example 7-11 to the top of *sentimentJournal.js*. (For more information about the `sentiment` package, visit the npm website (*https://oreil.ly/nwcs5*).)

Example 7-11. Adding import to sentimentJournal.js

```
import Sentiment from 'sentiment';          ❶
import SpellChecker from 'spellchecker';
import { SentimentScore } from './db.js';   ❷
```

❶ Import the `sentiment` and `spellchecker` packages to your project.

❷ Import the `SentimentScore` model from *db.js*.

With these libraries ready to use in your project, you begin creating the `Sentiment Journal` class by adding the code in Example 7-12. In this listing, the `Sentiment Journal` class structure is defined. You add fields for the sentiment analysis engine, an array of scores (to be loaded by the database), and a field to store the user's journal entry. Additionally, you add a class method called `correctSpelling`, which effectively uses the same code from your previous `correctSpelling` function. Only, this time the method can be called only in association with a `SentimentJournal` instance. Last, you export the class so you're able to use it in other parts of your project.

Example 7-12. Creating the `SentimentJournal` class in sentimentJournal.js

```
...
class SentimentJournal { ❶
  constructor () { ❷
    this.sentiment = new Sentiment();
    this.scores = [0];
    this.entry = '';
  }

  correctSpelling (inputString) { ❸
    const words = inputString.split(' ');
    const corrections = [];
    for (let word of words) {
      if (SpellChecker.isMisspelled(word)) {
        const options = SpellChecker.getCorrectionsForMisspelling(word);
        corrections.push(options[0]);
      } else {
        corrections.push(word);
      }
    }
    return corrections.join(' ');
  }
}
export default SentimentJournal; ❹
```

❶ Define the `SentimentJournal` class.

❷ Set up the class constructor to instantiate a new sentiment analysis object, initialize an array of scores to an initial score of 0, and define a field to store the user's entry.

❸ Define a class method, `correctSpelling`, to take an `inputString` parameter.

❹ Export the `SentimentJournal` class for use in other modules.

With this structure in place, you can start adding more methods to this class to support persisted storage and the original functionality you've built.

Add the class methods in Example 7-13 to your `SentimentJournal` class. `saveScore` is an `async` class method that uses the `SentimentScore` model and creates a new record using the `score` parameter that's passed into the method. The `fetchEntries`

Connecting a Database and Visualization | 129

async method waits for a database query of up to 100 recent records and assigns the scores from those results to the SentimentJournals *scores* state. You use `results.map(({score}) => score` because the initial results will contain more than just the score data, including record IDs and timestamps. This logic strips the results of the irrelevant data.

Example 7-13. Adding database queries to your class in sentimentJournal.js

```
...
async saveScore (score) { ❶
  await SentimentScore.create({score});
}

async fetchEntries () { ❷
  const results = await SentimentScore.findAll({limit: 100}); ❸
  if (results.length) {
    this.scores = results.map(({score}) => score); ❹
  }
}
...
```

❶ Define an `async` method, `saveScore`, to create a new `SentimentScore` record in your database using the `score` parameter.

❷ Define an `async` method, `fetchEntries`, to pull all persisted scores from the database.

❸ Query the 100 most recent saved `SentimentScore` records.

❹ If `SentimentScore` records exist, take only the score values and assign them to the `scores` array field.

These are the only two methods you'll need to save and fetch from your database in this project. Next, you need to add your analysis logic.

Now that you're using a new sentiment analysis library, add the method in Example 7-14 to your class. You define your `analyzeSentiment` method to check whether you have an entry to analyze. If `this.entry` exists, you run `this.senti ment.analyze`, which uses the `sentiment` package's analyze function to generate a score for the provided journal entry. You destructure the `score` from this result and divide the score by 10, and force it within the range of –1 and 1.

---

130 | Chapter 7: Natural Language Processor Sentiment Analysis

To ensure a number always falls between a certain range, you can get the `Math.max` of the variable number and the minimum of your range. If your number is less than the minimum, it will return that minimum value. Then wrap the result of that function in `Math.min`, with the other value being your range's maximum value. If your number is larger than the minimum, you take the minimum between it and your maximum allowed value. This way, your result always stays between your set range.

With your `normalizedScore` set, you can save it to the database as a new record by passing it to your `saveScore` method. You also add the score to your class instance's `scores` array to maintain state without having to query the database again.

Example 7-14. Adding database queries to your class in sentimentJournal.js

```
...
async analyzeSentiment () { ❶
  if (!this.entry || this.entry === '') return; ❷
  const { score } = this.sentiment.analyze(this.entry); ❸
  const normalizedScore = Math.min(Math.max(score / 10, -1), 1); ❹
  await this.saveScore(normalizedScore); ❺
  this.scores.push(normalizedScore); ❻
}
...
```

❶ Define your `analyzeSentiment` method.

❷ Check if the class instance `entry` field has an assigned value.

❸ Use the `sentiment` package's `analyze` function to process the entry and extract the score.

❹ Calculate a `normalizedScore` between –1 and 1.

❺ Wait for the score to save to your database.

❻ Add the new score to your class instance's scores array field.

Your class is now ready to analyze the sentiment of any input text. To get that input, you'll add the prompt module by adding the code in Example 7-15 to the top of *sentimentJournal.js*. Here, you import prompt, initialize the library with prompt.start(), and clear the prompt message.

Example 7-15. Importing and initializing the prompt in sentimentJournal.js

```
...
import prompt from 'prompt'; ❶
prompt.start();
prompt.message = '';
...
```

❶ Import the prompt package and initialize the library.

With the prompt library set up, add the function in Example 7-16 to your Sentiment Journal class. This method waits for the user's response to How do you feel? and assigns the resulting value to response. The response variable is passed through the class's correctSpelling method, where the resulting text is assigned to the class instance's entry field. With this method in place, you should be able to collect user responses, process an analysis score, save them to the database, and repeat.

Example 7-16. Adding a prompt method to your class in sentimentJournal.js

```
...
async promptEntry () { ❶
  const {response} = await prompt.get([{ ❷
    name: 'response',
    description: 'How do you feel?',
  }]);
  this.entry = this.correctSpelling(response); ❸
}
...
```

❶ Define a promptEntry method for SentimentJournal.

❷ Wait for prompt.get to return the user's response to your prompt.

❸ Assign the user's spelling-corrected response to this.entry.

To get this code to work, you'll need to create an *index.js* file and start using these class methods. Add the code in Example 7-17 to *index.js*.

In this file, you import your SentimentJournal class and create a new instance called journal. The journal variable allows you to access all methods defined in the class.

---

132 | Chapter 7: Natural Language Processor Sentiment Analysis

To begin, you call `journal.fetchEntries` to load any existing `SentimentScore` records from your database. You then enter an infinite `while (true)` loop, where each cycle prompts the user for a new journal entry using `journal.promptEntry`, then analyzes the entry using `journal.analyzeSentiment`. This loop continues indefinitely, allowing users to submit and process multiple entries in a single session.

Example 7-17. Set up your SentimentJournal in index.js *with a loop*

```
import SentimentJournal from "./sentimentJournal.js"; ❶

const journal = new SentimentJournal(); ❷
await journal.fetchEntries(); ❸

while (true) { ❹
  await journal.promptEntry(); ❺
  await journal.analyzeSentiment(); ❻
}
```

❶ Import the `SentimentJournal` class from your local module.

❷ Create a new instance of `SentimentJournal`.

❸ Fetch any saved journal entries from your data source.

❹ Begin an infinite loop to repeatedly prompt and analyze new entries.

❺ Prompt the user for a journal entry.

❻ Analyze the sentiment of the most recent journal entry.

Your *index.js* file is ready to start interactions on the command line. Before you test this, you need to add one more element to the output: a graph visualization.

For this project you can use the `asciichart` package (*https://oreil.ly/D_79r*), which can output a graph structure using ASCII characters. Run the command `npm install asciichart@^1.5.25` at the command-line prompt to install `asciichart` and add `import asciichart from 'asciichart'` to the top of your *sentimentJournal.js* file.

You can define custom configurations in `asciichart`, from color scheme to chart dimensions. Because you want the chart to show data between –1 and 1, add the code in Example 7-18 below your import lines in *sentimentJournal.js*. This `chartConfig` object defines the minimum and maximum values of the chart, as well as a comfortable line height for displaying this project's sentiment scores. You'll use this set of config values when you set up the chart logic.

Connecting a Database and Visualization | 133

Example 7-18. Adding a prompt method to your class in sentimentJournal.js

```
...
const chartConfig = { ❶
  min: -1,
  max: 1,
  height:  10,
}
...
```

❶ Define the configurations for your chart to display values between –1 and 1, with a line height of 10.

To actually print the chart, add the two methods in Example 7-19 to your Sentiment Journal class in *sentimentJournal.js*. The setChartColor method checks whether you have any recent sentiment scores. It then views the most recent score and assigns it to the recentScore variable.

If the recentScore is negative, you change the chart color to red in chartConfig. Otherwise, you assign the chart color to green, indicating a positive trend in scores. The printChart method performs three steps:

- Clears the command-line console of any previously printed charts
- Sets the chart color
- Prints the chart using asciichart.plot with your SentimentJournal instance scores and the previously defined chartConfig settings

Example 7-19. Adding asciichart methods to your class in sentimentJournal.js

```
...
setChartColor () { ❶
  if (!this.scores.length) return; ❷
  const recentScore = this.scores[this.scores.length - 1]; ❸
  if (recentScore < 0) { ❹
    chartConfig.colors = [asciichart.red]
  } else {
    chartConfig.colors = [asciichart.green]
  }
}

printChart () { ❺
  console.clear(); ❻
  this.setChartColor(); ❼
  console.log(asciichart.plot([ this.scores ], chartConfig)); ❽
}
...
```

❶ Declares the `setChartColor` method, responsible for setting the chart color based on the most recent score.

❷ Checks if there are any scores in `this.scores`. If the array is empty, the function exits to prevent errors.

❸ Retrieves the most recent score from `this.scores` by accessing the last item in the array.

❹ Checks if the recent score is negative, which will determine the color of the chart.

❺ Declares the `printChart` method, which will handle displaying the chart in the console.

❻ Clears the console to provide a clean view, removing any previous output.

❼ Calls `setChartColor` to update the chart's color based on the latest score before printing.

❽ Plots and logs the chart to the console using `asciichart.plot`, displaying the scores with the current color configuration.

With these final methods in place, your sentiment journal is ready to analyze text and show the results in a visually appealing way. In *index.js* add `await journal.printChart()` as the first line in your `while` loop. This will ensure that a chart is printed as soon as your app starts and previous sentiment score records are fetched.

 When you start the app for the first time there will be no previous scores; only the default score of 0 set in the constructor of your class.

Now, restart your app and start adding journal entries. When you type This terrible day is the worst! you'll notice the chart immediately updates to show a negative score (Figure 7-4).

Connecting a Database and Visualization | 135

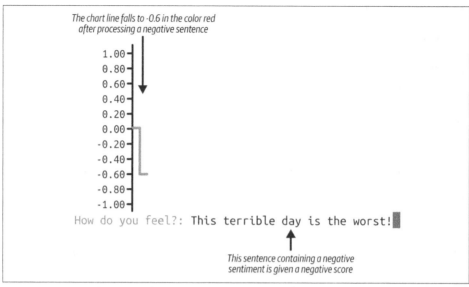

Figure 7-4. Console output showing a negative sentiment score and red chart drop after inputting a negative journal entry

As soon as you add a new entry, the chart will update again. If the sentiment is still negative, the chart will remain red. Otherwise, the chart will show a green line as soon as a positive statement is made. Try this out by typing `This amazing day is excellent!`. Notice the jump to 0.8 in the chart, as seen in Figure 7-5.

 If you want to erase your database, it is as simple as deleting the *journal.sqlite* file in your project's folder.

With your app effectively complete, you can start demonstrating its use with the therapy practice. With the database set up, clients can choose to add journal entries whenever they'd like without losing track of previous sentiment scores. Moreover, this app can be extended as an API, a web app that patients can use on their browsers, or rebuilt to work with any interface.

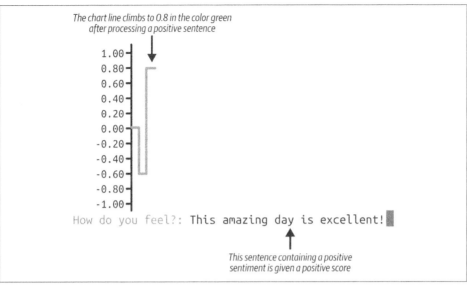

Figure 7-5. Console output showing a positive sentiment score and green chart rise after inputting a positive journal entry

Chapter Exercises

1. Enhance the spelling correction with fallback logic:

   a. Update your `correctSpelling` method to check whether the `SpellChecker.getCorrectionsForMisspelling` function returns any suggestions.

   b. If it returns an empty array (i.e., no correction was found), fallback to keeping the original word unchanged.

   c. Add logging inside the loop to verify which words were corrected and which were left as is.

   d. Try it out with an input like `"i feeeeel fine but not grte"` and confirm your app still produces a usable output.

    The spellchecker library doesn't always have a fix for every word, so fallback logic ensures your app won't crash or drop tokens unexpectedly.

Connecting a Database and Visualization | 137

2. Add sentiment labels to chart output:

   a. Modify the `printChart()` method to print a labeled sentiment category (e.g., "Positive", "Neutral", "Negative") alongside each new sentiment score.

   b. Use the final `normalizedScore` value to assign a label:

      - Score > 0.3: "Positive"

      - Score < –0.3: "Negative"

      - Otherwise: "Neutral"

   c. Display this label clearly under the chart so the user can interpret their last entry's result at a glance.

   d. Test with various journal entries to make sure each label corresponds appropriately to the score.

These exercises improve your app's resilience and clarity. Spelling fallback keeps the analysis running smoothly, and labeled chart feedback offers a more human-readable interpretation of the user's mood progression.

Summary

In this chapter, you:

- Learned how to build a Node app around an ML model

- Created your own text preprocessing flow

- Persisted data in a SQL table via an ORM

- Built a command-line app for tracking sentiment scores

CHAPTER 8

Marketing Mailer

This chapter covers the following:

- Sending emails from a Node app
- Setting up a scheduler to run tasks
- Verifying accounts and tracking email engagement

In this chapter, you'll build an app that sends emails and manages the logic for the receiving users. You learned in Chapter 1 how HTTP is one protocol for communicating across the internet. Here, you'll explore some of the protocols that are widely used for email servers and clients to support communication in another way. Just as Node can be used to deliver full-fledged APIs and web servers, it can be used for micro tasks, such as sending emails.

Throughout the chapter, you'll add incremental pieces to support some of the most common functionalities used in an email marketing service. You'll start by configuring a well-known package for sending mail externally. Then, you'll build an API to support collecting emails and verifying them. At the end, you'll add logic to automatically schedule marketing emails to select groups of subscribers to your product.

Tools and Applications Used in This Chapter

Before you get started, make sure to install and configure the tools and applications required for this project. Installation instructions for Node.js, Fastify, and VS Code are provided in Chapter 1, while project initialization steps, such as setting up your directory structure, configuring *package.json*, and using modern syntax, are covered in Appendix A. Once completed, return here to continue. Building a project from scratch helps deepen your understanding of each component, giving you greater control and flexibility as you progress.

Your Prompt

There's been hype around a virtual gym, Inn Box, which will allow participants to learn mixed martial arts and boxing techniques from their home. The startup has already raised money for their innovative idea, but wants to start collecting emails of prospective participants. They've hired you to put together a Node app equipped to send membership information, gym updates, and promotions. This way, Inn Box can start to engage with their growing audience.

Get Planning

You plan to deliver an app that can collect and verify email addresses, send emails, and determine which promotional campaigns prove most effective. By the end of this project, your app should be able to send outgoing emails with customizable content and store all relevant marketing information to a database.

You begin by sketching out a diagram detailing the flow of information from each subscriber through your app. In Figure 8-1 you establish that a user (the gym subscriber) will sign up with their email address. The email addresses will be collected by an API endpoint using the Fastify framework in your Node app. The email address is then registered in your database. You'll build a service in your app to send outgoing emails. As users receive the emails in their personal email clients, they'll be able to interact with linked content to verify their account or engage with promotions.

140 | Chapter 8: Marketing Mailer

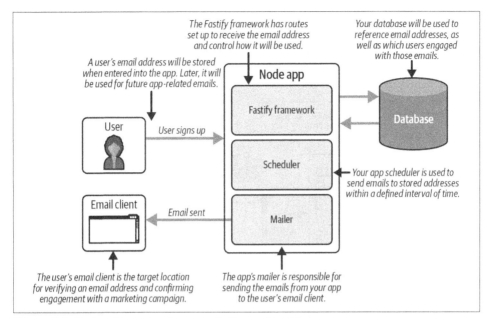

Figure 8-1. Project blueprint for a marketing mailer Node app

Links in the outgoing emails will trace back to the Node app, allowing you to save information about the user's engagement. Last, you'll build a service in your app to periodically schedule and send out emails automatically.

Diving deeper into the app logic, you focus on three crucial parts:

Fastify
   This is the core of how your app handles outgoing and incoming interactions with your users across the web.

Scheduler
   This is where you'll define the specifics of automatically running tasks, such as when to send out emails.

Mailer
   This lies at the core of how emails can be successfully sent out from your app and arrive in your users' inboxes.

As users register with your app, you'll be able to store data like their email address, verification status, and marketing campaigns they've engaged with (Figure 8-2). Collectively, this information provides Inn Box with a valuable dataset of prospective leads, including verified email addresses and engagement behavior, to guide future outreach and growth.

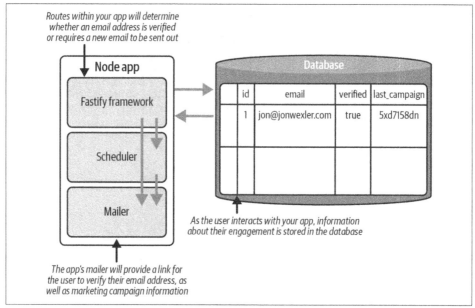

Figure 8-2. Diagram displaying how data is saved in your database

With this structure in place, you're ready to start building an app.

Get Programming

To start developing your app, create a new folder named `marketing_mailer`. Navigate to your project folder on your command line and run `npm init`. This command initializes your Node app. You can press Enter throughout the initialization steps. The result of these steps is the creation of a file called *package.json*. This file will instruct your Node app of any configurations or scripts needed to operate.

Next, create a file called *index.js* within your project folder. This file will act as the entry point for your app.

With your Node app initialized, you begin by installing your app's first npm package: nodemailer. In your project's root directory, run npm install nodemailer@^7.0.4 in your command line. The nodemailer package offers a comprehensive set of tooling to set up a mailing service for Node apps. For more information on how to use nodemailer, visit the Nodemailer website (*https://oreil.ly/4o_R6*).

Add the following import line to the top of *index.js* to import the createTransport function from nodemailer:

```
import { createTransport } from "nodemailer";
```

This import line destructures the createTransport function from the nodemailer package, allowing you to directly use the function to instantiate a mailer object.

Next, you need to add particular configurations to the createTransport function in order to start using a nodemailer instance for sending mail.

If you'd like to explore building your own SMTP mail server, try out the smtp-server and mailparser packages for setting up the necessary configurations to send outgoing mail and read incoming mail. A word of caution: setting up a custom mail server has many obstacles around security and configurations. Alternatively, you may build your own Haraka mail server, which offers everything you need to send and receive emails in Node. See more at the Haraka website (*https://oreil.ly/-vZfQ*).

Example 8-1 shows you what options are needed to configure your transporter object. nodemailer itself is not a mail server, but instead depends on an existing server to send your emails.

When configuring your mailer transporter, you'll find fewer obstacles working with the configuration options of a known mail server. As your mail will pass through a series of security protocols across the internet, a trusted mail server is likely to guarantee successful delivery of your mail.

In this example, you can use the business's email account or your personal Google email account to test.

Setting Up Your Mailer with Google

Logging in to your email from just about anywhere is convenient, but has its tradeoffs. For one, if you plan to sign in to your Gmail account across multiple devices, you're typing your password into each of those devices, risking your main password leaking to the public or being misused. Your email client password is a sacred password, and as such has become more protected under changes made by Google and other email platforms alike.

There are two recommended strategies for logging in to your email account from a potentially unsecure app:

Sign in with Google
> This approach usually has you click a link to sign in directly with Google without having to type your password directly into the risky app.

Using an app password
> App passwords are dedicated passwords generated by Google for your use in third-party apps. By using these passwords, you gain access to your email through another service without exposing your sacred main password.

Because you're building an app that hasn't quite met all the security standards needed for an email service, you may have to set up an app password for use in development. To do this with your Gmail account, follow Google's online instructions (*https://oreil.ly/osgw3*). From here you'll be guided to manage your app passwords and create a new one for the app you're building (Figure 8-3). You can give any app name here to help you identify its association with the generated app password.

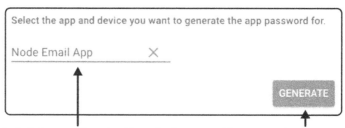

Figure 8-3. Register a Gmail API app

Once your app is registered, you are prompted with a specially generated password, as seen in Figure 8-4. In this figure, the X's represent where your app password will show on your web browser.

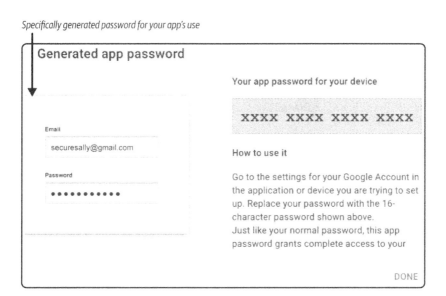

Figure 8-4. Retrieve a Gmail API token password

When this process is complete, you can use the generated app password along with your Gmail email address to sign into your account from your project.

For the `service` key, enter a value that matches your personal email service. In this case, you may use `gmail`. The `auth` key maps to an object containing your `user` (email address), and `pass` (app password) in Example 8-1.

Example 8-1. Configure your mail transporter in index.js

```
...
const transporter = createTransport({ ❶
  service: "gmail", ❷
  auth: { ❸
    user: "jon@jonwexler.com",
    pass: "kdsnndsoonxxjsd",
  },
});
```

❶ Assign the `createTransport` instance to `transporter`.

❷ Add a mail service to your configuration.

❸ Add an email and app password to your configuration.

Get Programming | 145

Next, you set up an object with options for email's contents. Example 8-2 shows the from, to, subject, and text keys to indicate that a welcome email will be sent from the Inn Box business account to your personal email address. The email's content will be plain text for now.

Example 8-2. Adding the nodemailer package to index.js

```
. . .
const mailOptions = { ❶
  from: "jon@innbox.jonwexler.com",
  to: "jon@jonwexler.com",
  subject: "Welcome to Inn Box!",
  text: "Confirm your email",
};
```

❶ Assign mailOptions to contain the email's content and criteria for a welcome message.

The last step is to create an async function to actually send the email. Add the code in Example 8-3 to the bottom of *index.js*. In this code, you create a sendMail function that uses the transporter.sendMail function, along with your mailOptions, to send an outgoing email. You wrap this function call in a try-catch to ensure the app does not fail in case an exception is thrown during the email generation process. At the end of the file, you call sendMail() to run the function and send an email as soon as the app starts.

Example 8-3. Adding the nodemailer package to index.js

```
. . .
const sendMail = async () => { ❶
  try { ❷
    const info = await transporter.sendMail(mailOptions); ❸
    console.log(`Email sent: ${info.response}`); ❹
  } catch (e) {
    console.log(`An error occurred: ${e.message}`); ❺
  }
};

sendMail(); ❻
```

❶ Define a sendMail function to send out an email.

❷ Use a try-catch block to gracefully handle any errors.

❸ Send an email with transporter.sendMail and wait for sending to complete.

146 | Chapter 8: Marketing Mailer

❹ Indicate a successfully sent email in a log to your console.

❺ Catch any error and log the message to your screen.

❻ Invoke the `sendMail` function.

Navigate to your project's root level in your command line and run your app by entering `node index`. After a moment, you'll see `Email sent: 250 2.0.0 OK 1662692125 m18-20006b929a2bsm475205qkn.3 - gsmtp`, or a similar variation of text. You may now confirm that an email was sent to the correct address by visitng your email client directly. There you'll find a new email from Inn Box in your inbox, as shown in Figure 8-5.

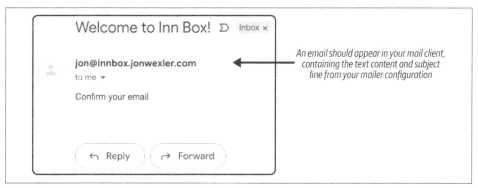

Figure 8-5. Display the successfully sent email in your mail client

 If you are not able to send the email correctly, try to troubleshoot by reading the error message output to your console. If the email was sent but never received, you may try sending to another email address or check your spam folder.

Notice that the email contains only plain text: `Confirm your email`. Because there is no link in this email, there's also no way for the user to confirm or verify their account with this example. However, you may spruce up the email by swapping out plain text for richer HTML content. Add the code in Example 8-4 above your `mail Options` definition in *index.js*. This block of HTML will display the same text, but in a bigger and bolder way, utilizing the `h1` HTML header tags.

Last, replace the `text` key and value in `mailOptions` with `html`. In this case, `html` is both the new key and value represented by the `html` variable.

Example 8-4. Define a block of HTML for your mailer in index.js

```
...
const html = ❶
`<html>
  <body>
      <h1>
      Confirm your email
      </h1>
  </body>
</html>`;
...
```

❶ Define HTML content and assign it to `html`.

When you change the mail options to use `html`, run your app again and notice the change in your next received email. As shown in Figure 8-6 you will see the same text as before, but displayed in an HTML tag. From here you may add more HTML structure and styling to enhance the look and feel of the email.

In the next section you'll introduce an API to collect email addresses and dynamically send emails instead of using your hardcoded values.

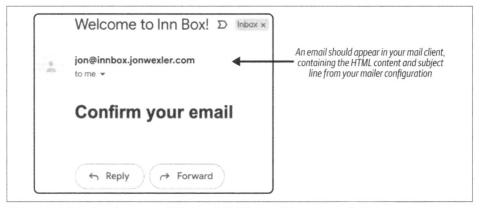

Figure 8-6. Display the successfully sent HTML email in your mail client

Adding a Framework for Your Mailer Service

You've successfully sent emails from your Node app. Now you need those emails to go to prospective customers. To accomplish that, you'll need an API to collect emails and feed them to your `sendMail` function. Before you get started with the API, you make space in the *index.js* file by moving its current contents. Create a new folder called `services` at your project's root level. Within that folder create a file called *mailer.js* and move all of the code from *index.js* into that file.

Because you'll be using the contents of *mailer.js* to send emails, you'll want to export the `sendMail` function. First, move the `mailOptions` variable definition into the `sendMail` function and add `html` and `to` as function parameters. This will allow you to dynamically call `sendMail`, passing in custom HTML and outgoing email addresses, as you can see in Example 8-5.

You can add more parameters to make any part of the email contents dynamic. Or, if you choose, you may pick a more generic subject line that works for all emails, like `Email from Inn Box!`

Example 8-5. Modifying and exporting `sendMail` *in* mailer.js

```
...
export const sendMail = async (to, html) => {   ❶
  const mailOptions = {
    from: "jon@innbox.jonwexler.com",
    to,
    subject: "Email from Inn Box!",
    html,
  };
  try {   ❷
    const info = await transporter.sendMail(mailOptions);
    console.log(`Email sent: ${info.response}`);
  } catch (e) {
    console.log(`An error occurred: ${e.message}`);
  }
};
```

❶ Export the `sendMail` function to take `html` and `to` (email) arguments.

❷ Attempt to send the email using the configured transporter and log the result or error message.

Now your *mailer.js* service module is ready to be used in other files. As a next step, you may create a module to contain your email HTML templates. Create a new file called *mailTemplates.js* at the root level of your project. In this file you'll define the various email templates used for sending outgoing mail. Because all of your email will use the standard HTML structure, you may remove the `html` block from *mailer.js* and wrap it in a new function called `htmlTemplate` in *mailTemplates.js*. This function takes an argument `content` and is used to generate an HTML template with any body content you'd like.

Add the code in Example 8-6 to define the `htmlTemplate` and a `welcomeMail` function, which passes text wrapped in HTML as content in your `htmlTemplate` function.

As you think of new emails to send, you can call `htmlTemplate` and pass in your custom HTML body content to generate the full email contents.

Example 8-6. Adding a dynamic HTML template function in mailTemplates.js

```
const htmlTemplate = (content) => { ❶
  return `<html>
  <body>
    ${content} ❷
  </body>
</html>`;
};

export const welcomeMail = () => { ❸
  const content = ` <h1>Welcome to Inn Box!</h1>`;
  return htmlTemplate(content);
};
```

❶ Define `htmlTemplate` to take body content as an argument.

❷ Fill HTML content in the middle of your standard structure.

❸ Define and export `welcomeMail` to return a simple HTML welcome email.

With your mailer logic moved to its own service, it's time to build the server you'll use to collect emails and invoke the mailer. For this project, you'll use Fastify, a lightweight and high-performance server framework. Install Fastify by running `npm install fastify@^5.4.0` at the root level of your project in the command line. Then, create an `app` instance of `Fastify` to represent your app and all its logic for handling external requests, as seen in Example 8-7.

If you plan to handle `application/x-www-form-urlencoded` input—such as form submissions or curl commands using the `-d` flag—you'll also need to register the `@fastify/formbody` plugin. Install it using `npm install @fastify/formbody@^8.0.2` and register it on your app to allow Fastify to parse URL-encoded bodies.

Example 8-7. Adding `fastify` *in* index.js

```
import Fastify from "fastify"; ❶
import formBody from "@fastify/formbody"; ❷

const app = Fastify(); ❸
await app.register(formBody); ❹
```

❶ Import `Fastify`.

❷ Import the @fastify/formbody plugin to handle URL-encoded form data.

❸ Instantiate an app from Fastify as app.

❹ Register the form body parser to allow POST requests with application/x-www-form-urlencoded data.

Your app is now configured and ready to define API routes for external communication. Add a single *route* called app.post("/subscribe"), which will handle incoming HTTP POST requests to /subscribe with an email in the request's body.

A route in Fastify is a way for your app to distinguish different requests to your app. A POST request implies that content will be submitted to the app, like a form. From here, you may look at the request's contents, or body, to collect any data needed in your app.

Add the route in Example 8-8 to receive a posted email address and log it back to the screen. You use res.json to send JSON content back to the requestor to indicate the end of the function. This simple experiment will help you determine whether your app is reachable via HTTP POST.

Example 8-8. Adding a POST route in index.js

```
...
app.post("/subscribe", async (request, reply) => { ❶
  const { email } = request.body; ❷
  console.log(`Received ${email}`); ❸
  reply.send({ message: "ok"}); ❹
});
```

❶ Define a POST route for the /subscribe path.

❷ Destructure email from the request's body.

❸ Log the posted email to your console.

❹ Return a JSON message in the response.

Last, define a port on which your app will run locally on your computer and set up your app to listen for incoming requests. Add Example 8-9 to the bottom of *index.js* to either use a port number predefined on your computer's environment variables (process.env.PORT), or default to port 3000. app.listen will start your app and listen for incoming requests at `localhost:3000` or your defined port. This version uses `async`/`await` at the top level, which is supported in ECMAScript modules.

Example 8-9. Adding listener function for your app in index.js

```
...
const port = process.env.PORT || 3000;  ❶

try {
  await app.listen({ port });  ❷
  console.log(`Server running at http://localhost:${port}`);  ❸
} catch (err) {
  console.error('Error starting server:', err);  ❹
  process.exit(1);
}
```

❶ Assign a port number from your environment or default to `3000`.

❷ Start the server using `await app.listen({ port })` at the top level.

❸ Log a message when the server is running successfully.

❹ Log any errors if the server fails to start.

With your server set up, start your app and notice the text `Server running at local host:3000` logged to your console. With your server running, you may now submit a POST request to test your app route. Open a new command-line window and run `curl -X POST -d "email=jon@jonwexler.com" http://localhost:3000/ subscribe`. This command will submit a POST request to the `/subscribe` route, containing an email address as a part of the request body. You will see `{"message":"ok"}` as a response in your second command-line window. Your first command-line window, with your server running, will display `Received jon@jonwexler.com`.

You may now connect your mailer to send an email out whenever a POST request is received. Import your `welcomeMail` template function and `sendMail` function to *index.js*, as shown in Example 8-10. These two functions may now be used within your route callback function.

Example 8-10. Importing mailer modules in index.js

```
...
import { sendMail } from "./services/mailer.js";  ❶
import { welcomeMail } from "./mailTemplates.js";
...
```

152 | Chapter 8: Marketing Mailer

❶ Import the sendMail function and welcomeMail HTML template function.

To use these functions, your route callback must be async to support awaiting mail to send. Add the async keyword ahead of your callback function. Then add await send Mail(email, welcomeMail()) right above the reply.send line. This new line will invoke the sendMail function and pass in the email address received in the POST request, as well as the welcomeMail HTML content. Rerun your app, and try to run the curl command for a POST request in your command line again. Notice the email you receive in your mail client with the subject Email from Inn Box! and content Welcome to Inn Box!.

Your app can now receive email addresses through this API endpoint and dynamically send outgoing emails. In the next section, you'll connect a database to start saving these email addresses.

Connecting a Database

Setting up a database is a way to ensure that retrieved content can be used and revisited as the company, Inn Box, grows. For this project, you use SQLite3 and the Sequelize object relational mapper (ORM) to structure and save your data. Install these two packages by stopping your app in the command line and running the command npm install sqlite3@^5.1.7 sequelize@^6.37.7.

With these two packages installed, create a new file called *db.js* at the root level of your project directory. By the end of this section, your project directory structure should look like Example 8-11.

Example 8-11. Project directory structure with a database

```
marketing_mailer
  |
  - index.js
  - services
    |
    - mailer.js
  - db.js ❶
  - database.sqlite ❷
  - package.json
  - node_modules
```

❶ Add the database configuration file, *db.js*, at the root level.

❷ The *database.sqlite* file will automatically generate once your database is set up and connected.

Connecting a Database | 153

Within *db.js*, import the `Sequelize` module by adding `import { Sequelize } from "sequelize"` to the top of the file. Then add the necessary configurations for `Sequelize` to connect to a `sqlite` database. Use `new Sequelize` to instantiate a new database connection. `dialect` will be `sqlite`, indicating the type of database you'll be connecting to. `storage` is *database.sqlite*, which will result in a file called *database.sqlite* generating at the root level of your project when the app starts. After, use `db.authenticate()` to establish a connection with your database. Add the code in Example 8-12 to *db.js*.

It's important to wrap this logic in a `try-catch` to ensure that any database connection issues are properly logged to the console.

Example 8-12. Set up the database in db.js

```
...
const db = new Sequelize({ ❶
  dialect: "sqlite",
  storage: "./database.sqlite",
});

try {
  await db.authenticate(); ❷
  console.log("Connection has been established successfully.");
} catch (error) {
  console.error("Unable to connect to the database:", error); ❸
}
```

❶ Instantiate a new `Sequelize` database using `sqlite`.

❷ Try to connect to your database.

❸ Catch and log any errors that occur.

With your database configured, you still need a table to store the contents of data used by Inn Box. Create a new `Sequelize` model called `Lead` to represent the new subscribers that may eventually become paying gym members. Add the code in Example 8-13 to *db.js* to define that model with three fields. The `email` field is set to be unique so no duplicate email addresses are found in the database. You also add a validation rule, `isEmail`, that comes with Sequelize to ensure the structure of the email matches the traditional structure. This will reduce the noise from text that won't even process during the email sending stage. The `lastCampaign` field is a string that will keep track of the campaign key used for that `Lead`. If Inn Box sends emails offering a 30% discount, the campaign key might be `30promo` (Example 8-13).

Example 8-13. Define and export the `Lead` model in db.js

```
...
const Lead = db.define( ❶
  "Lead",
  {
    email: { ❷
      type: Sequelize.STRING,
      unique: true,
      validate: {
        isEmail: true,
      },
    },
    verified: { ❸
      type: Sequelize.BOOLEAN,
      defaultValue: false,
    },
    lastCampaign: { ❹
      type: Sequelize.STRING,
    },
  },
  {}
);

Lead.sync(); ❺

export default Lead; ❻
```

❶ Define a new `Sequelize` model: `Lead`.

❷ Add a unique and conformant `email` field.

❸ Add a `verified` field to default as `false`.

❹ Add a `lastCampaign` field.

❺ Sync the model with your database upon connecting.

❻ Export the `Lead` model as the default module export.

With your `Lead` model in place, you're ready to start saving email addresses as they arrive at your `/subscribe` POST route. In your *index.js* file, import the `Lead` model at the top of your file by adding `import Lead from "./db.js"`. Within the `/subscribe` route, add the code in Example 8-14 to wrap your `sendMail` call in a `try-catch`

Connecting a Database | 155

block, and attempt to save a `Lead` record to your database with `Lead
.create({ email })`. Waiting for the database to save this record will hold off on
sending the email to that address until after it is saved.

Example 8-14. Save a new Lead in index.js

```
...
try { ❶
  await Lead.create({ email }); ❷
  await sendMail(email, welcomeMail());
} catch (e) {
  console.log("Could not save the Lead", e.message);
}
...
```

❶ Wrap your database call in a `try`/`catch` block.

❷ Create a new `Lead` record with the request body's email address.

Now, restart your app. You'll notice your console displays more logs this time to indicate the connection of your database. In a separate command-line window, run your curl POST command to see your record saved and a new email sent to your email client. To test the email validation, try saving the same email address a second time or submitting malformed text in place of a real email address. You will notice that the record will not save in this case, but instead will log: `Could not save the Lead Validation error`.

> Clearing your SQLite database is as easy as deleting the *database.sqlite* file in your project folder.

With your database connected, add a new route to support verifying your email address. Your new route should listen for GET requests containing the email address looking to be verified. Within the route, logic will check to see if the email address exists in your database. Then, if the `Lead` exists, you modify the `verified` field and save the `Lead` record. You add two different `res.json` lines, depending on the success of verifying the email (Example 8-15).

Example 8-15. Adding a verification route in index.js

```
...
app.get("/verify/:email", async (request, reply) => { ❶
  const { email } = request.params; ❷
```

```
  try {
    const lead = await Lead.findOne({ where: { email } }); ❸
    if (lead) { ❹
      lead.verified = true; ❺
      await lead.save(); ❻
      console.log(`${email} is verified`);
      reply.send({ message: "Verified!" }); ❼
    }
  } catch (e) {
    console.log("Could not verify the Lead", e.message);
  }
  reply.send({ message: "Unable to  verify." }); ❽
});
...
```

❶ Add a new route to handle email addresses as a URL parameter.

❷ Destructure the `email` from the request's `params`.

❸ Search for a `Lead` by the email address in the request.

❹ Check whether a `Lead` was found.

❺ If a `Lead` is found, modify its `verified` field.

❻ Save the modified `Lead` instance.

❼ Confirm to the user that their email was verified.

❽ Notify the user if their email is not able to be verified.

One way to test this new route is by modifying the `welcomeMail` template to include a link to this route. Add a new function, `confirmationMail`, in *mailTemplates.js* that will dynamically wrap your email text in a link. When the user clicks that link, they will be directed to your `/verify:email` route, whereupon their email address will be verified (Example 8-16).

Example 8-16. Adding a new dynamic confirmation template in mailTemplates.js

```
...
export const confirmationMail = (url) => { ❶
  const content = `<a href="${url}"><h1>Confirm your email</h1></a>`; ❷
  return htmlTemplate(content);
};
...
```

Connecting a Database | 157

❶ Add a new mail template function to take a `url` parameter.

❷ Create a link to the `url` argument to confirm the user's email.

In *index.js*, import the `confirmationMail` template function and use it in your `/subscribe` route in place of the `welcomeMail` template function. The new function will take in a URL. In this case, `confirmationMail(http://localhost:3000/verify/${email})` points to your local app and dynamically passes the email address.

To properly test this new route, you'll need to deploy your app to the internet. Once an email is received by your email client, like Gmail, it doesn't necessarily have a way to open a link to your locally running web server at `localhost:3000`. Once the app is in production, you may change the URL to reflect the public location, and clicking on the confirmation link will lead to a verification on your server and in your database.

Now that you have a way to dynamically create a link within your outgoing emails, you can start to create marketing campaigns for Inn Box and track which leads are interested.

Implementing a Marketing Pixel for Email Engagement

Email marketing is a huge business, generating billions of dollars a year across every industry. Part of what makes it so successful is learning more about the readers of the emails and whether they're engaging with your product. With your email client being a personalized and private space for your mail, this can be a challenging task.

Luckily, technology offers both the tools to reach your customers and the creativity to understand their engagement with your emails. One way marketing services track whether a lead opened their email is by adding a *tracking pixel*, also known as a *marketing pixel*. This pixel is a literal single pixel image pulled from the marketing service's servers. The trick is that the image's URL contains enough information so that when the image is requested to load from the server, the server can also record which lead opened the email and which campaign was promoted in that email.

In this way, companies can determine which emails are being opened, which drives decisions about the marketing campaigns that are working, ultimately feeding the company more paying customers. You already established a model that supports saving campaign strings for each lead. Following a similar approach to the `confirmationMail` template's dynamic URL, you'll create a new route to serve loaded content in your marketing campaign emails.

Add the code in Example 8-17 to define a new GET route for /campaign/:campaign Key/user/:email/image.png. This route path contains a campaignKey used to identify which promotions are in the sent email. An email parameter is also used to map this link to the targeted user's email in the database. The route ends with image.png to give the illusion that an image will be loaded by the server. Within the callback function, you pull the email and campaignKey values from the request. Then you search for a user by the given email address and update the respective record's last Campaign field to match the marketing email's campaignKey. In this way you can quickly track which users opened the most recent marketing emails and help the business determine the success of their email promotions.

Example 8-17. Adding a campaign tracking route in index.js

```
...
app.get("/campaign/:campaignKey/user/:email/image.png", async (request, reply) => { ❶
  const { email, campaignKey } = request.params; ❷
  try {
    const lead = await Lead.findOne({ where: { email } }); ❸
    if (lead) {
      lead.lastCampaign = campaignKey; ❹
      await lead.save();
      console.log(`${email} opened ${campaignKey}`); ❺
    }
  } catch (e) {
    console.log("An error occurred", e.message);
  }
  reply.send({ message: "ok" }); ❻
});
...
```

❶ Add a new campaign tracking route to take campaignKey and email params.

❷ Destructure the email and campaignKey from the request's params.

❸ Check if a Lead with the provided email exists.

❹ If the Lead exists, modify their lastCampaign to be the campaignKey and save the record.

❺ Log whether the email contents were viewed for the given campaign.

❻ Respond with a simple JSON message.

In *mailTemplates.js*, create a new function called campaignMail to create a new template for an email promotion (Example 8-18).

Implementing a Marketing Pixel for Email Engagement | 159

Example 8-18. Adding a campaign mail template in mailTemplates.js

```
...
export const campaignMail = (campaignText, campaignKey, email) => { ❶
  const content = ` ❷
<h1>${campaignText}</h1>
<img src="http://localhost:3000/campaign/${campaignKey}/user/${email}/image.png"
    style="display:none">
  `;
  return htmlTemplate(content);
};
```

❶ Add a new mail template function with dynamic text, a campaignKey, and the user's email.

❷ Add an image tag to fetch from your dynamic campaign tracking route.

To run this function, import campaignMail at the top of *index.js* and add send Mail("jon@jonwexler.com", campaignMail("Special Promotion", "promo1", "jon@jonwexler.com")) above the app.listen block in *index.js*. Just make sure to test the code with your own email addresses. As soon as you restart the Node app, an email will be sent with a hidden tracking image link. The email you receive in your email client will read Special Promotion, though you won't be able to immediately see the campaignKey tracked. Similar to the issues with confirming an email address in a development project, you'll first need to deploy this app to see the email tracking logic work and save to your database.

In the meantime, you can send a curl request to mimic the image URL call by opening a new command-line window and running curl http://localhost:3000/campaign/promo1/user/jon@jonwexler.com/image.png. In that same window, you'll see a response of {"message":"ok"}. Your server will log jon@jonwexler.com opened promo1 to its console window along with logs from a database query indicating an updated record.

With your app ready to verify emails and track email campaigns, the last step is to automate the emailing process. In the next section you'll use a scheduling package to help send emails out at specified times.

Integrating a Task Scheduler

Your app is set up to handle most of what a business needs to get started with email marketing. The functionality is bare, but opens the door for creatively formatted emails and a tracking system to help identify the business's paying market. Automating the sending of emails isn't required, but will ultimately make the process

160 | Chapter 8: Marketing Mailer

smoother from a management perspective. Like everything else in Node, there's a package to help manage tasks on a specified time basis.

At the root level of your project folder in your command line, run `npm install node-schedule@^2.1.1` to install the `node-schedule` package. This package provides functions with a variety of syntaxes for scheduling tasks to run. Instead of sending the campaign email as soon as the app starts, you can move it to a scheduler to better manage when the email is sent.

Create a file in your `services` folder called *scheduler.js*. This file will handle the scheduling and execution of tasks. Import the `scheduleJob` function directly from this package by adding `import { scheduleJob } from "node-schedule"` to the top of *scheduler.js*. Below that, add the code in Example 8-19 to define a function, `schedule`, to initiate a scheduled task. For now, you may have that task be a logged statement that runs according to the `timeOptions` you provide.

Example 8-19. Adding a task scheduler function in scheduler.js

```
...
export const schedule = (timeOptions) => { ❶
  scheduleJob(timeOptions, () => { ❷
    console.log("Time to send an email."); ❸
  });
};
```

❶ Define and export a `schedule` function that accepts a `timeOptions` argument.

❷ Run `scheduleJob` with the given time configurations.

❸ Log a message to your console during the execution of your scheduled job.

Now import the `schedule` function from the scheduler module in *index.js* by adding `import { schedule } from "./services/scheduler.js"` to the top of the file. Below that, add `schedule({ seconds: 30 })` to run your scheduled console log every minute at the 30-second mark of that minute. Restart your app and notice how `Time to send an email.` prints to your console once every minute.

Next, you copy the imports for `campaignMail` and `sendMail` to *scheduler.js* and send your `campaignMail` template from the `schedule` function instead of *index.js*. Now, your `schedule` callback function has become `async` as it handles sending campaign emails. Every time you call the `schedule` function, the emails won't be sent out immediately, but only at their scheduled time (Example 8-20).

Integrating a Task Scheduler | 161

Example 8-20. Running an email campaign from a scheduled job in scheduler.js

```
...
import { scheduleJob } from "node-schedule";
import { sendMail } from "./mailer.js"; ❶
import { campaignMail } from "../mailTemplates.js";

export const schedule = (timeOptions) => {
  scheduleJob(timeOptions, async () => { ❷
    await sendMail( ❸
      "jon@jonwexler.com",
      campaignMail("Special Promotion", "promo1", "jon@jonwexler.com")
    );
  });
};
```

❶ Adjust the module imports relative to the *scheduler.js* file location.

❷ Change the `scheduleJob` callback function to be `async`.

❸ Send an email at the scheduled time.

After saving this file and restarting your app, you'll notice an email is sent out to your specified recipient every minute. You can change the scheduled job time in *index.js* by changing {`second: 30`}. For example, the email may be scheduled to send every Monday at 1 PM, in which case the `timeOptions` would be {`dayOfWeek: 1, hour: 13 `}. To learn more about `node-schedule` and its scheduler configurations, visit the npm website (*https://oreil.ly/rJjyT*).

With your scheduler up and running, you've put together a comprehensive foundation for Inn Box's marketing campaign app. From here you may make some of the functions more dynamic or start decorating the HTML of your campaign emails.

Chapter Exercises

1. Add unsubscribe support to your email campaigns:

    To add unsubscribe support to your email campaigns, start by creating a new GET route /unsubscribe/:email in your server that updates the corresponding Lead record by setting a new unsubscribed field to true. Modify your Lead model to include this unsubscribed field with a default value of false. Then, update your email templates to include a visible unsubscribe link pointing to /unsubscribe/:email at the bottom of each message. Finally, ensure your application checks this field before sending emails—preventing re-subscription or scheduled emails from reaching users who have opted out.

Giving users an option to unsubscribe helps avoid spam complaints and keeps your mailing list healthy.

2. Track clicks on promotion links inside emails:

To track clicks on promotional links, add a new GET route such as `/click/:campaignKey/user/:email` that logs when a user clicks a link in your email. Update your `Lead` model to include a new `lastClickedCampaign` field to store this information. Modify one of your campaign email templates to include a visible button or hyperlink that points to the new tracking route. When the link is visited, update the corresponding user's `lastClickedCampaign` field and log a confirmation message to the console.

While open rates are helpful, click-through rates often give a clearer signal of user interest and intent.

Summary

In this chapter, you built a full-featured marketing mailer using Node. You learned how to:

- Programmatically send emails with rich, dynamic HTML content
- Collect and validate email addresses through an API endpoint
- Verify user accounts using confirmation links in emails
- Track user engagement by logging email opens and campaign interactions
- Schedule and automate outgoing emails with a customizable task scheduler

CHAPTER 9

Web Scraper

This chapter covers the following:

- Scraping contents from an HTML website
- Running a headless browser
- Collecting scraped data and offering it as an API

In this chapter, you'll build a web scraper to collect contents of HTML websites and process them in your Node server. *Web scraping* is the process of extracting data from a website and has existed for nearly as long as the internet itself.

Before APIs were made public and accessible by businesses, the only way to get updated product pricing, immediate news headlines, and static web content was by manually visiting a web URL and looking directly at the resulting web page; kind of like how we still mostly use the internet today.

There are now more ways to process and use data than ever before, but still not enough APIs to feed those processing systems. Even where APIs exist, restrictions in the type of data an end user has access to may be limited. For example, a food delivery service may provide an API for the top restaurants in a neighborhood, but not allow for filtering by dietary restrictions. To get that data, you could, alternatively, visit the URL for results filtered by dietary restriction and scrape the resulting contents. In this chapter, you'll explore the options available within the Node ecosystem to allow for scraping web pages and using that data in your own application.

165

Tools and Applications Used in This Chapter

Before you get started, make sure to install and configure the tools and applications required for this project. Installation instructions for Node.js, Fastify, and VS Code are provided in Chapter 1, while project initialization steps, such as setting up your directory structure, configuring *package.json*, and using modern syntax, are covered in Appendix A. Once completed, return here to continue. Building a project from scratch helps deepen your understanding of each component, giving you greater control and flexibility as you progress.

Your Prompt

As an active participant in an online tech forum, *Node Dojo*, you are tasked with helping to collect articles and tutorials related to Node. After scouring the internet, it's decided that you should collect the top Node articles available at *https://medium.com*. Though Medium offers an API (*https://oreil.ly/iqrgk*), you decide to develop a web-scraping tool to get the article titles and links for the top Node articles.

Get Planning

You plan to deliver an app that effectively visits a web page automatically and returns article titles and URLs. In this way, when new Node articles are published, you will be able to scrape data from Medium's site and provide your tech forum with the most engaging articles and tutorials to read.

To start, you'll target a specific URL and fetch its HTML contents. Initially, those contents could be parsed as plain text, where you'll find the articles' content you're looking for. Later, you'll incorporate powerful npm packages designed to fetch a web page's contents and help you parse the element of that page more efficiently. By the end of the development process, your app will even allow users to search specific keyword terms and return matching articles from Medium's site.

You begin by sketching out a diagram detailing the relationship between your app's logic and how external sites are scraped. In Figure 9-1 you establish that a user will initiate your app, whereupon the target external site is fetched and scraped. The returned HTML contents are then processed in your app so you may select only the article titles and links. Last, you return those values back to the client that started the application.

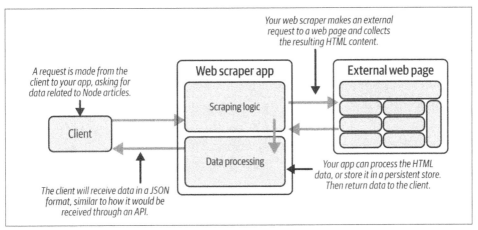

Figure 9-1. Project blueprint for a web-scraping Node app

This application has two parts:

Accessing and scraping
    Because there isn't necessarily another way to access the website's data, it's important that you are able to reach the site itself. If the site is blocked by an authentication layer, or is otherwise inaccessible, scraping won't work.

Filtering
    After making contact with the site, you'll receive the site's contents as HTML data. HTML offers a predictable structure that you may leverage to target only the data you need. If your app is designed well, there shouldn't be a need for much maintenance down the road.

With this structure in place, you're ready to start building an app.

Get Programming

To start developing your app, create a new folder named `site_scraper`. Navigate to your project folder on your command line and run `npm init`. This command initializes your Node app. You may press Enter throughout the initialization steps to accept the defaults. The result of these steps is the creation of a file called *package.json*. This file will instruct your Node app of any configurations or scripts needed to run correctly.

Next, create a file called *index.js* within your project folder. This file is the entry point for your app.

With your Node app initialized, you may navigate to the *index.js* file to start coding. Without installing any additional packages, you're already equipped to fetch a website's HTML contents using the built-in `fetch` API. Add the code in Example 9-1 to use `fetch` to make a GET request to *https://medium.com/tag/nodejs*. You'll receive a response object from the site, on which you can call the `text()` method to convert the response HTML to plain text. Then, log the resulting text using `console.log`.

This example uses top-level `await`, a modern JavaScript feature supported in Node 18 and later when your project is configured as an ECMAScript module. If your environment does not support top-level `await`, you can wrap your logic in an `async` function instead.

Example 9-1. Fetching HTML content from an external page in index.js

```
const URL = "https://medium.com/tag/nodejs"; ❶

try { ❷
  const response = await fetch(URL); ❸
  const text = await response.text(); ❹
  console.log(text); ❺
} catch (e) { ❻
  console.log("error", e.message);
}
```

❶ Assign the URL variable to the top Node articles Medium link.

❷ Wrap your code in a `try/catch` block to handle potential errors.

❸ Make a GET request to the specified URL using `fetch`.

❹ Convert the response to plain text.

❺ Output the plain HTML to your console.

❻ Catch and log any errors that occur during the request.

Navigate to your project in your command line and run node index to start your app. Depending on your connectivity, the fetch call may take a few seconds. When complete, you'll see hundreds of lines of HTML output to your screen similar to the content that follows:

```
<!doctype html>
<html lang="en">
<head>
  <title data-rh="true">The most insightful stories about Nodejs...</title>
  <meta data-rh="true" charset="utf-8"/>
  <meta data-rh="true" name="viewport" content="width=device-width,..."/>
  <meta data-rh="true" name="theme-color" content="#000000"/>
  ...
</head>
</html>
```

If you aren't seeing any output content, make sure your console log statement is written correctly. If any errors occur, you'll see the error message logged to the screen and may debug from that printed statement.

This output is typical HTML source code for a web page. Within the response you'll find HTML tags like <div> or <a> marking individual elements. These are the blocks of HTML that define the structure of the web page on your browser.

A Brief Word on HTML

If you're new to frontend development, or software development in general, you may not be familiar with how web pages are constructed. Just as JavaScript code depends on a certain syntax and structure, the visual construction of a website has its own rules.

Hypertext Markup Language (HTML) is the makeup of nearly every web page or web app you've visited on the internet. When you visit a URL on your web browser, you'll see a visual representation of data blocks known as HTML elements, in a formation accessible by your client-side JavaScript, known as the Document Object Model (DOM). Through this relationship, each element represents a part of the visual page you see. Some of those elements contain paragraphs of text. Others may contain ads or links. Figure 9-2 displays the home page for *https://www.oreilly.com*. In this example, you may notice how visual aspects of the page are actually self-contained HTML elements under the hood.

Get Programming | 169

Figure 9-2. Example HTML page breakdown for www.oreilly.com

Each HTML element has an opening and a closing HTML tag. The <div> tag is the most used HTML tag (though it arguably is generally misused). You may find that the title of an online article is found in a <div> tag. Some elements contain a class name or id to help differentiate between other elements. For example, an article title may appear in an element marked with a title class like this: <div class="title"></div>. Other times you may get the title implicitly from the type of tag used for that element. For example, an <h1> (or heading 1-level tag) is typically used to wrap title text content. These tags make it easier to target when searching through HTML output to collect the specific information you seek.

Later in this section, you'll explore the HTML response from an externally fetched page to further dissect a web page while scraping for content.

To learn more about HTML, read the MDN documentation (*https://oreil.ly/wuBXF*).

After confirming that you're able to retrieve HTML content from the source URL, it's time to explore the web page and identify elements worth scraping. In Figure 9-3 you'll find an example of what the browser page looks like for trending Node articles on Medium. Visually, it's easy to separate the title at the top of the page, Nodejs, from the list of article sections below. These will be indicators you may use to target their related HTML elements.

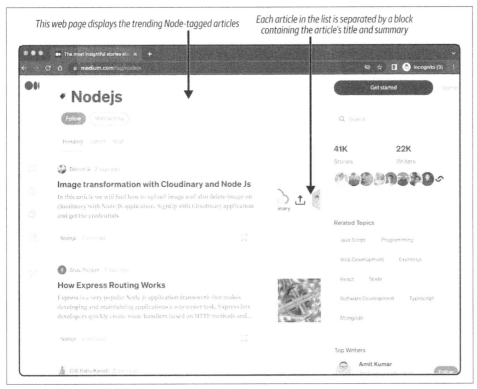

Figure 9-3. Example HTML page breakdown

To explore the HTML elements for one of these listed articles, you may right-click the article section and select Inspect from the tooltip menu. Figure 9-4 demonstrates what that menu looks like in the Chrome browser.

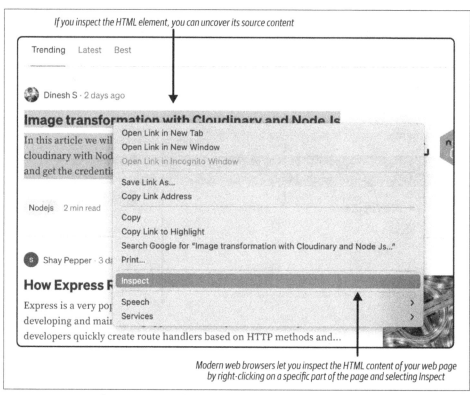

Figure 9-4. Example HTML page breakdown

Last, you see a window at the bottom of the browser with viewable HTML, as seen in Figure 9-5. Notice the article title appears within an <h2> tag. That tag also appears within an anchor tag, <a>, which is used to link to the article. These are two indicators that you may use on the server side when scraping this page.

Only one problem remains: parsing the resulting HTML from your `fetch` call. Despite the tree-like structure offered through HTML, you are left with only a plaintext version in your call's response. You may use a fancy regular expression to select the <h2> and <a> tags. However, there's a simpler solution using the npm packages, explored in the next sections.

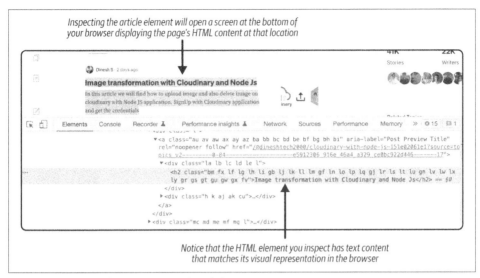

Figure 9-5. Example HTML page breakdown

Parsing with HTML-Friendly Tools

You've used the `fetch` API to retrieve HTML content from a web page and log it as plain text. You can use basic JavaScript string functions to inspect that text and make sense of the underlying HTML. For example, adding `text.split("><")` to your code in *index.js* will effectively separate the HTML elements of your page into an array. This process is crude and inefficient, though, leaving you only with more obstacles in your parsing journey.

Another option is to explore npm packages that work with HTML as plain text. A popular package is `cheerio`, which may be installed by running `npm install cheerio@^1.1.2` at the root level of your project directory in your command line. The `cheerio` package is a server-side implementation of the jQuery library. Whereas the jQuery library has been used for years to simplify JavaScript interactions with the HTML DOM, `cheerio` helps you parse HTML as plain text and target specific elements in the same way. To learn more about the `cheerio` package and API, visit the cheerio website (*https://oreil.ly/CVjmq*).

In your *index.js* file, add `import { load } from "cheerio"` to start using the package. Then add the code shown in Example 9-2, which uses the `load()` function to convert your plain-text HTML content in `text` to a `cheerio` object. This object is assigned to `$`, a variable name as used in jQuery to refer to the whole HTML DOM. You may now use the `$` variable to locate specific elements within the page. As seen in Example 9-2, article titles are found in `<h2>` tags. It also happens that those titles are nested within `<article>` tags. Using these two together in `$("article h2")` allows you to target all the article titles on the page. Then you loop over each of the resulting elements to log the title text using `$(element).text()`.

Example 9-2. Using `cheerio` to parse HTML content in index.js

```
...
const $ = load(text); ❶
const elements = $("article h2"); ❷
elements.each((i, element) => { ❸
  console.log($(element).text()); ❹
});
...
```

❶ Convert your HTML plain text to a `cheerio` object.

❷ Target all of the `<h2>` tags within an `<article>` tag.

❸ Iterate over each found element using Cheerio's `.each()` method.

❹ Log the inner text of the `<h2>` tags to your console.

Run your app to see a list of the top 10 trending article titles appear on your console. In this example, the same `fetch` call is executed. Only this time, you're parsing the result to only pull the titles. Try modifying your logic by targeting the `<article>` tag alone, then using the `find()` function to further target the `<h2>` and `<a>` tags nested within (Example 9-3). Notice, in addition to the title text, you're also collecting the `href` attribute belonging to the `<a>` tag. This is where the article URL lives.

Example 9-3. Targeting article titles and URLs in index.js

```
...
const elements = $("article"); ❶
elements.each((i, element) => { ❷
  const title = $(element).find("h2").text(); ❸
  const url = $(element).find("a").attr("href"); ❹
  console.log(title, url); ❺
});
...
```

174 | Chapter 9: Web Scraper

❶ Target all of the `<article>` elements.

❷ Iterate over each found element using Cheerio's `.each()` method.

❸ Find the article title and assign it to the `title` variable.

❹ Find the article URL and assign it to the `url` variable.

❺ Log the title and URL for each article to your console.

Now when you run your app, you'll see both the article title and link logged for all top 10 trending articles. However, the URLs listed are not complete. Although you could make sense of how to construct the URL from this output, you may not always depend on the page's source HTML to have a fully generated URL that you may use. Moreover, modern web apps and single-page applications (SPAs) may not even generate the majority of their HTML unless it is loaded in a browser. For that reason, you'll need an additional package, which you'll learn about in the next section.

Scraping Web Pages with a Headless Browser

To this point, you've been able to fetch and parse a web page's HTML. This process is sufficient for the majority of websites on the internet, though most modern apps and progressive websites are moving to a different style of content loading.

With the advent of web components and frontend libraries like React, Vue, and Angular, it is not guaranteed that your first impression of a loaded web page contains its fully loaded contents. That means a fetch call may result in a fairly empty response, relative to what you'd see in a web browser. This is partly why *headless browsers* were created.

A headless browser is a web browser without a visual component. A browser instance is created and may load a web page, its cookies, and document positioning. It may even maintain state and browser history. The best part is that it may run on the server. Figure 9-6 demonstrates the difference between content fetched via a traditional HTTP request and a headless browser. For web pages that lazily load their content, or have some immediate restriction on showing visual content, a `fetch` call may return only a shell of the HTML page, whereas a headless browser retrieves content reflecting the real human experience without a real person's manual verification.

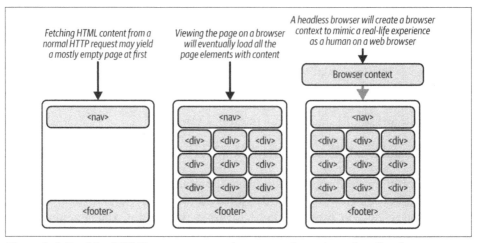

Figure 9-6. Fetching HTML page source code compared to using a headless browser

In your project, you'll use the `puppeteer` Node library to create a browser instance and retrieve article titles and URLs. Install the npm package by running `npm install puppeteer@^24.15.0` at your project's root level in the command line.

Starting with version 22, Puppeteer no longer downloads the Chromium browser automatically during installation. To install the correct browser version manually, add the following script to your *package.json* file: `"install-browser"`: `"puppeteer browsers install chrome"`. Once added, run the script by executing `npm run install-browser` in your command line. This will download the correct version of Chromium that Puppeteer uses to run your headless browser.

> ## Working with Puppeteer
>
> When a website is the only source for visualizing and accessing certain datasets, it may be challenging to rely on that data for your own application. Although it's increasingly common to see dedicated APIs made available to software engineers, the majority of content across the internet is still accessible only via your web browser. This limitation is particularly challenging for building and testing your own web applications. How may you test the visual output of your site without a tool that can "see" the generated output?
>
> Luckily, this problem is a shared concern across the tech community, and new solutions are being designed to assist. One of those tools is Puppeteer—a Node library that creates a browser context using Chromium (derived from the Chrome web browser). From within your Node server, the `puppeteer` npm package uses browser dev tools to re-create the browser experience for a web page. The library loads a new browser instance, virtually opens a new window, and visits the URL you choose. In effect, there are four main steps:

1. `const browser = await puppeteer.launch()`
   Launches a browser instance and assigns its value to a variable

2. `const page = await browser.newPage()`
   Creates a new page, from which to load a web page

3. `await page.goto(url)`
   Visits that web page, as you would in a normal browser

4. `browser.close()`
   Completes the task and shuts down the browser instance

Before closing the browser, you're able to use the Puppeteer API to evaluate and navigate the visited page. For example, you may select elements based on their class names or ID attributes, wait for them to load with `page.waitForSelector`, and click them using `page.click`, as you would in a graphical representation. Puppeteer also lets you take screenshots and save the resulting images to your filesystem.

This tool's flexibility in automating frontend tasks is why it's also one of the leading libraries used in end-to-end testing for web apps. You can learn more about Puppeteer on the Puppeteer website (*https://pptr.dev*).

With `puppeteer` installed, you now have access to a whole web browser within your Node server. Add `import puppeteer from "puppeteer"` to the top of your *index.js* file. Then replace the code with the code in Example 9-4. In this code block, you initialize a `puppeteer` browser and create a new browser page.

These objects are used to fulfill a browser-initiated web request. The actual request occurs in `page.goto(URL)`, in which a request is made to see the fully loaded contents of the requested URL. A user-agent string is added to ensure the response matches what a typical browser would receive. A short delay gives time for JavaScript-rendered content to appear. The `page.$$` syntax is used to run `document.querySelectorAll`, which collects all `<article>` elements from the DOM.

Each cl containing the content of an `<article>` element is iterated over. The `$eval` function is used on the selection to extract the `<h2>` element's text content and the `<a>` element's `href` attribute. Because the browser has rendered the page fully, the `href` contains a complete, usable link. After each iteration, the extracted `title` and `url` values are logged to your console.

Example 9-4. Using puppeteer to scrape HTML content in index.js

```
const URL = "https://medium.com/tag/nodejs";

const browser = await puppeteer.launch(); ❶
const page = await browser.newPage(); ❷
```

Scraping Web Pages with a Headless Browser | 177

```
await page.setUserAgent( ❸
  "Mozilla/5.0 (Macintosh; Intel Mac OS X) AppleWebKit/537.36 " +
  "(KHTML, like Gecko) Chrome/118 Safari/537.36"
);

await page.goto(URL, { waitUntil: "networkidle2" });  ❹

(await page.waitForTimeout?.(3000)) ?? ❺
  (await new Promise((r) => setTimeout(r, 3000)));

const articles = await page.$$("article"); ❻

for (const el of articles) { ❼
  const title = await el
    .$eval("h2", (el) => el.textContent.trim())
    .catch(() => null);

  const url = await el
    .$eval("a", (el) => el.href)
    .catch(() => null);

  if (title && url) {
    console.log(title, url);  ❽
  }
}

await browser.close();
```

❶ Create a new Puppeteer browser instance.

❷ Open a new page (tab) in the browser.

❸ Set a realistic user-agent to avoid blocked or stripped responses.

❹ Load the Medium tag URL and wait until the network is idle.

❺ Wait briefly to allow JavaScript-rendered content to appear.

❻ Select all `<article>` elements from the page.

❼ Loop through each article element to extract title and URL.

❽ Log the result to the console only if both values are found.

puppeteer runs by default as a headless browser. This is useful for running tests and bulk logic automatically. Because a full web browser is still being loaded under the hood, you may opt to see that browser run graphically. To do that, add { headless: false } as an argument in your puppeteer.launch function.

When you run your app this time, you'll notice it takes a bit longer than a standard fetch command. That's because a full Chromium browser is starting and loading your desired web page. You'll then see those same top 10 trending article titles and links appear in your console. The links will be functional, complete with the *medium.com* domain.

With this scraper in place, you've now taken your first steps toward extracting and using structured data from complex, JavaScript-driven websites. Whether you're building tools for content aggregation, testing visual layouts, or simply exploring how modern sites deliver content, Puppeteer gives you the flexibility of a full browser—right inside your Node app. In the next chapter, you'll expand on this foundation by turning your scraper into a reusable API service that can power frontend interfaces or downstream automations.

Chapter Exercises

1. Automate article keyword filtering:

    Write a function that accepts a keyword (e.g., "performance") as input and filters out any article titles that don't contain the keyword. After scraping the list of article titles and URLs, apply this function to display only the matching articles in your console. This encourages users to tailor their results to specific learning goals or topic preferences.

     Use .includes() on the title string for basic keyword matching. Be sure to normalize to lowercase for case-insensitive comparison.

2. Write scraped results to a JSON API:

    Instead of logging your scraped article titles and URLs to the console, create a new route such as /api/articles that returns the scraped results as a JSON object. This will allow your scraper to serve as a backend service for other apps or a frontend UI.

Store the results in a local array and return that array as the response body from your new route.

Summary

In this chapter, you learned how to:

- Access the contents of an HTML page from a Node server
- Target data elements of a website
- Collect and process data from a headless browser

CHAPTER 10

App Authentication

This chapter covers the following:

- Designing login authentication logic
- Using the Passport.js library to authenticate users and manage session or token-based strategies
- Using JSON web tokens to authenticate across APIs

In this chapter, you'll build authentication logic for a Node application. No matter the type of core application you decide to build, user authentication remains a vital component in securing your application data. With the expansion of the accessibility and availability of the internet, so too have applications become more vulnerable to attacks.

Applications have come a long way from verifying your identity via an email address and plain-text password. Most have implemented basic encryption or a hashing function to save only jumbled text versions of your passwords. Others have taken security to a new level with multifactor authentication (MFA), ensuring that a user may only log in with their password if they also verify their account with an additional code sent to their phone or email.

Each year, the tech community faces new user security and authentication problems, with many companies investing in dedicated teams to solve them. Luckily, most businesses have a mutual interest in protecting their clients' account data, resulting in industry standards for creating new accounts and processing incoming requests. These best practices are extended beyond the standard web page to mobile clients and Application Programming Interfaces (APIs), which may not have a UI login form. In the following sections, you'll build an authentication system and iterate over

181

improved versions to put some of these common authentication strategies into practice.

Tools and Applications Used in This Chapter

Before you get started, make sure to install and configure the tools and applications required for this project. Installation instructions for Node.js, Fastify, and VS Code are provided in Chapter 1, while project initialization steps, such as setting up your directory structure, configuring *package.json*, and using modern syntax, are covered in Appendix A. Instructions for installing and using Postman can be found in Appendix B. For a deeper explanation of SQLite concepts, see Appendix C. Once completed, return here to continue. Building a project from scratch helps deepen your understanding of each component, giving you greater control and flexibility as you progress.

Your Prompt

You've built a successful travel-planning app, Journey Doc, and the user base is steadily growing. The only problem is, while users may create new itineraries, they were never required to create their account with a secure password. This is both a security risk and an inconvenience because their saved itineraries are publicly accessible, leaving users unsure if they can trust your platform. As a remediation and development project, you decide to iterate on a number of authentication measures, requiring users to log in and authenticate their account before creating new travel plans or accessing existing travel data.

Get Planning

While a large portion of your app is already built and running, you decide to tackle your authentication challenge from scratch. By the end of this project, you'll have a dedicated app and API for creating user accounts complete with a username and encrypted password. The goal of the project is to use available tools to design the most efficient and secure logic to handle many new account requests and frequent password verification requests. For that reason, you'll use Node and Fastify to build an app server to handle HTTP requests, and a SQLite database to save relevant account information.

Figure 10-1 details the flow of information from user interaction on a web browser. First, the user will sign up with their account information, effectively registering their account and storing their username and associated password information in the database. Your registration logic handles the process of securing the account passwords, so only necessary information is stored. Later, when users log in to your web page, they'll be prompted with a similar login screen. Upon submitting the login form, the user's request is handled by a Fastify route handler that invokes authentication logic. This logic compares the incoming username and password combination to determine whether an account may be accessed.

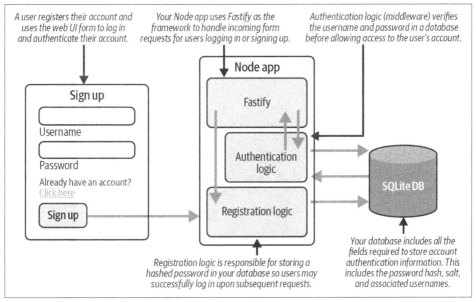

Figure 10-1. Project blueprint for a login authentication Node app

To start, you create a server with the minimum API endpoints needed to create and verify new user accounts and a single login page as a visual reference for user login activity. You connect a database to store username and password information and use the passwords in that database to verify whether user login attempts should be authenticated. You'll work with the Passport.js library, which contains many of the standard authentication protocols used across major web apps, packaged in a set of easy-to-use classes and functions.

Once you have a working authentication process, you'll address securing APIs that do not necessarily have a web browser client. These APIs may be used by a wide array of clients, from progressive web apps to mobile devices. A common strategy here is to generate authentication tokens that get passed between the client and your server to verify your users' identities.

With your app design sketched out, you move on to building out the server framework logic and API endpoints in the next section.

Get Planning | 183

Get Programming

To start developing your app, create a new folder named `app_authentication`. Navigate to your project folder on your command line and run `npm init`. This command initializes your Node app. You may press Enter throughout the initialization steps to accept the defaults. The result of these steps is the creation of a file called *package.json*. This file will instruct your Node app of any configurations or scripts needed to run correctly.

Next, create a file called *index.js* within your project folder. This file is the entry point for your app.

With your *index.js* file ready, you may install the main server framework, template engine, and supporting plugins used in this project. Run `npm install fastify@^5.0.0 @fastify/formbody@^8.0.0 @fastify/view@^10.0.0 handlebars @^4.7.8` to install Fastify, the Handlebars template engine, and the required Fastify plugins for handling form data and server-side rendering. These packages allow your app to parse incoming form submissions and dynamically render HTML templates based on user-specific data.

Building Templates with Handlebars

In addition to routing and API structure, Fastify offers server-side rendering (SSR) through the `@fastify/view` plugin. SSR is the process of building an HTML page from dynamic data on the server and serving that file to a user over the internet. A template language allows for variables to act as placeholders within an HTML template and later compile into a static HTML file. This process enables applications to serve web pages with distinct information as it relates to unique users. For example, every user should get the same "welcome page," but with only *their* own username inserted into the page: "Welcome, Jon!".

Figure 10-2 demonstrates how Fastify passes request data into a route handler that renders the Handlebars template. When Fastify is ready to return a webpage to the user, it will pass data, such as the user's name or email, into the Handlebars file, which will compile the file into a static HTML page.

The resulting HTML file is served from the backend server. This means the user will receive a response containing a full HTML page. However, each user can be assured that their personal information appears only for them as their account information is authenticated and processed into a Handlebars template.

---

184 | Chapter 10: App Authentication

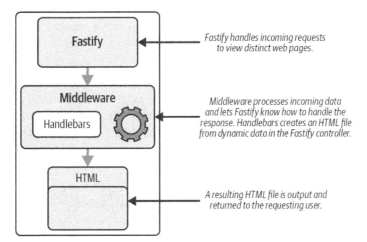

Figure 10-2. Building an HTML file with Handlebars templates

Handlebars.js is a popular JavaScript library that provides a simple, flexible way to generate HTML templates and build dynamic, interactive web applications. The library is often used in combination with a web framework, such as Fastify.js, to build server-rendered web applications.

The Handlebars library contains a few syntactical expressions to use in your templates. To display a variable within an HTML div, you simply wrap the variable within double braces: <div> {{nameVar}} </div>. Additionally, you may wrap a block of HTML within a condition. That condition may be represented within double braces and the addition of a hash symbol: {{#if boolStatement}}. In this way, Handlebars enables your template file to make dynamic decisions about what information to display before rendering the final HTML result.

To learn more about the Handlebars library, visit the Handlebars website (*https://handlebarsjs.com*). To learn more about template languages supported by Fastify, visit the Fastify documentation (*https://oreil.ly/EouiP*).

You start building out your main app logic by importing `fastify` into your project and configuring your app to receive incoming requests properly (Example 10-1). After importing `Fastify` at the top of *index.js*, you instantiate your `app` object from the `fastify` module. You define a constant named `PORT` and assign it the value 3000, which will be used to start your server locally.

This `app` object acts as your main running server. It is responsible for starting your server, interpreting incoming requests, and handling all operations related to authentication.

In Fastify, routes are defined directly on the app instance using methods like `app.get(...)` and `app.post(...)`. To handle incoming form data, you register the `@fastify/formbody` plugin, which parses `application/x-www-form-urlencoded` data. Fastify also handles `application/json` body parsing automatically for JSON-formatted requests.

 Fastify handles request processing through its plugin architecture and route lifecycle hooks. These hooks allow you to run code at various stages such as before validation, before handler execution, or after the response is sent, making it easy to extend functionality and enforce consistent logic across routes.

To ensure Fastify can locate your Handlebars template files, configure the `root` option when registering the `@fastify/view` plugin. This points to the folder containing your *.hbs* files—typically named *views*.

Example 10-1. Configuring your app in index.js

```
import Fastify from "fastify"; ❶
import fastifyFormbody from "@fastify/formbody"; ❷
import fastifyView from "@fastify/view"; ❸
import handlebars from "handlebars"; ❹

const app = Fastify(); ❺
const PORT = 3000; ❻

await app.register(fastifyFormbody); ❼
await app.register(fastifyView, { ❽
  engine: { handlebars },
  root: "views",
});
```

❶ Import the `fastify` module to create your web server.

❷ Import the `@fastify/formbody` plugin to support URL-encoded form data.

③ Import the @fastify/view plugin to support templating engines.

④ Import handlebars as your template engine implementation.

⑤ Instantiate the app from Fastify.

⑥ Define the port you'll use to reach your web server as 3000.

⑦ Register the formbody plugin to parse application/x-www-form-urlencoded payloads.

⑧ Register the view plugin and configure Handlebars as your rendering engine.

With your app configured to create routes and use SSR, you define your first route for the home path, /. To test that your app is working, you simply respond with a "Welcome!" message using reply.send. Last, you set up app.listen to watch for incoming requests at port 3000. Add the code in Example 10-2 to the bottom of your *index.js* file.

Example 10-2. Adding a route and starting the server in index.js

```
...
app.get("/", async (request, reply) => { ❶
  reply.send("Welcome!"); ❷
});

try {
  const address = await app.listen({ port: PORT, host: "127.0.0.1" }); ❸
  console.log(`App listening on ${address}`);
} catch (err) {
  console.error(err);
  process.exit(1);
}
```

❶ Define a route to receive GET requests to your default path using Fastify's app.get method.

❷ Respond with a plain-text value using reply.send.

❸ Start the server using await app.listen(...) and log the address when it's ready.

Get Programming | 187

Your app is ready to run and accept requests. Navigate to your project folder in your command line and start your app. In your web browser, navigate to *http://localhost:3000*, where you'll see the `Welcome!` message appear.

If you do not see a message appear, first ensure that your server is running correctly. Next, make sure you have added the necessary route and that all files have been saved.

It's great to see your app working, but plain-text messages don't offer much to support app authentication. In the next section, you create a UI page to serve back to your users.

Building a Login Form

To create a UI for your app, you set up a folder called `views` at the root level of your project and add a file called *index.hbs*. The *.hbs* file extension signifies it as a Handlebars file containing both HTML and Handlebars syntax.

Fastify expects template files to live in a folder called `views`. In this way, the framework helps you organize your files and makes it easier to locate relevant files that require compiling into HTML.

Within the *index.hbs* file, add the boilerplate HTML content in Example 10-3. This content imports the Bootstrap CSS library for immediate styling results, and creates the standard HTML `<head>` tag as well as custom styles.

Example 10-3. Adding the foundational structure in index.hbs

```
<html lang="en">
  <head>
    <meta charset="UTF-8" />
    <title>Journey Doc Login</title> ❶
    <link
      rel="stylesheet"
      href="https://cdn.jsdelivr.net/npm/bootstrap@5.2.3/dist/css/bootstrap.min.css"
      crossorigin="anonymous"
      referrerpolicy="no-referrer"
    /> ❷
    <style>
      body { padding: 50px; display: flex; align-items: center; justify-content:
      center; height: 100vh; }
      form { width: 500px; margin: 0 auto; }
```

```
    </style> ❸
  </head>
</html>
```

❶ Add a title tag for the login page you are rendering.

❷ Add a link tag to load Bootstrap CSS.

❸ Define custom styles for your login page.

With this foundation set, you may now add the body of the page with dynamic variables. Add the body defined in Example 10-4 after your closing </head> tag. The contents in this block of code create a form for submitting authentication information. The method of most forms is POST, as information is submitted to the server in the body of the request. The form's action refers to the app route you are targeting. That route may be the authentication or account creation route, depending on whether an account has already been registered. For that reason, the action will be dynamically linked to the value of the route variable. This variable is one of a few whose values will be determined on the server.

You display the title of the form by displaying the title variable within braces. Next, you generate two form inputs and their labels. One input is for the user's username, and the other is for their password.

HTML offers specific input types to meet the expectations of the input content. For example, the email input type expects a value in the format "*abc@xyz.com*," and the password input type will replace the password characters with bullets on the UI by default.

At the end of the form, there's a section to display a message from the server, such as a login error or confirmation, and a link the user can follow to switch pages. This link adds a query parameter (?page=...) to the home page URL, allowing the server to determine which content to render.

The value switchPage will help the server determine what the user wants to see. Last, you add the title variable as the text for the submit button. That way, a title of "Log in" will appear both at the top of the form and as the submit button too. All of these variables effectively act as placeholders for values to be determined on the server. Before rendering this page as HTML, the variables are replaced with their associated values.

Example 10-4. Adding an authentication form in index.hbs

```
...
<body>
  <form method="post" action="{{route}}"> ❶
    <h2>
      {{title}} ❷
    </h2>
    <div class="form-outline mb-4"> ❸
      <input
        type="text"
        name="username"
        id="usernameInput"
        class="form-control"
      />
      <label class="form-label" for="usernameInput">
        Username
      </label>
    </div>
    <div class="form-outline mb-4"> ❹
      <input
        type="password"
        name="password"
        id="passwordInput"
        class="form-control"
      />
      <label class="form-label" for="passwordInput">
        Password
      </label>
    </div>
    <div class="row mb-4">
      <div class="col">
        {{message}} ❺
        <a href="/?page={{switchPage}}"> Click here</a> ❻
      </div>
    </div>
    <button type="submit" class="btn btn-primary btn-block mb-4">
      {{title}} ❼
    </button>
  </form>
</body>
```

❶ Create a an HTML form with a dynamic action defined in the route variable.

❷ Display the title variable within a header tag.

❸ Create a form input for the user's username.

❹ Create a form input for the user's password.

190 | Chapter 10: App Authentication

❺ Display the message variable contents.

❻ Add the switchPage variable as a query parameter in the anchor tag's href value.

❼ Display the title variable as the text on your submit button.

The output of this rendered HTML file results in a form containing username and password inputs. Because this form is used for both account registration and login authentication, you add an additional optional input for password confirmation. This way, when the user is creating their account, they may type their password twice to ensure both passwords match when initially creating and saving their account.

A lot of authentication steps may be run on the web client ahead of reaching the server. HTML provides some useful tools for ensuring text is formatted correctly. Client-side JavaScript is often used to verify that password match and other form inputs are typed correctly to save the server from having to process a malformed request.

Add the code in Example 10-5 to add a conditional input field below the regular password field. The {{#if showExtraFields}} statement uses the Handlebars conditional syntax to check whether the showExtraFields variable is true, and an extra password field should display.

Example 10-5. Adding a conditional password input in index.hbs

```
...
{{#if showExtraFields}} ❶
  <div class="form-outline mb-4">
    <input
      type="password"
      name="confirmPassword"
      id="confirmPasswordInput"
      class="form-control"
    />
    <label class="form-label" for="confirmPasswordInput">
      Confirm Password
    </label>
  </div>
{{/if}}
...
```

❶ Add a field to conditionally show the "Confirm Password" field.

You may now define the required variables before your first defined route in *index.js*, as shown in Example 10-6. The variables live in the `loginFormVars` object and contain different values for the login and sign up pages. Notice the difference in titles and messages shown to the user. Also notice the route for `signup` sends form submissions to `/account`, whereas the `login` route value is `/auth`. These are two routes that need to be created to handle the form requests.

Example 10-6. Defining the authentication page variables in index.js

```
...
const loginFormVars = {
  signup: { ❶
    title: "Sign up",
    message: "Already have an account?",
    route: "/account",
    switchPage: "login",
    showExtraFields: true,
  },
  login: { ❷
    title: "Log in",
    message: "Need to create an account?",
    route: "/auth",
    switchPage: "signup",
    showExtraFields: false,
  },
};
...
```

❶ The `signup` key maps to all the page variables required to display on the sign-up page.

❷ The `login` key maps to all the page variables required to display on the login page.

To render the *index.hbs* page with these variables, update the default / route with the contents in Example 10-7. You start by checking whether a query parameter was passed in the URL. You check the request's `query` field and destructure to pull out the `page` value. This value (`switchPage`) will only be passed to the server when switching between the sign-up and login pages. Next, you define your `formVars` to match the set of page variables for the page you're displaying, or default to the `signup` variables. Last, you use `res.render` to pass these variables to the *index.hbs* page and compile it into an HTML file to send back to the user's web browser.

192 | Chapter 10: App Authentication

Example 10-7. Render the index.hbs *page from* index.js

```
...
const { page } = request.query;  ❶
const formVars = loginFormVars[page] || loginFormVars.signup;  ❷
return reply.view("index", formVars);  ❸
...
```

❶ Destructure the `page` key from your request's query parameters.

❷ Define your `formVars` as the values that match your query parameter for `page`, or default to the `signup` page values.

❸ Render the *index.hbs* page with your selected dynamic values.

With these changes in place, you may rerun your app and navigate to *http://localhost:3000* where you'll see a page similar to Figure 10-3. This form displays the variable values for the title, message, and submit button. When submitted, the form will also post data to the `/account` route. That route has not yet been set up, so for now you'd see an error on the screen instead.

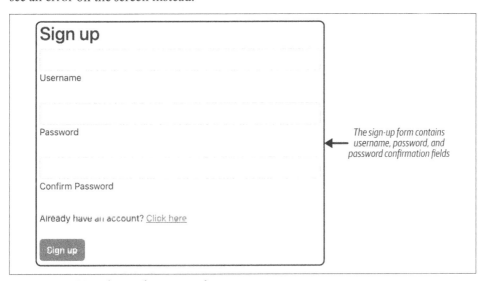

Figure 10-3. Visualizing the sign-up form

The final step to make use of this form is to define the `/account` and `/auth` routes. These routes will handle sign up and account creation, and login authentication, respectively. Because you are going to be saving new users and their passwords, you'll need a place to store them. For now, you store them in an object in memory. That means you will save new users while your app is running and clear the list of users

Building a Login Form | 193

each time you close your app. Add `const users = {};` above your routes in *index.js* as an in-memory store for saved users. Then add the code in Example 10-8 to define the remaining routes.

Both new routes use `app.post` and are `async` because they accept posted information and eventually will run I/O operations. For the `/account` route, you'll collect the user name and password fields from the request body and save the user account by adding a key by that `username` in the `users` object, and mapping it to the `password` value.

Right away, this approach has many flaws as it stores a plain-text password that can be overridden by the same username sign-up action. However, this logic is an intermediary step toward saving your passwords in a more practical way.

In the first route that you set the `username` and `password` in, the `users` object represents the creation of a new account. After that, you use `reply.send` to send a message of validation back to the user. The `/auth` route behaves similarly. Only, this route does not save a new user account, but instead checks whether a `username` key is found in the `users` object. If the username is found and the stored password matches the request body password, then we consider the account authenticated and respond with a message signifying a successful login attempt. Otherwise, we redirect the user to the `login` page to try again.

Example 10-8. Define the /account and /auth routes in index.js

```
...
const users = {};

app.post("/account", async (request, reply) => { ❶
  const { username, password } = request.body; ❷
  users[username] = password; ❸
  return reply.send({ message: "Account created." }); ❹
});

app.post("/auth", async (request, reply) => { ❺
  const { username, password } = request.body;
  if (users[username] && users[username] === password) { ❻
    return reply.send({ message: "Logged in." }); ❼
  }
  return reply.redirect("/?page=login"); ❽
});
...
```

❶ Create a POST route handler for /account to accept new user data.

❷ Extract username and password from the incoming request body.

❸ Store the provided password in the users object using the username as the key.

❹ Send a JSON response confirming account creation.

❺ Create a POST route handler for /auth to authenticate existing users.

❻ Verify that the username exists and the password matches the stored value.

❼ Respond with a success message if login is valid.

❽ Redirect the user to the login page if authentication fails.

Now your app is ready to both render the sign up and login forms, and accept their form submissions. Start your app and enter a username and password into the sign up form inputs. Then click "Sign up." You'll then be navigated to a page with a message indicating your successful account creation. Next try to log in.

You can navigate one back in your browser history and try clicking the "Click here" link to switch to the login page. Clicking the link will add the page query parameter to the route request, specifying the login page variables. Those variables are used to repopulate the page on the server and render the form again, ready to post data to the /auth route (Figure 10-4). Enter the same username and password and click "Log in".

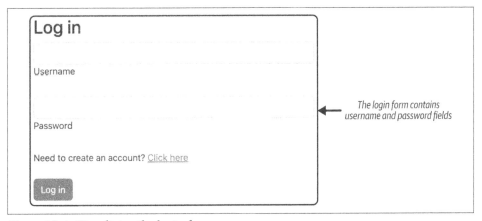

Figure 10-4. Visualizing the login form

If your login information is correct, you'll receive a JSON response with a message that says "Logged in." Otherwise, you'll be redirected to the login page to try again.

This app is a fun starting point, but requires a bit more work to secure your users' privacy and login identities. In the next section you'll incorporate the Passport.js library to assist with that.

Saving and Securing User Accounts

You've built an authentication system from scratch. The bad news is that it's not very secure and clears all of your users' information on app restart. This calls for a password security strategy and a database to persist your user accounts. Luckily, these two steps can be built together as a part of defining an Account model in your app. Your Account model defines fields that are needed to register an account, authenticate it with Passport.js, and save the user account values to a SQLite database through the Sequelize library.

This book uses the @fastify/passport plugin to integrate into your Fastify app. It provides a drop-in authentication system similar to Express but adapted for Fastify's lifecycle.

Figure 10-5 shows some of the functions the Account class will handle. In addition to registering and authenticating, it will also incorporate to serialize and deserialize account data. The class will extend a Sequelize Model class, enabling it to define persistent fields and run query functions on a SQL database.

Serialization is the process of taking a data object and converting it into a format that's compatible with a response object. This typically means converting a complex object into a large string. Deserialization is the reverse, in which a large or encoded string is rehabilitated into a JavaScript object.

To get started, you install the sequelize, sqlite3, passport, and passport-local packages. Navigate to the root level of your project folder on your command line and run npm i sequelize@^6.37.7 sqlite3@^5.1.7 passport@^0.7.0 passport-local@^1.0.0. The passport-local package works with the passport package to help you define a custom authentication strategy (as opposed to authenticating with a third-party service like Facebook or Google).

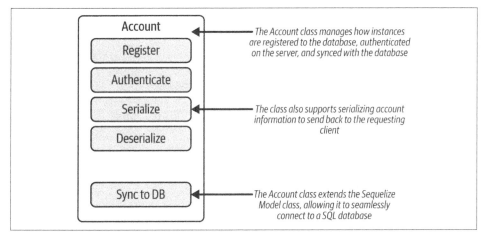

Figure 10-5. Overview of the Account *model class*

To get started, you install the sequelize, sqlite3, passport, and passport-local packages. Navigate to the root level of your project folder on your command line and run npm install sequelize@^6.37.7 sqlite3@^5.1.7 passport@^0.7.0 passport-local@^1.0.0. The passport-local package works with the passport package to help you define a custom authentication strategy (as opposed to authenticating with a third-party service like Facebook or Google).

After installing these packages, you create a new file, *db.js*, at the root level of your project to hold your database configurations. Add the code in Example 10-9 to *db.js*. This file imports the Sequelize library and instantiates a new database object, db, for a SQLite database stored within a db folder at the root level of your project. You then run db.authenticate to connect to the database. At the end of the file you export the database instance and Sequelize module for use in other parts of the app.

Example 10-9. Setting up your SQLite configurations in db.js

```
import { Sequelize } from "sequelize"; ❶

const db = new Sequelize({ ❷
  dialect: "sqlite",
  storage: "./db/database.sqlite",
});

try {
  await db.authenticate(); ❸
  console.log("Connection has been established successfully.");
} catch (error) {
  console.error("Unable to connect to the database:", error);
}
```

```
export default { ❹
  Sequelize,
  db,
};
```

❶ Import `Sequelize` to create a new database instance.

❷ Define db to connect to a SQLite database stored in a file called *database.sqlite*.

❸ Connect to the database with `db.authenticate`.

❹ Export the database and `Sequelize` module.

After configuring the database, you're able to work on the model that will persist on the database. Start by creating a folder called `models` and adding a file called *Account.js* (Example 10-10). This file imports the database configurations where you can access all of the functions and classes within `Sequelize`. Set up a JavaScript class for `Account` that extends `Sequelize.Model`. You may also define any other functions you'd like within this class. You add a class function to search for an account by its username, `findByUsername`. This function modifies the function parameter to lowercase and uses the `Sequelize findOne` function to search for a return of a single account by that `username`. The function's static keyword signifies that it is a class-level function (not an instance method). Later, it may be accessed by calling `Account.find ByUsername` and passing a `username` string.

Example 10-10. Creating your `Account` class in Account.js

```
import dbConfig from "../db.js"; ❶
const { Sequelize, db } = dbConfig; ❷

class Account extends Sequelize.Model { ❸
  static async findByUsername(username) { ❹
    const lowerCaseUsername = username.toLowerCase();
    return await this.findOne({ where: { username: lowerCaseUsername } }); ❺
  }
}
```

❶ Import the database configurations from *db.js*.

❷ Destructure dbConfig to access `Sequelize` and your db instance.

❸ Define your `Account`, which extends `Sequelize.Model`, giving the class `Sequelize` query functions.

❹ Add a class function to search for accounts by username.

❺ Run a `Sequelize` `findOne` query to find a single account record in the database.

This class is ready for full integration with `Sequelize`. To accomplish this, you'll add the code in Example 10-11 to the end of *Account.js*. In this code you run `Account.init` to initialize the fields for the `Account` model and register the model in your database. Here, you define the `username` field as a string that must have a valid value and not have a duplicate in the database. Next, you add fields for a `hash` and `salt`, both as strings that must not be null.

Hashing Passwords

Storing plain-text passwords is a sure way to have accounts hacked and sensitive information stolen. For that reason, it is an industry standard to never store an actual password on the database or server. Yes, a plain-text password must pass through the server with the incoming request, but when persisting or verifying account information, you are better off with other techniques.

A modern approach to storing password information is to hash a password and store the `hash` value and `salt` string. A `hash` is generated by running a hashing function on the original plain-text password. Hashing functions use an algorithm to convert the password into an unintelligible string. The key is to create a custom cryptographic `salt`, or random assortment of bits for each generated `hash`. The combination of a `salt` and hashing algorithm results in a string that cannot be converted back into the original password. So why do we store the `hash` and `salt`?

Figure 10-6 demonstrates how an incoming plain-text password is passed into the hashing function, along with the account's custom `salt`. The end result is a password `hash`. Account authentication verifies username and password information by checking that the request body's password, when combined with the username's account `salt`, results in a `hash` that matches the account's `hash` value. If the two hashes match, the account is verified.

In this way, the app never truly knows its users' passwords. In the event of a hacked database, hackers would only get a series of hash and salt values, unable to retrieve the original plain-text passwords.

Saving and Securing User Accounts | 199

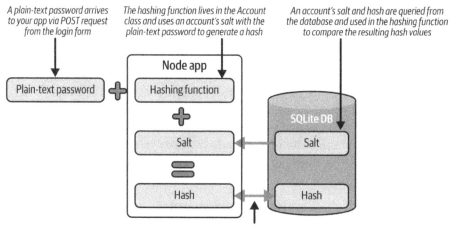

Figure 10-6. Flow of information for hashing an account's password

In this project you use the `crypto.pbkdf2` hashing algorithm. This algorithm is considered to be secure and fast. To learn more about the `crypto` API, refer to the Node documentation (*https://oreil.ly/IdyVQ*).

In addition to `crypto.pbkdf2`, several other password hashing algorithms are widely used in modern applications, each offering different trade-offs in terms of speed, security, and resistance to various types of attacks:

Argon2
: This is a key derivation function that was designed to be resistant to various types of attacks, such as GPU cracking and dictionary attacks. It is considered to be one of the most secure hashing functions currently available. Read more on the npm website (*https://oreil.ly/EZ7e0*).

bcrypt
: This is a password hashing function that uses a technique called adaptive hashing to make it resistant to brute-force attacks. It is widely used in web applications and is considered to be a very secure option. Read more on the npm website (*https://oreil.ly/KqB4V*).

scrypt
: This is designed to be a general-purpose key derivation function and is generally slower than `pbkdf2` due to its added resistance to hardware acceleration and dictionary attacks. Read more in the Node documentation (*https://oreil.ly/zmMYC*).

At the end of the file, you make use of a Sequelize hook, beforeCreate, which is executed before the account is saved to the database. This is a built-in Sequelize function. In this case you reassign the username to be a lowercase value. Last, you run Account.sync to sync the model with the database by creating the Accounts table if it doesn't already exist.

Example 10-11. Setting up your Account Sequelize model in Account.js

```
...
Account.init( ❶
  {
    username: { ❷
      type: Sequelize.STRING,
      allowNull: false,
      unique: true,
    },
    hash: { ❸
      type: Sequelize.TEXT,
      allowNull: false,
    },
    salt: { ❹
      type: Sequelize.STRING,
      allowNull: false,
    },
  },
  {
    sequelize: db, ❺
    modelName: "Account",
  }
);

Account.beforeCreate((account) => { ❻
  account["username"] = account["username"].toLowerCase();
});

Account.sync(); ❼
export default Account;
```

❶ Initialize the Account class to work with Sequelize.

❷ Define a username field of type STRING.

❸ Define a hash field of type TEXT.

❹ Define a salt field of type STRING.

❺ Specify the database instance and model name.

Saving and Securing User Accounts | 201

❻ Use the beforeCreate hook to make all username values lowercase.

❼ Sync the Account model to the database.

With the data model set up, you move on to incorporate password setting and authentication functions. First, import the passport-local module by adding import { Strategy as LocalStrategy } from "passport-local" to the top of *Account.js*. This library will help you define your authentication strategy. LocalStrategy refers to an authentication process using only username and password. In Example 10-12, you add the register and setPassword functions, which are used to create new accounts with hashed passwords.

The register function accepts username and password parameters and first checks if an account exists by the username. If an account does not exist, then you may continue to create an account. Unlike the in-memory users object from earlier in this chapter, you may not create duplicate accounts or override existing ones. The Account model's this.build function creates a new instance of an Account with the username field.

> The build function does not make an I/O operation, and so it is not a function in need of the async-await keywords.

With your Account instance, account, you set the account password by calling the setPassword function on that new instance. This function will handle all of the hashing operations. Last, you call account.save to officially save the account to your database.

Example 10-12. Defining your Account creation function in Account.js

```
...
static async register(username, password) { ❶
  const existingAccount = await this.findByUsername(username); ❷
  if (existingAccount) { ❸
    throw new Error("Account already exists");
  }
  const account = this.build({ username }); ❹
  account.setPassword(password); ❺
  return await account.save(); ❻
}
...
```

❶ Define a register function that accepts a username and password.

❷ Check your database for an existing Account record.

❸ Throw an error if an account already exists.

❹ Build a new virtual Account instance with the provided username.

❺ Call the setPassword function to save a hashed version of your password.

❻ Save and return the registered account object.

For the register function to work, you need to create the setPassword function within your Account class. Add the code in Example 10-13 below the register function in *Account.js*. This function accepts a password as the parameter. It first checks that the password has a value before continuing to the hashing function.

With the advent of async-await, coding has gotten a lot more succinct and easy to read. Under the hood, all awaitable functions are only functions that return a Promise. A Promise returns an eventual value, allowing your server logic to continue unblocked until that value is ready. For functions that have synchronous operations or have yet to support an awaitable return value, you may create your own Promise. Wrapping logic in a Promise allows you to call that function with the async-await keyword.

Within your try-catch block you begin your hashing logic. Recall that a hashing algorithm may contain a few different components to ensure a resulting hash value that cannot be reverse engineered to the original password. One of the criteria for generating the hash is to create a custom (and randomized) salt value. Node comes prepackaged with the crypto library to assist with operations like this. You first import that library by adding import crypto from "crypto" to the top of *Account.js*. Then, within your setPassword function you use crypto.randomBytes to generate a random assortment of bytes.

You pass in 32 to reflect the number of characters you'd like the salt to be. There is no correct answer here, though a length of 32 or more is a widely accepted value for a secure salt string. To learn more, read the article "Password Salting" (*https://oreil.ly/kw7Mr*). After generating a random set of bytes, you convert them to a hexadecimal string using the bufferBytes.toString("hex") function. Next, your official hashing function is used. The crypto.pbkdf2Sync function synchronously generates a hash with the provided arguments. You pass in your plain-text password, the generated salt, 12000 as the number of hashing iterations, a byte length of 64, and the hashing digest algorithm.

Note also that this example uses the sha512 digest, which is preferred over sha1 for stronger cryptographic guarantees. You may refer to the Node documentation (*https://oreil.ly/dlYII*) to learn more.

The resulting hashRaw value is then converted to a hexadecimal string and saved to the account's hash field. The generated salt is also saved to the account's salt field. Because the entire process is synchronous, there's no need to wrap it in a Promise or use await.

Example 10-13. Defining your password hashing function in Account.js

```
...
setPassword(password) {    ❶
  if (!password) {
    throw new Error("No password supplied.");
  }
  try {
    const bufferBytes = crypto.randomBytes(32);    ❷
    const salt = bufferBytes.toString("hex");    ❸
    const hashRaw = crypto.pbkdf2Sync(password, salt, 12000, 64, "sha512");    ❹
    this.set("hash", Buffer.from(hashRaw).toString("hex"));    ❺
    this.set("salt", salt);    ❻
  } catch (e) {
    throw new Error("Unable to hash password.");    ❼
  }
}
...
```

❶ Define your setPassword function to take a plain-text password.

❷ Generate a random assortment of bytes for your salt.

❸ Assign the converted bytes string as your salt value.

❹ Generate a hash value from your password, salt, and hashing parameters.

❺ Save the string value of your hash to your account instance.

❻ Save the string value of your salt to your account instance.

❼ Throw an error if any issues occur in the hashing process.

With your account registration and hashing function out of the way, you add logic for authenticating a user logging in. Add the function in Example 10-14 to your Account class. The authenticate function is provided with the plain-text password that the user has entered. The function returns true if the password is correct, or false if it's incorrect. The function begins by extracting the salt and hash values from the this object, which is assumed to be an instance of a user account. If the salt value is not present, the function throws an error.

Because you call authenticate on the Account instance, and not the class itself, the this keyword refers to the instance. In this way, you may access all the fields of that instance.

Next, the function uses the crypto.pbkdf2Sync function to generate a hash from the provided password and salt values. It then compares the generated hash to the stored hash for the user account. If the two hashes match, the function returns true, indicating successful authentication. If the hashes do not match, it returns false. This design separates the password check from any surrounding control flow, like the done callback in Passport.js.

Example 10-14. Add an authenticate method to your Account class in Account.js

```
...
authenticate(password) {   ❶
  const { salt, hash } = this;
  if (!salt) {   ❷
    throw new Error("No salt found");
  }

  const hashRaw = crypto.pbkdf2Sync(   ❸
    password,
    salt,
    12000,
    64,
    "sha512"
  );
```

```
  const currentHash = Buffer.from(hashRaw).toString("hex");  ❹

  return currentHash === hash;  ❺
}
...
```

❶ Define the authenticate function that accepts a password as an argument.

❷ Verify whether the account has a valid salt before continuing.

❸ Generate the hashRaw value using the crypto.pbkdf2Sync hashing function.

❹ Convert the hashRaw value to a string called currentHash.

❺ Return true if the hashes match, otherwise return false.

With this authenticate method ready, you must make it accessible to the Passport.js library. Add the class function in Example 10-15 to your Account class. This code defines a static method called passportAuthenticate on the Account class. The pass portAuthenticate method returns an async function that takes three arguments: username, password, and done. It attempts to find an account with the specified user name by calling the findByUsername method. If an account is found, it calls the instance method authenticate with the provided password. If the password is valid, the function calls done with the account object. Otherwise, it responds with a failure message.

This design decouples password verification from callback invocation, making the authenticate method easier to test independently.

Example 10-15. Add a passportAuthenticate class method to your Account class in Account.js

```
...
static passportAuthenticate() {  ❶
  return async (username, password, done) => {  ❷
    try {
      const account = await this.findByUsername(username);  ❸
      if (!account) {
        return done(null, false, { message: "User not found" });  ❹
      }

      const isValid = account.authenticate(password);  ❺
      if (isValid) {
        return done(null, account);  ❻
      } else {
        return done(null, false, { message: "Password incorrect" });  ❼
```

```
    }
  } catch (err) {
    return done(err);  ❽
  }
};
}
...
```

❶ Define a static method that returns a strategy callback.

❷ This async function will be used by Passport.js for login attempts.

❸ Look up the user account by username.

❹ If not found, respond with a "User not found" message.

❺ Call the instance's `authenticate` method to validate the password.

❻ If valid, call `done` with the authenticated account.

❼ If invalid, call `done` with a failure message.

❽ Handle and return any unexpected errors.

This code concludes the authentication process. Though Passport.js comes with additional support to help maintain state between user requests, instead of requiring users to log in every time they request a new page, Passport.js sends data within each request confirming the account's authenticated state.

Example 10-16 adds two more methods to the `Account` class. The `serializeUser` and `deserializeUser` functions are used to serialize and deserialize user accounts for storing in a session. These functions are typically used in conjunction with a session middleware, such as `@fastify/session`. The `serializeUser` function takes `account`, the user account object that should be serialized, and `done`, a callback function that is called when the serialization process completes, as arguments. The function extracts the `username` property from the `account` object and passes it to the `done` callback as the second argument.

The `deserializeUser` function takes `username`, serialized user data used to find the user account, and `done`, the callback function that is called when the deserialization process completes, as arguments. This function calls the `findByUsername` method to find the `account` with the provided `username`, and then passes the found account to the `done` callback as the second argument.

Saving and Securing User Accounts | 207

> ## A Brief Session on Sessions
>
> In a web application, a session is a way to store user data between requests. When a user logs in, the server creates a new session and stores the user's data in the session. The server then sends a cookie to the client's browser, containing a unique identifier for the session.
>
>
>
> A browser cookie is a small piece of data that is stored on a user's computer by a web browser. It is used to identify the user's browser and track their movements within a website. Cookies are typically used to keep track of login sessions, store user preferences, and to personalize the user's experience on a website.
>
> On subsequent requests, the client sends the cookie back to the server, along with the request. The server uses the session identifier in the cookie to look up the user's data in the session store and retrieve the user's data for the request.
>
> In Node with Fastify, sessions allow you to keep track of a user's state as they navigate your application. To use sessions in Fastify, you must install and configure the @fastify/session and @fastify/cookie plugins. These work together to enable session creation and cookie handling.
>
> Passport.js integrates with Fastify through the @fastify/passport plugin. When a user logs in, Passport.js stores the user's data in the session so that it can be accessed on subsequent requests. This allows the user to remain logged in as they navigate the application.

Example 10-16. Add serializeUser *and* deserializeUser *class methods to your Account class in* Account.js

```
...
static serializeUser(account, done) {
  const { username } = account;
  done(null, username);
}

static async deserializeUser(username, done) {
  try {
    const foundAccount = await this.findByUsername(username);
    if (!foundAccount) {
      return done(new Error("User not found"));  ❶
    }
    done(null, foundAccount);  ❷
  } catch (err) {
```

```
    done(err);  ❸
  }
}
...
```

❶ Return an error if no matching account is found.

❷ Pass the found account to the Passport.js session deserializer.

❸ If a database error occurs, pass it to the done callback.

The last step required to enable Passport.js is to create a new login strategy. Example 10-17 defines the genStrategy function, which is used to create a new instance of the LocalStrategy class from the Passport.js library. The genStrategy function returns a new instance of the LocalStrategy class, with the passport Authenticate function as the callback. When the strategy is used to authenticate an account, the passportAuthenticate function will be called to handle the authentication process using a username and password.

> The LocalStrategy class takes an options object as an argument, which can include a variety of options such as the fields used for the username and password, as well as a callback function to handle the authentication process.

Example 10-17. Add a genStrategy class method to your Account class in Account.js

```
...
static genStrategy() {  ❶
  return new LocalStrategy(this.passportAuthenticate());  ❷
}
...
```

❶ Define the genStrategy class method to return a new LocalStrategy instance.

❷ Return a new LocalStrategy using your passportAuthenticate class method.

With this strategy function set up, you may add the remaining configurations to *index.js*. To use Passport.js with sessions in Fastify, ensure you have the required session and passport plugins installed:

```
npm install \
  @fastify/cookie@^10.0.0 @fastify/session@^11.0.0 @fastify/passport@^3.0.0
```

Then import the necessary modules at the top of *index.js*:

```
import fastifyCookie from "@fastify/cookie";
import fastifySession from "@fastify/session";
import fastifyPassport from "@fastify/passport";
import Account from "./models/Account.js";
```

Example 10-18 configures the Fastify-compatible session and passport plugins. It also registers serialization and deserialization functions, which are used to store and retrieve user data from the session. Fastify sessions require `@fastify/cookie` and `@fastify/session` to be registered first.

The `secret` used for session configuration should be a strong, random string and is typically stored in an environment variable.

Example 10-18. Add session and Passport middleware functions to your Fastify app in index.js

```
...
await app.register(fastifyCookie); ❶
await app.register(fastifySession, {
  secret: "a_very_secret_value_1!2@3#4$5%6^7&8*9(0)",
  cookie: {
    secure: false,
    maxAge: 1000 * 60 * 60 * 24
  },
  saveUninitialized: false,
  resave: false
}); ❷

await app.register(fastifyPassport.initialize()); ❸
await app.register(fastifyPassport.secureSession()); ❹


fastifyPassport.registerUserSerializer(async (user, request) => user.username); ❺
fastifyPassport.registerUserDeserializer(async (username, request) => {
  const account = await Account.findByUsername(username);
  if (!account) {
    throw new Error("User not found");
  }
  return account;
}); ❻

fastifyPassport.use("local", Account.genStrategy()); ❼
```

❶ Register Fastify's cookie plugin for parsing cookies.

❷ Register Fastify's session plugin with a secret and configuration including session duration.

❸ Register Passport's initialization middleware.

❹ Register Passport's session middleware (via `secureSession()`).

❺ Register an async serialization function that returns the username directly.

❻ Register an async deserialization function that throws on error.

❼ Register the custom local login strategy.

> The key difference from Express is that Fastify's serialization functions are async and return values directly rather than using callbacks. They also receive the `request` object as a parameter.

Your app is now fully configured to use the `Account` model and its methods to register and authenticate new accounts. The last step is to create entry points for new and existing accounts to interact with your Fastify server.

Example 10-19 defines two new routes. The first route is a POST route that listens for requests at the /account endpoint. When a request is received at this endpoint, the server extracts the `username` and `password` fields from the request body and calls the `Account` class's `register` method. This method registers a new account with the provided credentials. The server then responds with a JSON message indicating success or failure.

The second route is a POST route that listens for requests at the /auth endpoint. This route handles authentication by calling Passport's authenticate method within a try-catch block. Unlike Express, Fastify's Passport integration throws errors on authentication failure, which must be caught and handled appropriately.

Example 10-19. Define new /account and /auth endpoints with error handling in index.js

```
...
app.post("/account", async (request, reply) => { ❶
  const { username, password } = request.body; ❷
  try {
    await Account.register(username, password); ❸
    return reply.send({ message: "Account created." }); ❹
  } catch (e) {
```

```
      return reply.code(400).send({
        message: "Account creation failed.",
        error: e.message
      }); ❺
  }
});

app.post("/auth", async (request, reply) => { ❻
  try {
    await fastifyPassport
      .authenticate("local", { authInfo: false })(request, reply); ❼
    if (request.user) { ❽
      const { username } = request.user;
      return reply.send({ message: "Logged in.", username }); ❾
    }
  } catch (err) {
    return reply.code(401).send({ ❿
      message: "Authentication failed",
      error: "Invalid username or password"
    });
  }
});
...
```

❶ Define the route for account registration using Fastify's `app.post`.

❷ Extract `username` and `password` from the request body.

❸ Attempt to register a new account with the provided credentials.

❹ Respond with a success message upon successful registration.

❺ Respond with an error message and status code 400 if account creation fails.

❻ Define the authentication route that handles login attempts.

❼ Call Passport's authenticate method, which returns a function that processes the request.

❽ Check if authentication succeeded by verifying the user object exists.

❾ Respond with a success message and the logged-in username.

❿ Handle authentication failures with a 401 Unauthorized status.

Unlike Express, Fastify's Passport integration requires calling authenticate as a function that returns another function. Authentication failures are handled through try-catch blocks rather than redirect URLs.

Your code is now complete and ready to test with Passport.js in a Fastify application. Restart your app and create a new account by visiting the sign-up form or using the following cURL command:

```
curl -X POST http://127.0.0.1:3000/account \
  -H "Content-Type: application/x-www-form-urlencoded" \
  -d "username=testuser&password=securepass123"
```

You should receive a response like:

```
{"message":"Account created."}
```

After your account is created, you can test authentication. First, try logging in with incorrect credentials:

```
curl -X POST http://127.0.0.1:3000/auth \
  -H "Content-Type: application/x-www-form-urlencoded" \
  -d "username=testuser&password=wrongpassword"
```

You'll receive a 401 Unauthorized response:

```
{"message":"Authentication failed","error":"Invalid username or password"}
```

Now, try logging in with the correct password:

```
curl -X POST http://127.0.0.1:3000/auth \
  -H "Content-Type: application/x-www-form-urlencoded" \
  -d "username=testuser&password=securepass123"
```

A successful authentication will return:

```
{"message":"Logged in.","username":"testuser"}
```

Your application is now capable of accepting and persisting new user accounts and securely authenticating them via session-based login. The authentication flow in Fastify provides HTTP status codes and JSON responses suitable for both browser-based and programmatic clients.

The next section demonstrates how to add an additional authentication strategy to support stateless authentication for non-browser clients—such as mobile apps and third-party integrations—by issuing and verifying JSON Web Tokens (JWTs).

Using JWTs for API Authentication

Imagine your travel app becomes so successful that you start to support mobile apps and third-party clients. These platforms need to authenticate users just like your web application does. However, session-based authentication with cookies (used in your Fastify + Passport setup) does not work well in environments that cannot store cookies or maintain sessions.

Instead, a stateless, token-based authentication system is better suited for APIs. This is where JSON Web Tokens (JWTs) come into play.

JWTs are self-contained tokens that include all authentication details in the token payload. These are commonly used in stateless systems like mobile clients, SPAs, and microservices, where the server does not need to persist any session data. When a user logs in, the server generates a signed token containing their identity. That token is then sent by the client in the `Authorization` header for every subsequent request.

In contrast, session-based authentication stores the session state on the server and expects the browser to store a cookie with the session ID. This approach works well for traditional server-rendered web applications, but less so for distributed systems.

With Passport.js, you can support both authentication methods in parallel:

1. Install the required packages by running the following command in your terminal:

    ```
    npm install passport-jwt@^4.0.1 jsonwebtoken@^9.0.2
    ```

2. Import the necessary JWT modules at the top of *Account.js*:

    ```
    import { Strategy as JWTStrategy, ExtractJwt } from "passport-jwt";
    import jwt from "jsonwebtoken";
    ```

    The `ExtractJwt` helper provides functions for extracting a token from an HTTP request—commonly from the `Authorization` header using the Bearer scheme.

3. Add the JWT strategy and signing logic in your `Account` class. Example 10-20 shows the `genJWTStrategy` and `signJWT` methods. The strategy extracts the username from the decoded token and attempts to locate a matching account in your database. If successful, it authenticates the request.

In production, your JWT secret key should never be hardcoded. Use `process.env.JWT_SECRET` and store secrets securely in your environment or secrets manager.

Example 10-20. Define `genJWTStrategy` *and* `signJWT` *methods in* Account.js

```
static genJWTStrategy() { ❶
  return new JWTStrategy( ❷
```

```
    {
      jwtFromRequest: ExtractJwt.fromAuthHeaderAsBearerToken(), ❸
      secretOrKey: process.env.JWT_SECRET || "SECRET_KEY", ❹
    },
    async (jwtPayload, done) => {
      try {
        const account = await this.findByUsername(jwtPayload.username); ❺
        if (account) { ❻
          return done(null, account);
        }
        return done(null, false, { message: "User not found" }); ❼
      } catch (e) {
        return done(e); ❽
      }
    }
  );
}

signJWT() { ❾
  const { username } = this;
  return jwt.sign({ username }, process.env.JWT_SECRET || "SECRET_KEY"); ❿
}
```

❶ Define the `genJWTStrategy` method to return a new Passport JWT strategy.

❷ Return a new `JWTStrategy` instance for authenticating bearer tokens.

❸ Extract the JWT token from the request's `Authorization` header.

❹ Use a secure secret key to verify tokens.

❺ Search the database for an account matching the username in the token payload.

❻ If a match is found, authenticate the request.

❼ If no match is found, deny authentication.

❽ On error, call `done` with the error.

❾ Define `signJWT` to generate a signed token.

❿ Return a signed JWT that encodes the account's `username`.

Once this logic is in place, update your Fastify server to register the new JWT strategy alongside the local one. In your *index.js* file, add:

```
fastifyPassport.use("jwt", Account.genJWTStrategy());
```

This registers the "jwt" strategy with Passport.js. You can now create API routes that use `passport.authenticate("jwt", ...)` to protect access via token-based authentication.

In the next section, you'll define those API endpoints to issue and verify JWTs for mobile or API-based clients. Last, define new endpoints for use by non–web clients. Add the code in Example 10-21 after your existing routes in *index.js*. This code defines two Fastify routes: one for authentication and one for testing access to protected resources. Both use the Passport.js authentication middleware registered with Fastify.

The first route, `/api/auth`, is a POST route that authenticates an account using the local strategy. If successful, the route uses the `signJWT` method on the authenticated account to return a signed JWT to the client.

The second route, `/api/test`, is a GET route protected by the JWT strategy. The client must send a valid JWT token in the `Authorization` header. If the token is valid and corresponds to a user in the system, the route returns a confirmation that the user is authenticated. Otherwise, the request is rejected with a `401 Unauthorized` response.

Example 10-21. Define additional API routes in index.js

```
app.post(
  "/api/auth", ❶
  { preValidation: fastifyPassport.authenticate("local", { session: false }) }, ❷
  async (request, reply) => {
    const { user: account } = request;
    const token = account.signJWT(); ❸
    return reply.send({ token }); ❹
  }
);

app.get(
  "/api/test", ❺
  { preValidation: fastifyPassport.authenticate("jwt", { session: false }) }, ❻
  async (request, reply) => {
    return reply.send({ status: "Authenticated." }); ❼
  }
);
```

❶ Define the `/api/auth` API route for account login and JWT issuance.

❷ Use the `local` strategy to authenticate the username/password from the request.

❸ Use the account's `signJWT` method to generate a JWT.

❹ Send the token in a JSON response.

❺ Define the /api/test route to test JWT-protected access.

❻ Use the jwt strategy to validate the token sent in the request header.

❼ Send a confirmation message if authentication is successful.

You can now test this directly from the command line. First, authenticate with an existing user:

```
curl -X POST http://localhost:3000/api/auth \
  -H "Content-Type: application/json" \
  -d '{"username":"<username>","password":"<password>"}'
```

Replace <username> and <password> with your actual credentials.

If successful, the response will include a token:

```
{ "token": "eyJhbGciOiJIUzI1NiIsInR5cCI6IkpXVCJ9..." }
```

Next, use that token to access the protected route:

```
curl http://localhost:3000/api/test \
  -H "Accept: application/json" \
  -H "Authorization: Bearer <your_token_here>"
```

If the token is valid, you'll receive { "status": "Authenticated." }.

You've now successfully extended your app to support stateless API authentication with JWTs.

Chapter Exercises

1. Add logout functionality for session-based login users.

    a. Define a GET /logout route.

    b. In the route handler, call req.logout() and reply.redirect("/").

    c. Update your login success page (or view) to show a logout link when the user is logged in.

    d. Test it by logging in, clicking "Logout", and ensuring you can no longer access protected pages.

A good authentication flow always includes a way for users to manually end their session.

2. Restrict page access to authenticated users:
   a. Create a view called dashboard.hbs with a welcome message.
   b. In *index.js*, define a GET /dashboard route.
   c. In the route handler, use req.isAuthenticated() and conditionally reply.redirect("/?page=login") or render the dashboard.
   d. Update your login success logic to redirect users to /dashboard.

   This adds view-based access control, essential for session-secured web applications.

Summary

In this chapter, you:

- Explored common security vulnerabilities in Node apps and how implementing proper authentication is a developer's responsibility
- Used Node's built-in crypto module to securely hash passwords using salts and strong algorithms
- Integrated Passport.js with Fastify to manage authentication strategies in a modular, plugin-based architecture
- Implemented session-based authentication using cookies and @fastify/session to maintain login state for browser-based users
- Added stateless token-based authentication using JWTs to support mobile apps and API clients that do not use cookies

CHAPTER 11

Coffee Order Manager

This chapter covers the following:

- Designing a queuing system
- Using Redis as an in-memory queue management system
- Using RabbitMQ for more advanced and scaled queues

In this chapter, you'll create a couple of Node applications that use queues to manage workloads and enhance scalability. While Node is widely adopted across industries for its efficiency, it faces challenges when handling large-scale applications. Node's event loop allows it to process incoming requests asynchronously, delegating tasks to other processes to ensure smooth operations. However, as the number of requests increases, or if tasks are CPU intensive or synchronous, the event loop can become a bottleneck, delaying subsequent requests. Queues address this challenge by offloading tasks, organizing them for sequential or parallel processing, and ensuring that critical processes are not overwhelmed. By using queues, you can balance workloads, improve response times, and maintain the reliability of your Node applications, even under heavy demand.

An architectural solution to this problem is to introduce a queuing system to handle requests and task management. Just as the event loop utilizes primitive queues to add new tasks and listen for completion events, more complex queues help organize the flow of tasks through an application, ensuring that no single segment of the application process ever blocks data from reaching its ultimate target.

In this chapter, you'll explore ways in which a primitive queue can be used to manage tasks in a Node application. Then you'll use Redis as a pub/sub messaging system to offload your logic to its proven structure. Last, you'll use a popular queuing system, RabbitMQ, to support your application for an even greater scale. By the end of this chapter, you'll have a better sense of when to consider messaging queues and when you'd find a queue cumbersome.

Tools and Applications Used in This Chapter

Before you get started, make sure to install and configure the tools and applications required for this project. Installation instructions for Node.js, Fastify, and VS Code are provided in Chapter 1, while project initialization steps, such as setting up your directory structure, configuring *package.json*, and using modern syntax, are covered in Appendix A. Instructions for installing and using Postman can be found in Appendix B. For a deeper explanation of SQLite, as well as installation steps for Redis and RabbitMQ, see Appendix C. Once completed, return here to continue. Building a project from scratch helps deepen your understanding of each component, giving you greater control and flexibility as you progress.

Your Prompt

An online coffee delivery company called JavaShipped has been growing in popularity, with a mass influx of online coffee orders overwhelming the core servers. The JavaShipped team wants you to help implement a system to handle increased scale. They suggest a messaging system to manage incoming order requests and have tasked you to build that system using Node.

Get Planning

The JavaShipped team is happy with their coffee ordering platform and fulfillment process. However, their existing Node application has a bottleneck preventing new orders after a certain limit. They also want to improve their application to better handle inventory check to make sure there's enough coffee to deliver before accepting orders, as well as processing internal analytics for the product as a whole. You visualize the problem in Figure 11-1 by displaying incoming requests hitting a single application server endpoint. In this figure, the /order endpoint is the main entrypoint for new coffee orders. While Node is traditionally fast at handling millions of web requests a minute, the underlying application logic may run too slowly to process enough incoming orders in a timely manner. Because of this, your application's response might timeout; or worse, it could crash entirely.

220 | Chapter 11: Coffee Order Manager

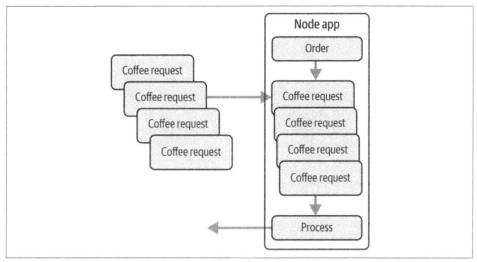

Figure 11-1. Existing JavaShipped application structure with a request bottleneck

To improve this design, you begin by diagramming a similar structure that depends on an internal queue to handle processing drink orders. Figure 11-2 demonstrates how a queue can be used to buffer incoming requests, giving the order processing logic a place from which to pull new order requests. While Node has its own internal queue that behaves in a similar manner, this explicit queue could help engineers determine new logic to manage orders better, or even notify end users of when the system is overwhelmed or when new orders are no longer being accepted.

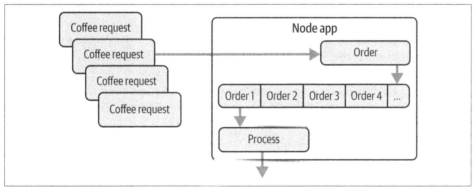

Figure 11-2. Adding an internal queue to handle new order requests

This approach is sufficient for smaller projects, but you'll soon discover that it does not scale well. Worse, your queue is still in the application's internal memory. That means if the application crashes before adding an order to persistent storage, all of your most recent order requests will disappear. For that reason, you diagram an improved system with your queue stored in a separate server. Figure 11-3 displays your application alongside a Redis server. The role of Redis here is to handle temporary storage of your order requests as they are processing. If your application crashes, your orders remain intact in your Redis storage (more on this later in the chapter).

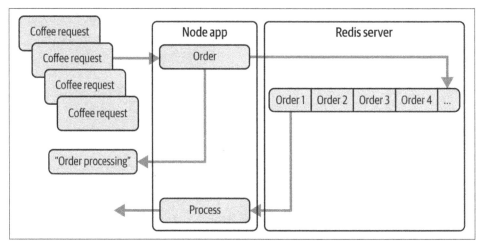

Figure 11-3. Utilizing a Redis server to manage order requests

You present your solution to JavaShipped and remind them that scalability is particularly important as their coffee delivery empire grows. You explain that the Redis solution is great, but that there are more robust ways to handle order requests on a global level. You introduce the RabbitMQ messaging queue architecture in Figure 11-4, which separates some of the application logic into separate services. These services depend on a RabbitMQ server to listen for relevant tasks and only issue them to the service as they become available. In this way, your application can offload both the queuing system and some of the application processing logic to separate services. Because these services are Node applications too, they may be hosted in isolated environments and continue to run, even if the main Node server crashes.

With your demonstration complete, you get the green light from JavaShipped to begin building out an improved Node application to handle the company's scalability problem.

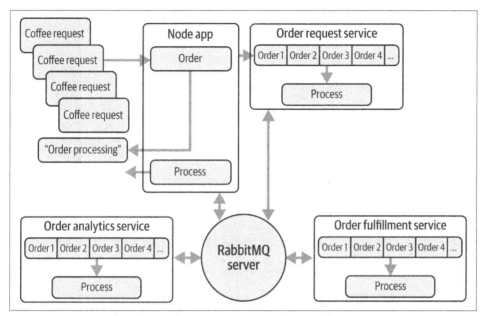

Figure 11-4. Upgrading the application structure with a RabbitMQ messaging queue server between services

Get Programming

To start developing your app, create a new project folder named `coffee_queue`. Navigate to your project folder on your command line and run `npm init`. This command initializes your Node app. You may press Enter throughout the initialization steps to accept the defaults. The result of these steps is the creation of a file called *package.json*. This file will instruct your Node app of any configurations or scripts needed to run correctly.

Next, create a file called *index.js* within your project folder. This file is the entry point for your app.

With your *index.js* file ready, you may install the main server framework used in this project. Navigate to the root of your project folder in your command line and run `npm install fastify@^5.4.0 @fastify/formbody@^8.0.2` to install Fastify as your web application framework. Then add the code in Example 11-1 which sets up a simple HTTP server using the Fastify framework. First, you import `fastify` and create an instance of the Fastify server, assigning it to the `app` variable. You define a constant variable `PORT` with the value of `3000`. This is the port number that the server will listen on for incoming requests.

> The `app` variable is used to configure the server and define the routes.

You register a plugin that parses incoming requests with URL-encoded payloads. This plugin is used to handle form data submitted in POST requests. Fastify handles JSON requests natively, so no additional middleware is required. Last, you write code which starts the server listening on port 3000 and logs a message to the console once the server is running.

> The `listen()` method takes a callback function that is executed once the server starts listening for incoming requests. In this case, it logs a message to the console indicating that the server is running on the specified port.

Example 11-1. Configure your application in index.js

```
import Fastify from "fastify"; ❶
import formbody from "@fastify/formbody"; ❷

const app = Fastify(); ❸
const PORT = 3000; ❹

await app.register(formbody); ❺

app.post("/slow-order", async (request, reply) => { ❻
  const { drinkOrder } = request.body; ❼
  for (let i = 0; i < 10000000000; i++) {} ❽
  console.log("ORDER PLACED"); ❾
  reply.send(`Drink order added to queue: ${drinkOrder}`); ❿
});

await app.listen({ port: PORT }); ⓫
console.log(`Server listening on http://localhost:${PORT}`); ⓬
```

❶ Import Fastify into your application.

❷ Import the plugin to handle form-encoded bodies.

❸ Create a Fastify server instance.

❹ Define a port value for incoming requests.

❺ Register the formbody plugin for handling URL-encoded form submissions.

❻ Add a POST route to handle incoming drink orders.

❼ Destructure drinkOrder from the incoming request body.

❽ Simulate a blocking operation with a long loop.

❾ Log when an order is placed.

❿ Send a response with the order confirmation.

⓫ Await the Fastify server to start listening (Node 18+ supports top-level await).

⓬ Log the server address to confirm it's running.

Before you run this application, it would help to add an endpoint at which you could submit requests to be processed. Because this project is dealing with scalability issues due to long order processing times, you create a route to mimic the waiting time for a placed order. This code defines a route handler for the POST HTTP method on the path /slow-order. From the request you extract the drinkOrder property from the request.body object, which contains the data that was sent in the request's body.

The request.body object is populated by Fastify's built-in support for JSON and registered formbody plugin. Make sure this plugin is registered before the route to ensure body content is available.

The next line creates a loop that iterates 10 billion times. This loop simulates a long-running process that might slow down the server's response time. In this case, the loop simply wastes CPU cycles and blocks other requests from processing to mimic an order being processed by JavaShipped. You log a message to the console indicating that an order has been placed, after the loop has finished executing. Last, you respond to the client with a message that their drink order was added to the internal queue.

You may run this application by navigating to your project's root directory in your command line and running node index. When your application starts, you'll see a log message indicating that the server is listening at *http://localhost:3000*. You may now post content to your app. Without a web interface, you may post a drink order by opening a new command-line window alongside your running server and running the following cURL command:

```
curl -X POST -H "Content-Type: application/json" \
  -d '{"drinkOrder":"latte"}' http://localhost:3000/slow-order
```

Notice that running this command takes roughly 10 seconds before a response of `Drink order added to queue: latte` is logged to your console. If a normally placed drink order takes this long, it can be a problem for new incoming orders. You begin to tackle this problem with a naive approach: building a simple queue to handle new order requests.

Because JavaScript does not natively support the queue data structure, you can simulate one using the built-in `Array` methods such as `push()` and `shift()` to add and remove items in a first-in, first-out (FIFO) manner.(JavaScript, queues in This project uses a simple array to manage the queue of drink orders. For more complex needs—such as job timeouts, retries, or concurrency—you might consider a dedicated library like the queue package on npm, which provides a more robust queue implementation.

Queues in JavaScript

While JavaScript does not have a built-in queue implementation, it is still possible to implement a queue data structure in JavaScript using arrays or linked lists. JavaScript was originally designed as a scripting language for the web, where queues may not be needed as frequently as they are in other types of applications. JavaScript was also designed to be lightweight and easy to use, and including a full suite of data structures may have made the language more complex. Array methods such as `push`, `shift`, and `slice`, can be used to implement a queue data structure using arrays. There has been demand for more robust data structures like queues in JavaScript, leading to the development of third-party libraries and packages.

The `queue` npm package is a simple implementation of a queue data structure for JavaScript. A queue is a collection of items that can be added to the back and removed from the front in a first-in, first-out (FIFO) order. You may use the `queue` package as a simple API for creating and manipulating queues.

The following are some methods you may use with a `Queue` instance:

`enqueue(item)`
    Adds an item to the back of the queue

`dequeue()`
    Removes the item at the front of the queue and returns it

`peek()`
    Returns the item at the front of the queue without removing it

`isEmpty()`
    Returns `true` if the queue is empty, `false` otherwise

`length()`
    Returns the number of items in the queue

---

226 | Chapter 11: Coffee Order Manager

> toArray()
>   Returns an array containing the items in the queue, in the order they were added
>
> For more information about the queue package, visit the npm website (*https://oreil.ly/uJlq0*).

Next, you add two new routes from Example 11-2 after your /slow-order route in *index.js*. These endpoints handle adding new drink orders and processing orders off the coffeeQueue. The first route listens for HTTP POST requests to the /order URL path. When a request is received, drinkOrder data is extracted from the request body using destructuring assignment and then pushed onto a coffeeQueue queue. The length of the queue is then logged to the console, and a response is sent back to the client with the message "Drink order added to queue".

The second endpoint listens for HTTP GET requests to the /process-order URL path. When a request is received, the next drink order is dequeued from coffeeQueue using the shift method. If there is a drink order in the queue, it is returned to the client as a JSON object using Fastify's reply.send() method. If there are no drink orders in the queue, a message "No drink orders in queue" is sent back to the client.

You may add the for loop from the /slow-order route to your /process-order route. This loop will continue to block new requests to the /order route. The benefit of the queue, however, is that processing logic may be extracted into a separate service, so your main Node application does not need to spend time on both incoming requests and processing orders.

Example 11-2. Adding routes to place order in your queue in index.js

```
app.post("/order", async (request, reply) => {  ❶
  const { drinkOrder } = request.body;
  coffeeQueue.push(drinkOrder);  ❷
  console.log(coffeeQueue.length);  ❸
  reply.send("Drink order added to queue");  ❹
});

app.get("/process-order", async (request, reply) => {  ❺
  const nextOrder = coffeeQueue.shift();  ❻
  if (nextOrder) {
    reply.send({ order: nextOrder });  ❼
  } else {
    reply.send("No drink orders in queue");  ❽
  }
});
```

❶ Define a POST route for the /order path using Fastify.

❷ Add the drinkOrder to your coffeeQueue queue object.

❸ Log the number of items in the queue.

❹ Respond with a message to the client that the order has been added.

❺ Define a GET route for the /process-order path.

❻ Pull an item from the queue and assign it to nextOrder.

❼ If there is an item in the queue, return that value using reply.send().

❽ If there is no item in the queue, return a message to the client.

You may run this application by rerunning node index in your command line. curl -X POST -H "Content-Type: application/json" -d '{"drinkOrder":"latte"}' http://localhost:3000/order adds a new latte drink order to your queue. Now, when you run the cURL command curl http://localhost:3000/process-order, you'll see the earliest drink order returned from your queue logged to your console. As orders come in, they are added to the queue, and as they are processed, they are dequeued from the queue. This type of approach is useful for managing large volumes of requests in a systematic and efficient way, ensuring that orders are processed in the order in which they were received.

You may build on this approach by adding new routes like the /order-count endpoint in Example 11-3. This route simply checks the number of items in your queue and logs that value in a message to your console.

Example 11-3. Adding a queue order count endpoint in index.js

```
app.get("/order-count", async (request, reply) => { ❶
  reply.send(`${coffeeQueue.length} drink orders in queue`); ❷
});
```

❶ Define a GET route for the /order-count path using Fastify.

❷ Return a message with the queue length to the client using reply.send().

Try running your application with this new route, adding two new drink orders and running curl http://localhost:3000/order-count in another command-line window. You'll see 2 drink orders in queue. Run curl http://localhost:3000/

---

228 | Chapter 11: Coffee Order Manager

`process-order` and then check the order count again to see that it has changed. In this way, your queue system already helps maintain the order state for your project. However, despite the improvement, you must still manually process orders from your queue via an endpoint. Moreover, if your application crashes, your queue, with all of its orders, disappears. In the next section, you'll solve this problem by adding a Redis server to support your application.

Adding a Redis Server

Your application is beginning to take shape structurally to manage drink orders at a pace that's comfortable for your business. However, a queue on its own still requires a function to manually process drink orders one at a time. For a business with an increasing number of requests, your application would benefit from real-time messaging, a queue that handles scale, and logic that is decoupled from your main Node server.

One solution is implementing Redis as a publish/subscribe (pub/sub) messaging pattern between your application and drink order data. Redis Pub/Sub allows for real-time messaging between clients and servers. This means that any updates or changes made to the server can be immediately pushed to clients subscribed to specific channels, without the need for clients to constantly poll the server for updates. These channels can be custom named. Figure 11-5 shows how one part of your application may publish data to Redis, and in turn, Redis will broadcast data on that specified channel to services that subscribed to that channel.

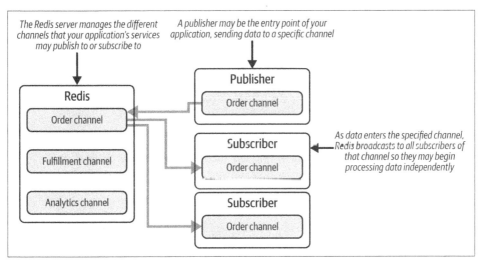

Figure 11-5. Redis broadcasting to its channel subscribers

This solution is designed to handle large volumes of messages and can be easily scaled to accommodate more clients and channels. This can help improve the performance and reliability of your application, especially as the number of clients and channels grows. Last, the application logic allows different parts of the system to communicate with each other through channels without requiring direct connections or dependencies on your main Fastify application.

More on Redis

Redis is an in-memory data store that is commonly used for caching and real-time data processing. As it runs on its own server, it supports storing a variety of data structures such as strings, hashes, lists, and sets outside of your main application. In a Node app, Redis is often used for caching previously requested data, user authentication keys for recent account activity, and, really, any other data that is frequently accessed. Its data management system is a popular choice across nearly every technical platform today.

Using Redis as a datastore helps reduce the load on your database and improve the performance and speed of your application. It can also be used to implement rate limiting in your application, helping to prevent abuse and improve the reliability of your service. The Redis Pub/Sub messaging system supports real-time messaging and event-driven architectures in your app. With pub/sub, you can publish messages to channels, and subscribers can receive those messages in real time.

For your project, you'll use the real-time messaging functionality through the following three methods:

`publish(channelName, message)`
> Publishes a message to a Redis channel. The `channelName` argument is a string that represents the name of the channel, and the `message` argument is the message to be published. When a message is published to a channel, Redis will distribute the message to all clients that are subscribed to that channel.

`subscribe(channelName)`
> Subscribes to a Redis channel. The `channelName` argument is a string that represents the name of the channel. When a client subscribes to a channel, Redis will add the client to a list of subscribers for that channel. The client will then receive any messages that are published to that channel.

`on(event, callback)`
> Registers an event listener for a Redis client. The `event` argument is a string that represents the name of the event to listen for, and the `callback` argument is a function that will be called when the event occurs. The message event is a commonly used event for Redis clients, and it is triggered whenever a message is received on a subscribed channel. When a message event occurs, the callback

230 | Chapter 11: Coffee Order Manager

function will be called with two arguments: the name of the channel where the
message was received, and the message itself.

After installing Redis, you may create a new Redis client and use these methods to
quickly send data to different parts of your application. In Node 18+ using ES modules, you may import Redis like this:

```
import { createClient } from 'redis';

const pub = createClient();
const sub = createClient();

await pub.connect();
await sub.connect();
```

Then use:

```
await pub.publish('orders', 'latte');
await sub.subscribe('orders', (message) => {
  console.log(`Received order: ${message}`);
});
```

For more information about Redis Pub/Sub, refer to the Redis documentation (*https://oreil.ly/keqA2*).

To introduce Redis to your application, install the redis npm package by running `npm install redis@^5.6.1` at the root level of your project directory in your command line. Then import that package by adding `import { createClient } from "redis"` to the top of your *index.js* file. You then need to create two Redis clients—one for subscribing and one for publishing—using the createClient method. After creating your Redis clients in *index.js*, add the code in Example 11-4 to set up the subscriber and publisher for your Redis Pub/Sub system.

Remember that Redis runs as an independent server and must be running alongside your Fastify application. Follow the instructions in Appendix C to start your Redis server.

This code sets up a Redis client for both subscribing and publishing, and then subscribes to the drink-order channel using the subscriber client. For both clients, you use the connect() method to establish a connection with the Redis server.

`await subscriber.subscribe("drink-order", (drinkOrder) => {...})` subscribes to the drink-order channel and sets up a listener for incoming messages on that channel. The callback function is triggered whenever a message is received, and the drinkOrder argument will contain the message payload. In this example, the callback logs a message to the console.

Because await is used before both the connect() and subscribe() methods, the code must be written using async/await syntax (supported in Node 18+ with top-level await).

Example 11-4. Adding a Redis Pub/Sub system in index.js

```
import { createClient } from "redis"; ❶

const subscriber = createClient(); ❷
await subscriber.connect();

const publisher = createClient(); ❸
await publisher.connect();

await subscriber.subscribe("drink-order", (drinkOrder) => { ❹
  console.log(`Received a new ${drinkOrder} order.`); ❺
});
```

❶ Import the Redis client creation method.

❷ Create a Redis client as a subscriber and connect it to your Redis server.

❸ Create a Redis client as a publisher and connect it to your Redis server.

❹ Subscribe to the drink-order channel and listen for messages.

❺ Log the message payload when a new drink order is received.

Then, in your /order route, add the line await publisher.publish("drink-order", drinkOrder) below the line where you destructure drinkOrder from the request body. This publishes the drink order value to the drink-order channel and immediately notifies all subscribers.

Open a new command-line window alongside your running Fastify server and run this cURL command:

```
curl -X POST -H "Content-Type: application/json" \
  -d '{"drinkOrder":"latte"}' http://localhost:3000/order
```

Immediately you'll see Received a new latte order. logged to your console.

Because your Redis server runs on its own port, you can create as many Node applications as needed to communicate with it across channels. For example, within the `subscriber.subscribe` block, you could add `await publisher.publish("fulfill-order", "latte")` to trigger another action.

You can also publish structured data using stringified JSON:

```
await publisher.publish("drink-order", JSON.stringify({
  drink: "latte",
  cost: 450,
  customer: "Jon Wexler"
}));
```

The subscriber would then need to parse it:

```
await subscriber.subscribe("drink-order", (message) => {
  const parsed = JSON.parse(message);
  console.log(`Received ${parsed.drink} for ${parsed.customer}`);
});
```

With your changes in place, you're able to create a distributed system of services that communicate through Redis. However, Redis has some limitations. Messages are not persisted by default—if a client is disconnected, it will miss messages. Redis also only supports simple, string-based payloads, and Pub/Sub operates on a single thread, which can limit throughput.

In the next section, you'll adapt more robust messaging patterns to overcome these limitations.

Integrating a Robust Messaging System

Your application can now handle a multitude of messages across a number of customized channels. Redis Pub/Sub is a powerful mechanism for building real-time communication systems. In your case, more channels may be added to communicate to other services about processing data along a chain of task dependencies. For example, an order may be placed, triggering a fulfillment service, which in turn publishes to another channel triggering an analytics service. Because you're trying to solve for scalability and reliability for a business that cannot lose customer orders, you decide to use a more advanced messaging system.

Similar to your simple queue and Redis Pub/Sub system, RabbitMQ offers a set of messaging features that enable you to build more complex message-based structures including message routing, acknowledgment, durability, and persistent queues. These features allow messages to be delivered reliably, routed based on rules, and acknowledged or retried if they fail. With RabbitMQ, you can maintain isolated, focused services that communicate through an internal pipeline—without overloading any single Fastify process or Node app.

To demonstrate this, you'll begin integrating RabbitMQ into your project by organizing your Node application into three services: the main entrypoint (which accepts

Integrating a Robust Messaging System | 233

orders), a fulfillment service (which processes them), and an analytics service (which tracks and logs them).

Ensure RabbitMQ is installed and running before executing any code. Like Redis, RabbitMQ runs as an independent server with its own port. See Appendix C for setup instructions.

Why RabbitMQ?

Once you've decided to use a robust queuing system, it's important to consider the available options and choices used across the industry. Which system you choose depends on the specific requirements and constraints of your app, such as scalability, durability, message guarantees, and operational complexity. The following are common options:

RabbitMQ
   A popular open source message broker that supports multiple messaging protocols (like AMQP). It's reliable, well-documented, and supports routing, queues, persistence, and acknowledgments.

ZeroMQ
   A lightweight messaging library geared toward extremely high-performance applications. Unlike RabbitMQ, it doesn't require a broker and focuses on raw speed and simplicity in distributed applications.

Kafka
   A distributed, high-throughput event streaming platform. Kafka is well-suited for use cases involving real-time ingestion and analysis of large-scale data streams.

Amazon SQS
   A fully managed, scalable message queue by AWS. It's durable and easy to scale, but adds cloud vendor lock-in and potential latency tradeoffs.

RabbitMQ is used for your project because it is open source, easy to set up locally, and ideal for scaling production systems. RabbitMQ allows you to decouple services, offload processing from your Fastify server, and establish asynchronous communication between services—all of which support fault tolerance and long-term scalability.

As you evaluate these tools, consider your goals, budget, and tolerance for complexity. RabbitMQ strikes a solid balance for mid- to large-scale apps that need reliability without heavy cloud dependencies. For more information, visit the RabbitMQ website (*https://www.rabbitmq.com*).

To get started with RabbitMQ, install the required package by running `npm install amqplib@^0.10.8` at your project's root level in your command line. Because you are building multiple services, you may begin by initializing the separate application folders for those services. These project folders can live alongside your main project folder. Initialize two new Node applications called `fulfillment_service` and `analytics_service`, install the `fastify` and `amqplib` npm packages, and ensure that the code in Example 11-5 exists at the top of each application's *index.js* file.

In this listing, you import the Fastify framework and the `amqplib` library, which is used to interact with the RabbitMQ message broker. After creating a new Fastify instance, you register Fastify's built-in body parsers to handle incoming JSON and URL-encoded requests. You also define the port number the server will run on using `process.env.PORT || 3000`. The last line declares two variables, `channel` and `connection`, which will be used to interact with the RabbitMQ message broker. Finally, the application uses top-level `await` to start listening on the designated port.

Example 11-5. Adding Fastify and RabbitMQ project configurations in index.js

```
import Fastify from "fastify"; ❶
import amqp from "amqplib";

const app = Fastify(); ❷
const PORT = process.env.PORT || 3000; ❸
let channel, connection; ❹

await app.listen({ port: PORT }); ❺
console.log("Server running at http://localhost:" + PORT);
```

❶ Import the `fastify` and `amqplib` libraries into your project.

❷ Create a Fastify application instance.

❸ Define the `PORT` number on which your server will listen for requests.

❹ Declare the `channel` and `connection` variables for RabbitMQ.

❺ Start your Fastify server using top-level await.

As this code is applied to your main application and your additional services, you need to change the `PORT` value to different values for each project so that they may run alongside each other. Update the default `PORT` value for the `fulfillment_service` to 3001, and 3002 for the `analytics_service`. At this point, you should have three project folders, each with their own *index.js* file and separately defined `PORT` values.

Integrating a Robust Messaging System | 235

RabbitMQ does not require a web server framework like Fastify, but using Fastify allows each service to expose its own routes and endpoints, which may be useful for debugging, health checks, or extending functionality. With your RabbitMQ server running, each application must connect to it to communicate across your application network. Add the code in Example 11-6 to the *index.js* file in each of your three Fastify-based Node applications. This code outlines the steps to follow:

1. Create an asynchronous function named `connect`.

2. Use `amqp.connect("amqp://localhost:5672")` to establish a connection to a RabbitMQ server running locally on the default port (5672). Assign the connection to the `connection` variable. The `amqp.connect()` method returns a promise, so use `await` to wait for the connection to be established.

3. Call `connection.createChannel()` to create a new channel on the RabbitMQ server. Assign the channel to the `channel` variable. Use `await` to ensure the channel is ready before proceeding.

 Channels are used to send and receive messages between clients and servers. Because connecting to an additional server is a process that takes an unknown amount of time, each of these lines uses `await` to ensure no further tasks are executed before a connection to RabbitMQ is made.

4. Call `channel.assertQueue("drink-order")` to verify that a queue named `drink-order` exists. If the queue doesn't exist, RabbitMQ will automatically create it.

5. Wrap the connection and channel creation logic in a `try-catch` block. Log or handle any errors that occur during the process.

6. Use the `drink-order` queue to register new drink orders from your main application entry point. In a separate `fulfillment_service`, read from the `drink-order` queue, and also connect to and write to the `analytics` queue for tracking purposes.

RabbitMQ runs on port 5672 by default. This port number was selected for the AMQP (Advanced Message Queuing Protocol) protocol, used by RabbitMQ for communicating across channels.

Example 11-6. Connecting to your RabbitMQ server in index.js

```
...
async function connect() { ❶
  try {
    connection = await amqp.connect("amqp://localhost:5672"); ❷
    channel = await connection.createChannel(); ❸
    await channel.assertQueue("drink-order"); ❹
  } catch (err) {
    console.error(err); ❺
  }
}
...
```

❶ Define a function to set up a connection to RabbitMQ and your selected queue.

❷ Connect to the RabbitMQ server and assign the connection to `connection`.

❸ Create a new RabbitMQ channel and assign it to `channel`.

❹ Ensure the `drink-order` queue exists (or create it if it doesn't).

❺ Catch and log any errors during connection or channel creation.

With each service connected to your RabbitMQ server, you may begin passing data from one queue to another. To do this, add the function in Example 11-7 to *index.js*. This function uses `channel.sendToQueue` to send a JavaScript object as binary data to the `drink-order` queue. The `Buffer.from` method converts the object into a binary buffer so that it can be transferred efficiently.

 Messaging systems like RabbitMQ expect binary data. Serialization via `Buffer.from(JSON.stringify(...))` ensures that structured data can be reliably reconstructed by the receiver.

This function is used in the main Fastify server and `fulfillment_service` only, since these are the systems that produce data for queues. In `fulfillment_service`, change the queue name from `drink-order` to `analytics`.

Integrating a Robust Messaging System | 237

Example 11-7. Adding a sendOrderData function in index.js

```
...
async function sendOrderData(data) { ❶
  await channel.sendToQueue("drink-order", Buffer.from(JSON.stringify(data))); ❷
}
...
```

❶ Define a function to publish data to RabbitMQ.

❷ Serialize the data and send it to the target queue.

You'll also need to call `connect()` to initialize the connection when your service starts. Add this line after the function definition.

To update your route to use RabbitMQ for sending drink orders, modify your Fastify route handler as shown in Example 11-8:

Example 11-8. Updating your route to send order data to the drink-order *channel in* index.js

```
...
app.post("/order", async (request, reply) => {
  const { drinkOrder: order, cost, customer } = request.body;
  const data = { ❶
    order,
    customer,
  };
  await sendOrderData(data); ❷
  console.log(`Drink: ${order} is being processed for ${customer}`); ❸
  reply.send("Order Processing"); ❹
});
...
```

❶ Create an object representing the incoming drink order.

❷ Send the object into the messaging pipeline via RabbitMQ.

❸ Log the transaction to the console.

❹ Respond to the client with a confirmation.

238 | Chapter 11: Coffee Order Manager

In your `fulfillment_service`, be sure to update `sendOrderData` to use `channel.sendToQueue("analytics", ...)` so that data continues flowing through your system pipeline. Within your `connectQueue` function in the `fulfillment_service` project folder, add the code in Example 11-9 to process incoming data. First, you establish connections to both the queue you'll read from, `drink-order`, and the queue you'll write to, `analytics`, using `channel.assertQueue`. Just as `channel.sendToQueue` sends data to a queue, you use `channel.consume` to read data from a specified queue. This method sets up a consumer that listens for messages on the `drink-order` queue. As messages become available, this listener will consume the message data.

You then extract the `content` property—the message body—from the `data` object. The `content` is converted from binary to a string and parsed as JSON, from which you extract the `order` and `customer` values. A message is logged to the console to indicate the order is being fulfilled. `channel.ack(data)` sends an acknowledgment to RabbitMQ, letting it know the message was handled successfully and should be removed from the queue. Finally, the order data is passed to `sendOrderData` for forwarding to the next queue.

In RabbitMQ, a consumer must acknowledge that it has successfully processed a message. If not acknowledged, RabbitMQ assumes the message has not been processed and leaves it in the queue, which may lead to duplicate processing.

Example 11-9. Connecting your `fulfillment_service` consumer in index.js

```
...
await channel.assertQueue("analytics"); ❶
await channel.assertQueue("drink-order");

channel.consume("drink-order", async (data) => { ❷
  const { content } = data; ❸
  const { order, customer } = JSON.parse(content.toString()); ❹
  console.log(`${order} being fulfilled for ${customer}`); ❺
  channel.ack(data); ❻
  await sendOrderData({ order, customer }); ❼
});
...
```

❶ Assert that the `analytics` and `drink-order` queues exist.

❷ Set up a consumer to listen for incoming messages on the `drink-order` queue.

❸ Extract the binary content from the message.

❹ Parse the message into a JavaScript object.

❺ Log the incoming order being fulfilled.

❻ Acknowledge the message so it is removed from the queue.

❼ Forward the message to the next processing queue.

The final step is to consume messages from the `analytics` queue. To begin, define an object in your `analytics_service` project that tracks the number of orders per drink: `const drinkMap = { latte: 0, coffee: 0, cappuccino: 0 }`. This object can be used to analyze how customers are ordering. Then, to read from the `analytics` queue and process that data, add the code in Example 11-10 to the bottom of your `connect Queue` function in *index.js*.

This setup mirrors the `fulfillment_service` logic: listen on a queue, extract the message, parse it, and perform an action. In this case, you increment the count of a drink in `drinkMap`, log the analysis step, and acknowledge the message.

Example 11-10. Connecting your `analytics_service` consumer in index.js

```
...
const drinkMap = { latte: 0, coffee: 0, cappuccino: 0 };

await channel.assertQueue("analytics"); ❶

channel.consume("analytics", (data) => { ❷
  const { content } = data; ❸
  const { order, customer } = JSON.parse(content.toString()); ❹
  if (drinkMap[order] !== undefined) { ❺
    drinkMap[order]++;
  }
  console.log(`${order} being analyzed for ${customer}`); ❻
  channel.ack(data); ❼
});
...
```

❶ Ensure the `analytics` queue exists.

❷ Start a consumer for the `analytics` queue.

❸ Extract binary message content.

---

240 | Chapter 11: Coffee Order Manager

❹ Parse the stringified message into usable variables.

❺ Check if the order type exists in the tracking map and increment it.

❻ Log the analysis step to the console.

❼ Acknowledge message receipt to RabbitMQ.

Your main server and both supporting services are now fully connected through RabbitMQ. To test them, open three terminal windows, one for each project folder: the main server, `fulfillment_service`, and `analytics_service`. In each window, run:

```
node index
```

Then, in a fourth terminal, run the following `curl` command to simulate a new drink order:

```
curl -X POST -H "Content-Type: application/json" \
  -d '{"drinkOrder":"latte", "cost":"4.50","customer":"Jon Wexler"}' \
  http://localhost:3000/order
```

Your output should look like this:

- Main server: `Drink: latte is being processed for Jon Wexler`
- Fulfillment service: `latte being fulfilled for Jon Wexler`
- Analytics service: `latte being analyzed for Jon Wexler`

This demonstrates an effective flow of asynchronous, distributed message handling from one service to the next using RabbitMQ queues. With this structure in place, you may now embellish the type of data processing you'd like to occur within each service. For example, you may want to verify that you have inventory before accepting and fulfilling a drink request in the `fulfillment_service`. You may also wish to enhance your analytics logic to display meaningful metrics in the `analytics_service` console output. Add the code in Example 11-11 to your *index.js* file in `analytics_service` to introduce a function that summarizes drink order percentages in real time.

This code defines a function called `processDrinkAnalytics` that calculates the percentage of each drink order out of the total number of drink orders received every 10 seconds. It uses `setInterval` to schedule repeated execution and iterates over the keys in `drinkMap`, which tracks the count of each drink. It calculates the total order count, computes percentages, formats the results, and logs them to the console. Additionally, a `setTimeout` resets the drink counts to zero every 5 minutes to keep the metrics fresh. Call `processDrinkAnalytics()` after defining it so the tracking starts as soon as the service is run.

Integrating a Robust Messaging System | 241

Example 11-11. Introducing an `analytics_service` analytics function in index.js

```
...
function processDrinkAnalytics() { ❶
  const FIVE_MINUTES_IN_MILLISECONDS = 5 * 60 * 1000; ❷
  const TEN_SECONDS_IN_MILLISECONDS = 10000;

  setInterval(() => { ❸
    const drinkNames = Object.keys(drinkMap); ❹

    const totalDrinkCount = drinkNames.reduce((total, drinkName) => { ❺
      return total + drinkMap[drinkName];
    }, 0);

    const drinkPercentages = drinkNames.map((drinkName) => { ❻
      const percentage =
        Math.floor((drinkMap[drinkName] / totalDrinkCount) * 100) || 0;
      return ` ${drinkName}: ${percentage}%`; ❼
    });

    console.log(`Drink orders: ${drinkPercentages}`); ❽

    setTimeout(() => { ❾
      drinkNames.forEach((drinkName) => {
        drinkMap[drinkName] = 0;
      });
    }, FIVE_MINUTES_IN_MILLISECONDS);
  }, TEN_SECONDS_IN_MILLISECONDS);
}

processDrinkAnalytics(); ❿
...
```

❶ Define a function that handles drink order analytics.

❷ Set two timing constants: one for resetting and one for logging.

❸ Schedule drink percentage logs to print every 10 seconds.

❹ Collect the list of drink names being tracked.

❺ Calculate the total drink count.

❻ Map drink counts to percentages.

❼ Format the percentage string per drink.

❽ Log the drink percentage breakdown.

❾ Reset the drink counts every 5 minutes.

❿ Start the analytics logging when the service runs.

Run your `analytics_service` again and send a variety of drink orders using the `curl` command:

```
curl -X POST -H "Content-Type: application/json" \
  -d '{"drinkOrder":"latte", "cost":"4.50","customer":"Jon Wexler"}' \
  http://localhost:3000/order
```

Observe the live percentage breakdowns in the console. For example, after sending only latte orders, you'll see something like: `Drink orders: latte: 100%, coffee: 0%, cappuccino: 0%`.

From here, you can expand your system with additional services, endpoints, databases, or more detailed order handling logic. This chapter demonstrated how to design a queue-based messaging system that can scale with demand and improve reliability.

Chapter Exercises

1. Add an inventory tracking service using Redis:

   a. Create a new Node app called `inventory_service` and install the `redis` package.

   b. In *index.js*, connect to Redis and subscribe to the `drink-order` channel.

   c. Define an `inventory` object (e.g., `{ latte: 10, coffee: 10, cappuccino: 10 }`) that tracks available stock for each drink.

   d. On each incoming order, decrement the corresponding drink's inventory.

   e. Log a warning if stock drops below 3 (e.g., `"Low stock for latte: 2 remaining"`).

   f. Use `setInterval` to reset inventory back to 10 every 5 minutes.

Use `JSON.parse(drinkOrder)` to extract data from Redis messages.

Integrating a Robust Messaging System | 243

2. Requeue failed messages in RabbitMQ:

    a. In your `fulfillment_service`, modify the consumer for the `drink-order` queue.

    b. Simulate a failure for every third order (e.g., `orderCount % 3 === 0`).

    c. Use `channel.nack(data, false, true)` instead of `ack()` to requeue failed messages.

    d. Log a retry message each time this happens.

    e. Optionally, track retry counts with a `retries` field in the message payload.

> Requeuing prevents lost orders, but be careful to avoid infinite retry loops.

Summary

In this chapter, you:

- Explored how Node applications handle high demand and throughput using asynchronous patterns and queues
- Built queue-based systems to manage incoming tasks and improve request handling
- Used Redis as an in-memory queue to buffer and broadcast messages across services
- Leveraged Redis Pub/Sub to enable real-time event communication between decoupled parts of the application
- Integrated RabbitMQ to implement robust, scalable message queues with durable service-oriented architecture

CHAPTER 12

Music Label Blockchain Market

This chapter covers the following:

- Building your own blockchain architecture
- Designing a marketplace with a tokenized ledger
- Integrating Web3 for scalable and secure transactions

In this chapter, you'll build a Node application that explores the blockchain architecture and how it can be adapted with JavaScript. Through a bare-bones implementation, you'll learn how to conceptualize a blockchain and incorporate its fundamental methods. You'll build a prototype marketplace that supports blockchain transactions and learn about how your Node application facilitates a decentralized network of exchanges through a distributed ledger. By constructing the foundational elements of a blockchain, such as the smart contract, cryptographic puzzle, consensus logic, and general ledger, you will better understand how Node and JavaScript help make this architecture possible.

In the latter half of the chapter, you'll use industry-standard tools like Web3, the Ethereum blockchain network, and Solidity to create smart contracts and integrate your Node application to a wider audience. You'll better grasp how blockchain is used today and how its use in a marketplace is differentiated from its prominent use in cryptocurrency exchange. If you're already familiar with blockchain, this chapter will reinforce your knowledge on the technical side. Otherwise, this short and sweet exposure will get you up and running with blockchain and eventually "mining your own business."

245

Tools and Applications Used in This Chapter

Before you get started, make sure to install and configure the tools and applications required for this project. Installation instructions for Node.js, Fastify, and VS Code are provided in Chapter 1, while project initialization steps, such as setting up your directory structure, configuring *package.json*, and using modern syntax, are covered in Appendix A. Once completed, return here to continue. Building a project from scratch helps deepen your understanding of each component, giving you greater control and flexibility as you progress.

Your Prompt

A music studio, DeSoundTralized Studios, wants to partner with major artists to sell previews of songs and albums before their official release. They want to develop a marketplace where customers can purchase the rights to listen to high-quality audio files from the limited and authenticated collection. They want to allow buyers to resell the songs after listening and limit the number of resells before the rights expire when the music is released to the public. Moreover, they do not want to manage the continuous series of sales—only the initial purchase, and then let the market decide the prices thereafter. The delivery of the audio file and how it's listened to by the buyer will be handled by another platform and is out of scope for this project.

Get Planning

This problem requires a system that can securely and efficiently provide a real-time market for audio file sales, where a sale depends on the authenticity of the song and its sale history. That means that when a song is made available for one month and up to five resells, your application must verify the transfer of ownership from one buyer to the next, keep track of the number of transfers, and remove ownership from the final buyer at the time of expiration. Additionally, the music studio does not want to manage transactions and distribution beyond the initial sale. Together, these criteria call for an application that securely and cryptographically signs transactions to ensure authenticity, with a decentralized and distributed database. These conditions measure up to a good recipe for blockchain. See Figure 12-1 to better visualize this architecture.

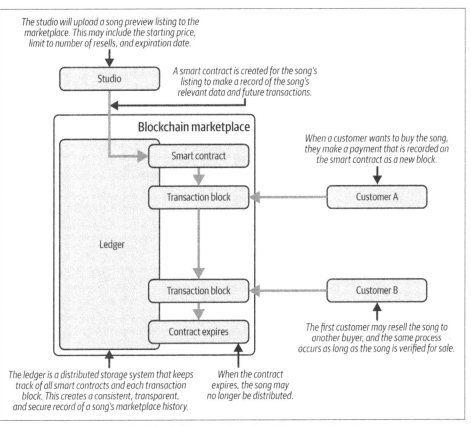

Figure 12-1. Visualizing the blockchain marketplace for music distribution

Blockchain in a Nutshell

Blockchain is a digital and transparent record of transactions without a central administration. To explain it further, consider a public library's existing system for lending books. As patrons borrow books, the library keeps an internal record and attempts to notify the readers when their book is due for return. Certain criteria are followed to ensure that a book may be borrowed, such as the borrowing period of the book, its availability, the number of reservations made to borrow the book, and even its current location. All of this information is typically managed by the library and is prone to human error, system mistakes, and lost information. This, in turn, may lead to books never being returned or perpetually being ineligible to borrow.

Blockchain solves this problem because it is both decentralized and has a transparent record of every book's history at the library. Imagine the standard library borrowing system, but one that shares every book's history of being borrowed (like a long list of dates, names, and locations) to all patrons, and which automates the borrowing

Get Planning | 247

process by checking this public history and verifying whether a book is eligible to borrow or whether it needs returning.

If someone wants to borrow (`transaction`) `Node Projects`, the system would check the blockchain records (`ledger`). This process scans the chronological collection of transactions (`block`) and verifies the borrowing criteria (`smart contract`) before creating a new borrowing transaction. This transaction is then made publicly available for others in the library network to approve. Library patrons rush to validate the transaction by solving a riddle (`cryptographic puzzle`) and agreeing on the answer (`consensus`), so that the transaction may be codified in a block and added to the transparent ledger. This process depends on a collective network.

The cryptographic puzzle can range in complexity and often requires exerting computational power to solve. One reason for this requirement in validating transactions is to prevent malicious attacks or false transactions from accessing the ledger. In the library example, patrons who solve the riddle may receive rewards in exchange for their effort. Likewise, a digital blockchain system may reward solvers of the puzzle and those that verify the solution. The solving and validation of the puzzle is generally automated and performed by participants in the network with dedicated computers tied to the network.

The following are a part of blockchain's core terminology:

Blockchain
　　The blockchain in this system would be a distributed ledger technology that allows for secure, transparent, and immutable recording of all book borrowing transactions on the network.

Transaction
　　A transaction in this system would be the act of borrowing a book from the library. This would involve the borrower initiating the transaction by sending a request to the smart contract on the blockchain network, which would then validate and verify the request before recording the details on the ledger. The transaction would also involve the borrower returning the book to the library, which would trigger a new transaction to be recorded on the blockchain network.

Smart contract
　　A smart contract in this system would be a self-executing program that enforces the rules and conditions of the book borrowing process. It would be written in code and deployed on the blockchain network to automate the lending process.

Consensus
　　Consensus in this system refers to the process of verifying and validating the book borrowing transactions on the blockchain network. This is typically done

through a consensus algorithm, such as proof of work or proof of stake, which involves a network of nodes agreeing on the validity of the transactions.

Block
A block in this system would be a bundle of verified book borrowing transactions, which are added to the blockchain network in a chronological order.

Ledger
The ledger in this system would be a digital record of all book borrowing transactions on the blockchain network, including details such as the book title, borrower name, borrowing period, and return date. The ledger would be immutable and transparent, meaning that all transactions recorded on it could not be altered or deleted.

Because this system is decentralized, it depends on an active network of participants making transactions and verifying them. For this reason, successful blockchain platforms offer valuable incentives to encourage participation in maintaining the smart contract and consensus elements of approving and persisting a new transaction.

To better understand how the blockchain works, you build out the fundamental pieces in code, including the `Block`, `Blockchain`, `Transaction`, and `Node` classes. The `Node` class is used to register a new node, or participating server, on the blockchain network...

Get Programming

To start developing your app, create a new project folder named `blockchain_market place`. Navigate to your project folder on your command line and run `npm init`. This command initializes your Node app. You may press Enter throughout the initialization steps to accept the defaults. The result of these steps is the creation of a file called *package.json*. This file will instruct your Node app of any configurations or scripts needed to run correctly.

Next, create a file called *index.js* within your project folder. This file is the entry point for your app.

First, you create the foundational classes for your app. `MarketplaceNode`, `Block chain`, `Block`, and `Transaction`. Create a folder called `src` within your project directory. This is where the code for your classes will live. Create the *marketplaceNode.js*, *blockchain.js*, *block.js*, and *transaction.js* files within the `src` folder. Then you install the `fastify` package by running `npm install fastify@^5.4.0`, and within your *index.js* file, you initialize your web server, as shown in Example 12-1.

In this listing, you set up a `fastify` app and configure it to take a custom `PORT` value. The `PORT` may be assigned by a command-line argument that is passed in after the

Get Programming | 249

node index.js line. `process.argv.slice(2)` returns the values after the executable path only, and assigns that value to PORT. If no value is passed in, PORT defaults to 0.

> Setting the PORT to 0 tells `fastify.listen()` to choose a port value for you. This comes in handy when assigning mass values for various applications.

You configure the `fastify` instance to handle and parse JSON content using the built-in body parser. Last, you start the server by having it listen on your specified PORT value. If no PORT value exists, `fastify` assigns one for you. You reassign PORT to that number using `server.address().port` and log out the server's location on startup.

Example 12-1. Configure your web server in index.js

```
import Fastify from "fastify"; ❶
const fastify = Fastify(); ❷
let [PORT] = process.argv.slice(2); ❸
PORT = PORT || 0;

fastify.get("/", async (request, reply) => {
  reply.send({ message: "Marketplace running" });
}); ❹

await fastify.listen({ port: PORT }); ❺
PORT = fastify.server.address().port; ❻
console.log(`Running on http://localhost:${PORT}`); ❼
```

❶ Import the `fastify` library to your project.

❷ Create a Fastify instance.

❸ Retrieve command-line arguments and destructure the array to assign the first argument to the PORT variable.

❹ Example route to verify the server is running correctly.

❺ Start the server and listen on the assigned port.

❻ Update the PORT variable to the actual assigned port number.

❼ Log the server's location to your console.

Test out this server by running node index.js in your command line at the project's root level. Notice that each time you start your application, a new port number is assigned. Then run node index.js 3000 and notice that your application only runs on port 3000. Moving forward, port 3000 will represent your main marketplace node server location. This means that *http://localhost:3000* will act as the starting point for new nodes to participate in the blockchain marketplace. As new nodes enter the marketplace, they will need to broadcast their server location to all other nodes so that the community of nodes is known by all participants. To accomplish this, you start to build the MarketplaceNode class and provide it API endpoints to interact with other nodes.

Figure 12-2 demonstrates how new marketplace nodes enter the network. When a new node wants to participate, it will register its URI with the network. From there, the existing peer network will evaluate the incoming marketplace node and add it to the peer list. This list is then synchronized across all peer nodes so that the list of participants is consistent across the network.

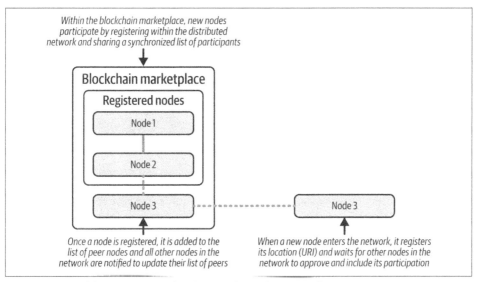

Figure 12-2. Adding a new marketplace node to the network

To accomplish this, you add the code in Example 12-2 to your *MarketplaceNode.js* file in *src*. This file will contain all of the logic for the MarketplaceNode class. In this code, you define the MarketplaceNode class with a constructor that takes three parameters: url, peers, and blockchain. These parameters represent the URL of the marketplace node (location of that network node), an array of peers (other nodes in the marketplace network), and a reference to the blockchain object, respectively.

The constructor also initializes other properties such as setting the node's `balance` to 50000 (this is $50 in cents). For now, you'll let each node in the network start with an initial fund to demonstrate the transactions within the network. `this.songs = {}` initializes an empty hash assigned to the songs property, which is used to keep track of songs purchased on the network. Last, `this.broadcastSelf()` invokes the `broadcastSelf` function to inform other nodes in the marketplace network about the existence of this node.

Example 12-2. Defining the `MarketplaceNode` class in marketplaceNode.js

```
class MarketplaceNode { ❶
  constructor(url, peers = [], blockchain) { ❷
    this.url = url;
    this.peers = peers;
    this.blockchain = blockchain;
    this.balance = 50000;
    this.songs = {};
    this.broadcastSelf();
  }
}
export default MarketplaceNode; ❸
```

❶ Define the `MarketplaceNode` class to represent a single node in the marketplace network.

❷ Initialize the node's properties, including its URL, peer list, blockchain reference, account balance, and local song store. Immediately broadcast the node to its peers.

❸ Export the `MarketplaceNode` class as the default module export so it can be imported elsewhere in the application.

At this time, you have a class with a reference to the `broadcastSelf` function. Broadcasting is an essential part of a functioning blockchain network as it informs all other nodes in the network of changes in the marketplace. Transparency and consistent delivery of changes in the distributed network is what separates blockchain from other transactional systems. For that reason, you'll first create a `broadcast` function that may be used by other functions to broadcast information across the network. Add the `broadcast` function shown in Example 12-3 to your `MarketplaceNode` class. This function uses `axios` to make an HTTP request to each peer node's URI and takes a specific `path` and `data` as arguments. The `path` will specify to which endpoint you are sending your data, and the `data` may represent any changes or updates to the network, such as new `MarketplaceNode` registration.

252 | Chapter 12: Music Label Blockchain Market

Within the function, you iterate over the `MarketplaceNode` peers, skipping your own node's URL and make a POST request to the specified path for that peer's location. Effectively, this makes an outgoing HTTP request to the same endpoint for each peer in the network. To get this to work, you need to install the `axios` package by running `npm install axios@^1.11.0` at the root level of your project folder in your command line, and importing the `axios` library (`import axios from 'axios'`) to the top of *MarketplaceNode.js*.

The `map` function is used to create an array of promises, and `Promise.all` ensures that all the promises are resolved before moving on.

Example 12-3. Adding a broadcast function in marketplaceNode.js

```
...
async broadcast(path, data) {            ❶
  await Promise.all(
    this.peers.map(async (peer) => {     ❷
      if (peer === this.url) return;     ❸
      try {
        await axios.post(`${peer}/${path}`, data);   ❹
      } catch (error) {
        console.error(error.message);
      }
    })
  );
}
...
```

❶ Define the `broadcast` async function to take a `path` and `data` argument.

❷ Iterate over the `MarketplaceNode`'s list of peer URLs.

❸ Skip the peer URL that matches the broadcasting node's URL.

❹ Make an `axios` POST request to the provided `path`, passing `data` in the request body.

With the `broadcast` function in place, it may be reused to broadcast information to all the other peer nodes in the network. Two such cases are `broadcastSelf`, to let other peer nodes know when you've joined the network, and `registerNode` to add other new participating nodes to your peers list. Add the functions in Example 12-4 to your `MarketplaceNode` class to make use of these functions. The `broadcastSelf` function is an async function that calls other peer nodes' `register-node` endpoints and passes its own marketplace node URI as data. The `registerNode` function receives new marketplace node URI information and adds it to the node's `peers` list. Then that node calls `broadcast` for the `sync-peers` endpoint, passing all of its peers as the data. The `sync-peers` endpoint will notify all other nodes in the network to align on the peer node data, so that every participant is in sync with one another.

Example 12-4. Adding broadcastSelf and registerNode functions in marketplaceNode.js

```
...
async broadcastSelf() { ❶
  this.broadcast("register-node", { url: this.url }); ❷
}

async registerNode(newNodeUrl) { ❸
  this.peers.push(newNodeUrl); ❹
  await this.broadcast("sync-peers", { peers: this.peers }); ❺
}
...
```

❶ Define the `broadcastSelf` function.

❷ Call the `broadcast` function on the `MarketplaceNode` object using the `register-node` path and the node's URL as data.

❸ Define the `registerNode` function that takes a `newNodeUrl` argument.

❹ Add the `newNodeUrl` value to your node's `peers` list.

❺ Add the `broadcast` function on the `MarketplaceNode` object using the `sync-peers` path and the node's `peers` list as data.

With these functions in place, you may now initialize a new `MarketplaceNode` instance. At the top of your *index.js* file, declare the `marketplaceNode` variable by adding `let marketplaceNode`. Then add the `initializeNode` function from Example 12-5 to *index.js*. This function is used to set the current node's URI, initialize the list of peer nodes (to start, your new nodes will always point to the same node before syncing its list to include all participants in the network). Last, you assign `marketplaceNode` to a new instance of `MarketplaceNode` using the node's URL and `initialPeers` array. You may then call `initializeNode()` immediately after Fastify finishes listening and a port is assigned.

254 | Chapter 12: Music Label Blockchain Market

It's important to call this function only after assigning the PORT value, otherwise your initialized node will not have a set URI.

Example 12-5. Adding an `initializeNode` *function in* index.js

```
...
const initializeNode = () => {   ❶
  const URL = `http://localhost:${PORT}`;   ❷
  const initialPeers = ["http://localhost:3000"];   ❸
  marketplaceNode = new MarketplaceNode(URL, initialPeers);   ❹
};
...
```

❶ Define the `initializeNode` function.

❷ Assign URL to your development URL and dynamically assigned PORT number.

❸ Set the `initialPeers` array to include the URI *http://localhost:3000*.

❹ Assign `marketplaceNode` to a new `MarketplaceNode` instance using the defined URL and `initialPeers` list.

With your MarketplaceNode initialized in *index.js*, the final step is to define the /register-node and /sync-peers endpoints. Add the code in Example 12-6 to the middle of *index.js*, after initializing the `fastify` variable.

Example 12-6. Adding `register-node` *and* `sync-peers` *API endpoints in* index.js *with Fastify*

```
fastify.post("/register-node", async (request, reply) => {   ❶
  const { url: newNodeUrl } = request.body;   ❷
  await marketplaceNode.registerNode(newNodeUrl);   ❸
  reply.send({ message: "Node Registered" });   ❹
});

fastify.post("/sync-peers", async (request, reply) => {   ❺
  const { peers } = request.body;   ❻
  marketplaceNode.peers = peers;   ❼
  console.log(`${marketplaceNode.url} synced ${marketplaceNode.peers}`);   ❽
  reply.send({ message: "Synced Peers" });   ❾
});
```

❶ Define the /register-node POST route using Fastify.

❷ Extract the url from the request body.

❸ Register the node in the current marketplaceNode.

❹ Return a message confirming registration.

❺ Define the /sync-peers POST route.

❻ Extract the incoming list of peer URLs.

❼ Replace the local peer list.

❽ Log the peer sync for debugging purposes.

❾ Confirm sync with a JSON message.

Your code is now ready to set up a marketplace network and take on new node participants. To test this, open a command-line window in your project's root directory and run node index 3000 to start your server. This will initiate the code in *index.js*, which creates a new MarketplaceNode. The first node will be set to *http://localhost: 3000*. Your command line should indicate that this node is online (Figure 12-3). Now open a second and third window from the same directory running node index and start your app a second and third time while the first server is running. Those two other servers will start up and immediately register into the network through the node at *http://localhost:3000*.

Figure 12-3. Command-line output for starting three node servers

You may log the list of peers by adding console.log(`${marketplaceNode.url} synced ${marketplaceNode.peers}`) in your /sync-peers route in *index.js*. This will help you see the sync in action. The last server that starts up will add to the end of the peers list for each participating node. The log message should look something like http://localhost:53896 synced http://localhost:3000,http://local host:53884,http://localhost:53896.

With the marketplace nodes connected, it's time to build the core structure of the marketplace itself, the blockchain.

Coding the Blockchain

The marketplace is largely reliant on the participating nodes' ability to exchange money and information across the network. This is made possible through the blockchain structure. As participants engage in the marketplace, more transactions are made, and the record of changes along the way are saved within the chain of blocks, synchronized across all the nodes in the network.

Figure 12-4 demonstrates how the network exists without a central authority. Each of the nodes in the network carry a copy of all changes and a list of all participating nodes. In this way, any node is able to initiate a transaction, and all other nodes may reference the same copy of the blockchain to verify its validity.

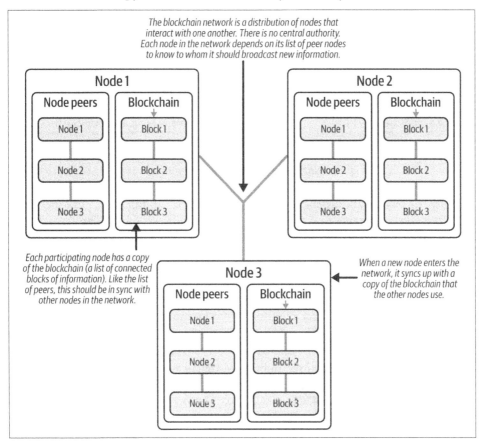

Figure 12-4. Visualizing the blockchain network of nodes

Further breaking down this structure, Figure 12-5 details the contents of the Blockchain, Block, and Transaction classes. The Blockchain class contains a collection of blocks. An instance of the Block class represents a collection of transactions and contains properties that distinguish it from other blocks in the chain. Individual transactions from the `Transaction` class make exchanges of songs for currency a possibility.

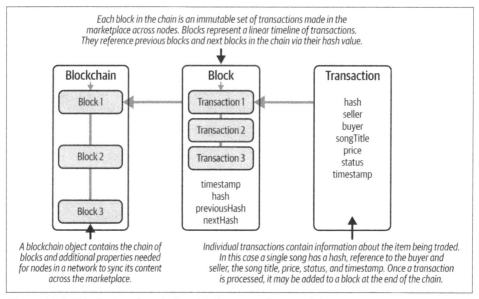

Figure 12-5. Displaying the relationship between data models

Because the blockchain depends on blocks, you start by building out the `Block` class. Add the code in Example 12-7 to *block.js* in your project's *src* folder. This code defines a class called `Block` that represents a block in a blockchain, preparing it to be linked with other blocks to form a chain. A `Block` contains `transactions` and has properties such as a `timestamp`, `previousHash`, `hash` (the current hash), and `nextHash` (a reference to the next block).

Initializing a new `Block` object requires a `transactions` array and an optional `previousHash` value. The timestamp is set to the current time using the `Date.now()` method. The transactions are assigned to the `transactions` property of the `Block` object. The previous hash is stored in the `previousHash` property. The current hash is calculated by calling the `calculateHash` method, which will be added shortly. The calculated hash is stored in the `hash` property, and the `nextHash` property is initially set to `null`, indicating that there is no reference to the next block yet.

Example 12-7. Defining the `Block` class in block.js

```
class Block {
  constructor(transactions, previousHash) { ❶
    this.timestamp = Date.now(); ❷
```

```
      this.transactions = transactions;     ❸
      this.previousHash = previousHash;     ❹
      this.hash = this.calculateHash();     ❺
      this.nextHash = null;                 ❻
  }
}
export default Block;                       ❼
```

❶ Accept transactions and a previousHash value when instantiating a new Block.

❷ Assign a timestamp property to the current datetime.

❸ Assign a transactions property to the argument array of transactions.

❹ Assign a previousHash property to the argument value pointing to the latest block.

❺ Assign a hash property to a new calculated hash value.

❻ Assign a nextHash property to a null value to start.

❼ Export the Block class for use in other parts of the application.

Next, you add the calculateHash function to your Block class by adding the code in Example 12-8. This code defines a method to compute and return the hash value of the block using the SHA-256 hashing algorithm. The method begins by calling the createHash function, which is part of the crypto library that comes with Node. You will need to add import { createHash } from "crypto" to the top of *block.js* to make use of this function. createHash creates a hash object, using the SHA-256 algorithm that will be used to calculate the hash value.

 SHA-256 is a widely adopted and standardized hashing algorithm, known for being computationally efficient and nearly impossible to reverse the hash value back to its original input. More importantly, it is extremely unlikely for two different inputs to produce the same hash value, making it a good candidate for generating a random hash identifier for your blocks.

Next, the update method is called on the hash object, using the block's previous hash, timestamp, and a JSON representation of the block's transactions as input data to be hashed. The digest method is called on the hash object, passing hex to generate the final hash value in hexadecimal format. In this way, you generate a unique hash value for each block. This hash value is an important component of blockchain technology, as it ensures the integrity and security of the data stored in each block.

Example 12-8. Creating the `calculateHash` *function in* block.js

```
...
calculateHash() { ❶
  return createHash("sha256") ❷
    .update( ❸
        this.previousHash +
        this.timestamp +
        JSON.stringify(this.transactions)
    )
    .digest("hex"); ❹
}
...
```

❶ Define the `calculateHash` function for generating an encrypted hash value.

❷ Use the `createHash` method to create a hash object using the `sha256` algorithm.

❸ Generate a hash value based on the input's previous hash value, timestamp, and array of transactions.

❹ Convert the value to a hexadecimal value.

With the `Block` class set up, you may start working on the `Blockchain` class. Create a file called *blockchain.js* in `src` and add the code in Example 12-9. This code imports the `Block` class from `block.js`. The `Blockchain` class initializes new `Blockchain` objects with optional `chain` and `pendingTransactions` parameters. If a `chain` is provided, it is assigned to the `chain` property. Otherwise, a new `chain` is created with a genesis block using the `createGenesisBlock` method. Similarly, the `pendingTransactions` will default to an empty array, unless an array of values is passed in. The constructor also initializes other properties such as the difficulty level, a list of pending transactions, and the mining reward.

Mining a Block

Mining is the process of adding new blocks to the blockchain by solving a computational puzzle. The goal of mining is to find a hash value that meets certain criteria so that the network of nodes can safely add a block to the blockchain in a decentralized manner. The `Blockchain` class works simultaneously as a storage of blocks and transactions, as well as a blueprint for how to codify new blocks into the chain. The following are key steps in the mining process as they relate to the `Blockchain` class:

Pending transactions
> A miner node collects a set of pending transactions that have not yet been included in any block.

---

260 | Chapter 12: Music Label Blockchain Market

Block formation

The miner assembles these pending transactions into a new block, along with other information like the previous block's hash and a timestamp.

Hash calculation

The miner calculates the hash of the block by applying the calculateHash to the block's data. The hash function takes into account all the block's contents, including the transactions, previous block's hash and timestamp.

Proof of work

The miner then adjusts a random numerical value repeatedly and recalculates the block's hash until they find a hash value that satisfies the computational puzzle. The specific criteria depend on the network's difficulty level, which is often represented by the number of leading zeros required in the hash.

Validating the proof

Once the miner finds a suitable hash value, they broadcast the block to the network. Other participants in the network can verify the proof of work by rehashing the block's data and confirming that the resulting hash meets the difficulty criteria. For this project, you may skip this step to reduce code complexity.

Block addition

If the proof of work is valid, the block is added to the blockchain, and the miner is rewarded with a predefined reward for their effort. The block is linked to the previous block through its hash, forming a chain of blocks.

Updating the network

After a block is added, the miner starts the process again, collecting new pending transactions and creating a new block to mine.

Through this process marketplace nodes in the network have an incentive to exchange goods and currency, while also playing a role in supporting the blockchain's distributed records and data reliability. The Blockchain class defines the difficulty level and miningReward for that reason.

The createGenesisBlock method creates a new genesis block, which is the first block in the blockchain if no chain is provided. It takes an empty array as the transactions parameter and sets the previous hash to null. The getLatestBlock method retrieves the most recent block in the chain by accessing the last element of the chain array. Last, the Blockchain class is exported for use in other files.

Example 12-9. Defining the Blockchain class in blockchain.js

```
import Block from "./block.js"; ❶
class Blockchain { ❷
  constructor(chain, pendingTransactions = []) { ❸
```

Get Programming | 261

```
    this.chain = chain || [this.createGenesisBlock()]; ❹
    this.difficulty = 4; ❺
    this.pendingTransactions = pendingTransactions; ❻
    this.miningReward = 100; ❼
  }

  createGenesisBlock() { ❽
    return new Block([], null);
  }

  getLatestBlock() { ❾
    return this.chain[this.chain.length - 1];
  }
}
export default Blockchain;
```

❶ Import the `Block` class, which is used to create new blocks in the chain.

❷ Define the `Blockchain` class, representing a distributed ledger of blocks.

❸ Create a new blockchain instance with an optional initial chain and list of pending transactions.

❹ If no chain is provided, initialize the chain with a genesis block.

❺ Set the mining difficulty, which determines how hard it is to mine a new block.

❻ Store any transactions waiting to be added to the next mined block.

❼ Set the mining reward given to a node for successfully mining a block.

❽ Define the `createGenesisBlock` method, which returns the initial block in the blockchain.

❾ Define the `getLatestBlock` method to retrieve the most recent block in the chain.

The genesis block is manually created or generated by the blockchain network as a starting point when a blockchain network initially gets up and running. When new nodes enter the network, they also create a new blockchain with a genesis block until other nodes in the network sync their most up-to-date blockchain.

Now that your `Blockchain` class is set up, you may access it in other files. Add `import Blockchain from "./src/blockchain.js"` to the top of *index.js* to import the Block

262 | Chapter 12: Music Label Blockchain Market

chain class. Then add `const blockchain = new Blockchain()` right above where you assign `marketplaceNode` in the `initializeNode` function, and add `blockchain` as the third parameter in instantiating your `MarketplaceNode` object. This will initialize a new `Blockchain` object alongside your `marketplaceNode` when you connect to the network.

The next steps for using these new classes are to set up the broadcasting functions and routes to sync your blockchain with other nodes in the network. Add the code in Example 12-10 to your `MarketplaceNode` class in *marketplaceNode.js*. This code defines `broadcastBlockchain`, which uses the `broadcast` function to sync a given node's `blockchain` across all other nodes.

Example 12-10. Creating the `broadcastBlockchain` function in marketplaceNode.js

```
...
async broadcastBlockchain() { ❶
  this.broadcast("sync-blockchain", { chain: this.blockchain.chain }); ❷
}
...
```

❶ Define the `broadcastBlockchain` function.

❷ Call the `broadcast` function with the `sync-blockchain` route path and `chain` as data parameters.

Next, define the route to accept the API call made to `sync-blockchain` by adding the code in Example 12-11 to *index.js*. This Fastify route handler receives a blockchain's chain of blocks via the request body. You pull that `chain` value and update your `marketplaceNode`'s blockchain with this `chain`. In doing so, each node in the network will have synced and up-to-date chains.

Example 12-11. Defining the `/sync-blockchain` route in index.js

```
...
fastify.post("/sync-blockchain", async (request, reply) => { ❶
  const { chain } = request.body; ❷
  marketplaceNode.blockchain = new Blockchain( ❸
    chain,
    marketplaceNode.blockchain.pendingTransactions
  );
  reply.send({ message: "Blockchain synced", blockCount: chain.length }); ❹
});
...
```

❶ Define the `/sync-blockchain` POST route using Fastify.

Get Programming | 263

❷ Destructure the `chain` value from the request body.

❸ Update the marketplace node's blockchain by passing the received chain and existing pending transactions.

❹ Send a JSON reply confirming that the blockchain was synced.

To test this, place `this.broadcastBlockchain()` in `registerNode` in your `Market placeNode` class and log out `console.log(`Syncing blocks ${JSON.stringify(ch ain)}`)` in your `/sync-blockchain` route in *index.js* to see the output of synced chains. The output should resemble `[{"timestamp":1686164334757,"transactions":[],"previousHash":null,"hash":"fd4b...","nextHash":null}]`. This confirms the genesis block is being synced across all newly connected nodes.

With your blockchain set, it's time to introduce transactions and enable nodes to use them across the blockchain network. With the new transaction verified, the code checks if the length of the `this.blockchain.pendingTransactions` array is greater than 4. If so, it calls the node's `mine` method (this method hasn't been defined yet) and logs the result to the console. Once complete, the `broadcastBlockchain` method is called to broadcast the updated blockchain to other nodes, and the function returns the string `"Processed transaction"` as the result of the `processTransaction` function.

Example 12-12. Defining the `processTransaction` method in marketplaceNode.js

```
...
async processTransaction(transactionHash) { ❶
  const transaction = new Transaction(transactionHash); ❷
  const id = transactionHash.id || transaction.id;
  if (transaction.type === "BUY") { ❸
    if (this.balance < transaction.price) return "Insufficient balance"; ❹
    this.balance -= transaction.price;
    try {
      await axios.post(`${transaction.sender}/payment`, { ❺
        price: transaction.price,
      });
    } catch (e) {
      console.log(e.message);
    }
    console.log({ bal: this.balance }); ❻
  }
  this.songs[id] = transaction; ❼
  this.blockchain.pendingTransactions.push(transaction); ❽
  if (this.blockchain.pendingTransactions.length > 4) { ❾
    console.log(await this.mine());
  }
```

```
  await this.broadcastBlockchain(); ❿
  return "Processed transaction"; ⓫
}
...
```

❶ Define the asynchronous `processTransaction` method to handle new transactions.

❷ Instantiate a new `Transaction` object from the provided hash.

❸ Proceed only if the transaction type is "BUY".

❹ Check if the balance is sufficient to complete the purchase.

❺ Send a payment request to the seller node with the transaction amount.

❻ Log the updated balance after deducting the price.

❼ Store the transaction in the local `songs` registry using its ID.

❽ Add the transaction to the list of pending blockchain transactions.

❾ Mine a new block if there are more than 4 pending transactions.

❿ Broadcast the updated blockchain to peer nodes.

⓫ Return a message indicating the result of the transaction.

In the blockchain marketplace application, transactions are handled within the routing logic defined in the *index.js* file. The system supports both `/sell` and `/buy` routes. When a user initiates a `/sell` transaction, they must specify the song title and its cost. Conversely, when a `/buy` transaction is triggered, the user provides the song ID, which also serves as the transaction ID. Both routes invoke the `processTransaction` function in the Node application. This function adds the transaction to the pending `Transactions` list within the Blockchain, where it awaits validation before being committed to the chain. Example 12-13 shows this in more detail.

Example 12-13. Defining the `/payment` route in index.js *using Fastify*

```
...
fastify.post("/payment", async (request, reply) => { ❶
  const { price } = request.body; ❷
  marketplaceNode.balance += price; ❸
  reply.send({ message: `New balance ${marketplaceNode.balance}` }); ❹
```

```
});
...
```

❶ Define the /payment POST route using Fastify.

❷ Extract the price value from the request body.

❸ Increase the node's balance by the amount received.

❹ Send a response indicating the updated balance.

While the implementation shown in Example 12-14 is intentionally streamlined and lacks production-level safeguards, it clearly illustrates the core exchange mechanism that powers the blockchain marketplace. The mineBlock method encapsulates the mining process, turning a collection of pending transactions into a validated block that gets permanently added to the chain. This not only simulates the proof-of-work concept used in real-world blockchains but also reinforces the idea that every transaction—whether a /sell, /buy, or /payment—must be formally mined and appended to the ledger to complete the exchange cycle and ensure consistency across the distributed network.

Example 12-14. Defining the mineBlock method in blockchain.js

```
...
async mineBlock() { ❶
  const targetPrefix = "0".repeat(this.difficulty); ❷
  let nonce = 0;
  let hash = "";

  while (hash.substring(0, this.difficulty) !== targetPrefix) { ❸
    nonce++;
    hash = createHash("sha256")
      .update(JSON.stringify(this.chain) + nonce)
      .digest("hex");
  }

  const previousBlock = this.getLatestBlock(); ❹
  const newBlock = new Block(this.pendingTransactions, previousBlock.hash); ❺
  previousBlock.nextHash = newBlock.hash;
  this.chain.push(newBlock); ❻
  this.pendingTransactions = []; ❼
}
...
```

❶ Define the mineBlock method to convert pending transactions into a new block.

❷ Set the target prefix based on the difficulty.

---

266 | Chapter 12: Music Label Blockchain Market

3 Loop until a hash starting with the correct prefix is found.

4 Retrieve the most recent block.

5 Create a new block from pending transactions and link it to the previous block.

6 Push the new block onto the blockchain.

7 Clear pending transactions after mining completes.

Example 12-15. Defining the mine *method in* marketplaceNode.js

```
...
async mine() { ❶
  const price = this.blockchain.miningReward; ❷
  const reward = new Transaction({ ❸
    sender: this.peers[0],
    recipient: this.url,
    price,
    transactionType: "MINE",
  });

  this.blockchain.pendingTransactions.push(reward);
  await this.blockchain.mineBlock(); ❹
  this.balance += price; ❺
  return "Mining complete"; ❻
}
...
```

1 Define the mine method to reward a node.

2 Store the mining reward amount.

3 Create a mining reward transaction.

4 Trigger the mining process.

5 Add the reward to the miner's balance.

6 Return a completion message.

Example 12-16. Defining the /sell *route in* index.js *using Fastify*

```
...
fastify.post("/sell", async (request, reply) => { ❶
  const { price, songTitle } = request.body; ❷
```

```
  await marketplaceNode.processTransaction({ ❸
    price,
    songTitle,
    sender: marketplaceNode.url,
    transactionType: "SELL",
  });
  reply.send({ message: "Song being listed" }); ❹
});
...
```

❶ Define the /sell POST route using Fastify.

❷ Extract price and songTitle from the request.

❸ Process the transaction as a "SELL" type.

❹ Respond to the client confirming listing.

Now your application is prepared to handle requests on participating nodes to sell songs on the blockchain network. When a node's endpoint is hit, its URL is used as the sender in the transaction.

Example 12-17. Defining the /buy route in index.js *using Fastify*

```
...
fastify.post("/buy", async (request, reply) => { ❶
  const { id } = request.body; ❷
  const transaction = marketplaceNode.songs[id]; ❸
  if (!transaction) {
    return reply.send({ message: "No song exists by that id" }); ❹
  }

  const result = await marketplaceNode.processTransaction({ ❺
    id: transaction.id,
    price: transaction.price,
    songTitle: transaction.songTitle,
    expiration: transaction.expiration,
    recipient: transaction.sender,
    sender: marketplaceNode.url,
    transactionType: "BUY",
  });

  reply.send({ message: result }); ❻
});
...
```

❶ Define the /buy POST route for purchasing songs.

268 | Chapter 12: Music Label Blockchain Market

❷ Extract the song ID from the request body.

❸ Look up the song from local registry.

❹ Respond with an error if the song doesn't exist.

❺ Process a "BUY" transaction with song and node details.

❻ Send back the result of the transaction processing.

To test this, use a tool like cURL or Postman to issue a /sell followed by a /buy request. Try submitting an invalid id on /buy to test error handling and observe that new songs are added only after being mined into a block. The availableSongs method in the MarketplaceNode class (Example 12-18) supports this functionality by returning a filtered array of songs that are currently listed for sale. It scans the node's songs object and extracts only those transactions marked with the "SELL" type, returning their ID, title, and price. This ensures that clients and interfaces can query which items are actually on the marketplace, avoiding confusion or invalid transactions.

Example 12-18. Defining the availableSongs method in marketplaceNode.js

```
...
availableSongs() { ❶
  return Object.values(this.songs) ❷
    .filter((transaction) => transaction.type === "SELL")
    .map(({ id, songTitle, price }) => [id, songTitle, price]);
}
...
```

❶ Define the availableSongs method in your MarketplaceNode class.

❷ Return an array of songs whose most recent transaction type is SELL.

To make the list of available songs accessible across the network, a /songs route is introduced to expose this data as a simple API endpoint (Example 12-19). When a GET request is made to this route, it invokes the availableSongs method from the marketplaceNode instance and returns the result as a JSON array. This allows clients or external interfaces to retrieve an up-to-date list of all songs currently listed for sale, each represented by its ID, title, and price.

Get Programming | 269

Example 12-19. Defining the /songs route in index.js

```
...
fastify.get("/songs", async (request, reply) => { ❶
  reply.send({ songs: marketplaceNode.availableSongs() }); ❷
});
...
```

❶ Define the /songs GET route to return all songs for sale.

❷ Return JSON with the list of available songs recorded in your marketplaceNode.

You can test the endpoint by first creating a song with the /sell route and then querying /songs to confirm the listing appears. If no songs are available, the response will be an empty array. This route is particularly well-suited for integration with a user-facing UI, where song listings can be dynamically fetched and displayed, enhancing discoverability and usability across the decentralized marketplace.

Running the Real-World Example

To run this example in a real-world distributed context, you'll need to ensure participating nodes remain in sync. This is partially handled by broadcasting blockchain state and shared song listings across peers. For example, calling await this.broadcast("sync-blockchain", { chain: this.blockchain.chain, songs: this.songs }); shares the latest chain and song data across the network. Receiving nodes can then merge new listings with their local store using logic like marketplace Node.songs = { ...marketplaceNode.songs, ...songs };.

However, the current implementation is simplified and leaves room for meaningful improvements. Future iterations should focus on securing the network by authenticating nodes before allowing them to join or contribute listings. Introducing support for reversible transactions could also help in cases of dispute or fraud, offering rollback mechanisms. More robust mining logic should mirror consensus algorithms used in production blockchains (e.g., proof-of-work or proof-of-stake), instead of instantly validating transactions with a local function call. Additionally, replacing plain HTTP communication with encrypted protocols like HTTPS or WebSockets can enhance privacy and reliability. Finally, handling listing expiration dates would help enforce realistic time-bound offers, making the marketplace more dynamic and practical.

Chapter Exercises

1. Add song expiration logic:

   a. Inside the `Transaction` class, define a method `isExpired()` that compares the current time to the `expiration` timestamp.

   b. In the `/songs` route handler, filter out any songs whose associated transaction has expired using `isExpired()`.

   c. Optional: Add a log to display expired songs that are being removed from the active marketplace.

   d. Test by creating a song with a short expiration and confirm it no longer appears after the expiry time has passed.

   Expiration logic is essential for managing time-sensitive assets like early-access audio in digital marketplaces.

2. Broadcast song listings with the blockchain:

   a. Update the `broadcastBlockchain` method in `MarketplaceNode` to also include `this.songs` in the broadcast payload: `await this.broadcast("sync-blockchain", { chain: this.blockchain.chain, songs: this.songs })`.

   b. In your `/sync-blockchain` route, merge the incoming `songs` hash into the local node's `songs` object using: `marketplaceNode.songs = { ...marketplaceNode.songs, ...songs };`

   c. Test by listing a song from one node and confirming that it appears in another node's `/songs` list after syncing.

This exercise enhances consistency across nodes by syncing shared song data alongside the chain state.

Summary

In this chapter, you:

- Built a decentralized music marketplace using Node
- Defined core components like `MarketplaceNode`, `Blockchain`, `Block`, and `Transaction` classes
- Managed transactions with cryptographic hashing and validation logic
- Implemented mining and consensus mechanics between distributed nodes
- Synced chain state and song listings across the network
- Explored enhancements like expiration, listing broadcasts, and smart contract integration with Web3 tools

CHAPTER 13

Building an AI-Powered Learning Assistant with Google's Gemini API

This chapter covers the following:

- Setting up a Node application to interact with Google's Gemini API
- Implementing AI-powered learning assistance for technical learning
- Integrating a user profile database to track learning progress

Large Language Models (LLMs) like Google's Gemini or OpenAI's ChatGPT are rapidly transforming the way applications interact with users, enabling more context-aware, intelligent, and adaptive experiences. AI-driven systems are no longer just about answering questions; they can now analyze user behavior, track learning progress, and provide personalized recommendations, making them invaluable for technical education and skill building. By integrating LLMs into applications, developers can create dynamic tools that enhance user engagement, educate more effectively, and adapt to individual learning and communication styles.

In this chapter, you'll create an AI agent application designed to assist users in interactively preparing for technical interviews and learning programming concepts. The AI-powered assistant will guide users through their learning process, adjusting to their strengths, weaknesses, and learning styles. You will learn about API integrations, context-aware AI interactions, and using a database to store user learning profiles.

273

> **Tools and Applications Used in This Chapter**
>
> Before you get started, make sure to install and configure the tools and applications required for this project. Installation instructions for Node.js, Fastify, and VS Code are provided in Chapter 1, while project initialization steps, such as setting up your directory structure, configuring *package.json*, and using modern syntax, are covered in Appendix A. Instructions for installing and using Postman can be found in Appendix B. For a deeper explanation of SQLite, see Appendix C. For guidance on setting up your Google Gemini account and obtaining an API key, refer to Appendix E. Once completed, return here to continue. Building a project from scratch helps deepen your understanding of each component, giving you greater control and flexibility as you progress.

Your Prompt

An online service called Interview Atlas that helps engineers master technical programming skills and prepare for interviews would like to integrate a smart assistant. They've hired you to design an AI tool with the help of existing AI APIs to help users navigate technical interviews and learning programming concepts. As users progress, the AI will guide them, offering explanations, practice questions, and insights into their learning patterns. The AI should also adapt based on users' needs, identifying areas where they struggle and making recommendations on how to improve.

Get Planning

The Interview Atlas team would like you to design a system that uses an existing external LLM. They suggest that you integrate a Node app with the Google Gemini API to create this AI assistant. In doing so, your app will communicate with the Gemini API during each user query and display that AI response back to the user. To start, you plan to create a simple Node app that connects to the Gemini API and returns a response. The app will be built using the Fastify framework, which is a lightweight and efficient web framework for Node (Figure 13-1).

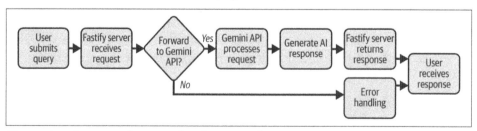

Figure 13-1. System architecture for phase one of AI assistant

274 | Chapter 13: Building an AI-Powered Learning Assistant with Google's Gemini API

Once the first phase is complete, you plan to curate the AI's responses to make them more relevant to the learning process. This involves designing a prompt that instructs the AI to act as a learning assistant, providing explanations, examples, and feedback on user queries (Figure 13-2). Each prompt sent to the AI will be *engineered* to match the context of a technical learning assistant.

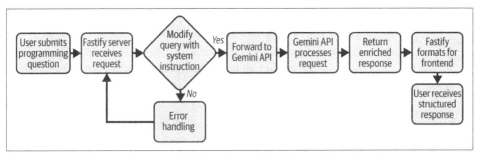

Figure 13-2. System architecture for phase two of AI assistant

To complete the setup, you include a database to store user profiles and track their learning progress over time. You also integrate a basic authentication measure so users may register, log in, and save their interaction history. In this way, users will be able to study engineering concepts, prepare for technical interviews, and receive personalized feedback on their learning journey (Figure 13-3).

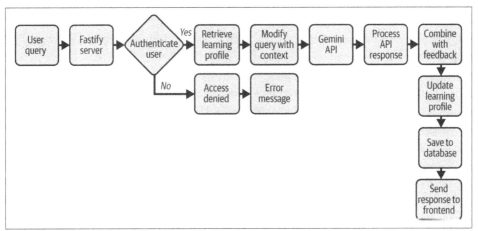

Figure 13-3. System architecture for phase three of AI assistant

With your project plan in place, you begin implementing the AI assistant as a Node app.

Get Programming

To start developing your app, create a new project folder named `interview_atlas_ai`. Navigate to your project folder on your command line and run `npm init`. This command initializes your Node app. You may press Enter throughout the initialization steps to accept the defaults. The result of these steps is the creation of a file called *package.json*. This file will instruct your Node app of any configurations or scripts needed to run correctly.

Next, create a file called *index.js* within your project folder. This file is the entry point for your app. For your first iteration, you will test your API connection to Google's Gemini API. To do this, you'll use the `axios` library to make HTTP requests. You will also use the `dotenv` library to manage your environment variables, such as your API key. Install the two libraries by running `npm install axios@^1.11.0 dotenv@^17.2.1` in your project's root directory on your command line.

In your text editor, add a file called *.env*. This file will store your environment variables (passwords and API keys) that allow your project to run as a server without revealing sensitive data within your code. Within this file add your API key for the Google Gemini API. You can find this key in your Google Cloud Console. The *.env* file should look like the following (for sample API key `GISaSrW-fsM3TNYp2UkmucNuSnkPKmGUtlsaDF4`):

```
GEMINI_API_KEY=GISaSrW-fsM3TNYp2UkmucNuSnkPKmGUtlsaDF4
```

This is the API key you'll use during each external API request made from your application.

This key is tied directly to your Google account and, just like other AI services, may incur charges with excess usage. Be sure to check your Google Cloud Console for any usage limits or billing information.

Next, navigate to your project's *index.js* file and add the code in Example 13-1. This code defines a function that sends user prompts to Google's Gemini AI model and returns a generated response. The `API_URL` is stored as a constant, embedding the API key securely from environment variables to prevent hardcoding sensitive credentials. The `generateResponse` function makes an asynchronous `POST` request using `axios`, formatting the user's prompt according to the API's required structure. The `POST` request body for the Gemini API is structured as an object containing a `contents` array, where each item represents a message exchange with the AI, specifying a `role` (e.g., "user") and a `parts` array containing the actual text input. This format is crucial because it allows for multiturn conversations, maintains context, and ensures that prompts are properly segmented for processing, enabling the model to generate context-aware responses.

Each AI API has its own structure for sending requests. The POST body format for the Gemini API is different from OpenAI's GPT-4 API. Be sure to check the API documentation for the correct format.

The response is then processed using optional chaining to extract the AI-generated text while providing a fallback message if no output is returned. If the request fails, the function handles errors gracefully by returning a detailed error message, preventing crashes and aiding debugging.

In previous versions of Node, you may have used an async Immediately Invoked Function Expression (IIFE) to call generateResponse(). In Node 18+ with ES module support, you can use top-level await instead.

Example 13-1. Testing an AI API request in index.js

```
import axios from "axios"; ❶
import dotenv from "dotenv";

dotenv.config();

const BASE = "https://generativelanguage.googleapis.com/v1beta/models";
const MODEL = "gemini-2.0-flash:generateContent";
const API_URL = `${BASE}/${MODEL}?key=${process.env.GEMINI_API_KEY}`; ❷

async function generateResponse(prompt) { ❸
  try {
    const { data } = await axios.post(
      API_URL,
      { contents: [{ role: "user", parts: [{ text: prompt }] }] }, ❹
      { headers: { "Content-Type": "application/json" } } ❺
    );

    return data?.candidates?.[0]?.content?.parts?.[0]?.text || "No response."; ❻
  } catch (error) {
    return `Error: ${error.response?.data || error.message}`; ❼
  }
}

const prompt = "In one sentence, explain Node."; ❽
const response = await generateResponse(prompt); ❾
console.log("AI Response:", response); ❿
```

❶ Imports `axios` for making HTTP requests and `dotenv` to load environment variables

❷ Stores the Gemini API URL, embedding the API key

❸ Defines an asynchronous function to send the request

❹ Sends a `POST` request with the user's prompt as the request payload

❺ Sets `Content-Type` to `application/json` to ensure proper request format

❻ Extracts the AI-generated response from the returned data

❼ Handles errors gracefully, returning a meaningful error message

❽ Defines the user prompt to send to the AI.

❾ Calls the `generateResponse()` function using top-level `await`.

❿ Logs the AI response to the console

Gemini model names may change over time. You can find the current list in the Google Gemini model reference (*https://oreil.ly/MuTFt*).

Now run `node index.js` in your project's root directory in your command line to execute this code. You should see a result that isolates the LLM response to your prompt, with a text output like `"AI Response: Node.js is a JavaScript runtime environment that allows developers to execute JavaScript code server-side, enabling the creation of scalable and efficient web applications."`

> ## Large Language Models and AI APIs
>
> Large Language Models (LLMs) are advanced AI systems trained on vast amounts of text data to understand and generate human-like language. They use deep learning techniques, particularly neural networks, to predict the most likely next words in a sequence based on given input. LLMs power AI APIs, which allow developers to interact with these models through programmatic requests.

A neural network is a machine learning model inspired by the human brain, consisting of layers of interconnected nodes (neurons) that process input data, learn patterns, and make predictions through weighted connections and activation functions.

Using an LLM is like asking a room full of billions of people for help instead of just one person—rather than relying on a single opinion, the AI draws from countless conversations, books, languages, and sources to give the most relevant response. It doesn't think like a human, but it predicts the best possible answer based on patterns learned from vast amounts of text.

When you send a prompt to an AI API, the request is processed by the model, which analyzes the text and generates a relevant response. AI APIs enable seamless integration of AI capabilities into applications, providing functionalities such as text completion, summarization, and question answering. The following are some of the key concepts and components involved in using LLMs and AI APIs:

Tokenization
LLMs break down input text into smaller units called tokens (words, subwords, or characters). The model processes these tokens and predicts the next token in the sequence to generate coherent responses.

Transformer architecture
Most modern LLMs use a transformer-based neural network, which relies on mechanisms like self-attention to understand the relationships between words, even across long passages of text.

Inference
When an AI API receives a prompt, the model runs an inference process, using its learned patterns to generate a probable response. This is different from training, as the model is applying existing knowledge rather than learning new information.

Temperature and max tokens
AI APIs often provide parameters to control response generation. temperature affects randomness (higher values make responses more creative), while max_tokens limits the response length

AI APIs like OpenAI's GPT-4, Google's Gemini, and Anthropic's Claude provide structured interfaces for accessing LLM capabilities in real-time applications.

For more details on AI APIs, visit the OpenAI API documentation (*https://oreil.ly/k90Xs*) or the Google Vertex AI documentation (*https://oreil.ly/QA2_K*).

With your AI API connection established, you can now customize the AI assistant to provide more relevant responses for learning programming and preparing for technical interviews. This involves modifying the request structure to include an instructional prompt that guides the AI's behavior.

Customizing the AI Assistant for Learning Assistance

Prompt engineering is the practice of designing precise and effective instructions to guide AI models like Gemini in generating useful and accurate responses. Since LLMs generate text based on input patterns, the way a prompt is structured significantly impacts the quality and relevance of the output. By carefully crafting a prompt, developers can control the AI's behavior, provide necessary context, and refine its response style.

> ### Prompt Engineering: Crafting Effective AI Instructions
>
> Using prompt engineering, developers can instruct the AI to take on a specific role, such as a teacher, programmer, or historical figure. For example, a prompt like `"You are an experienced software engineer. Explain recursion to a beginner."` will lead to a more structured and knowledgeable response than simply asking, `"What is recursion?"`. Additionally, prompts can include constraints, formatting requirements, or examples to fine-tune the output.
>
> A well-engineered prompt is like curating a cooking recipe differently for children than how you'd instruct adults. The resulting recipe should be suitable for the audience's comprehension and skill level.
>
> The following are some common techniques used in prompt engineering:
>
> *Role prompting*
> > Assigns the AI a persona, such as `"You are a cybersecurity expert"`, which helps shape responses based on expertise.
>
> *Context injection*
> > Provides background information within the prompt to help the model generate responses with relevant context.
>
> *Few-shot prompting*
> > Includes examples within the prompt to guide the AI's response style and expected output.

> *Format prompting (or output structuring)*
> Directs how the response should be formatted, such as "Provide a bullet-point summary" or "Explain using a simple analogy".
>
> Effective prompt engineering enhances AI usability, enabling more accurate, creative, and structured responses. It is a crucial skill for developers integrating AI into applications, chatbots, and automation workflows.
>
> For more on prompt engineering, refer to OpenAI's prompt engineering guide (*https://oreil.ly/wVWyZ*) or Google's Vertex AI documentation (*https://oreil.ly/ItGBu*).

To make sure the AI assistant provides learning-focused responses, modify the request structure to include an instructional prompt, as shown in Example 13-2.

In this code, you modify `generateResponse`, which sends a user prompt to Google's Gemini AI API and retrieves a generated response. You add an additional prompt content object that instructs the AI to act as a knowledgeable assistant focused on technical topics. This prompt is included in the request body, ensuring that the AI understands its role and provides relevant answers. The AI's response is then extracted and returned to the user.

Example 13-2. Guiding AI to teach programming in index.js

```
...
async function generateResponse(prompt) {
  try {
    const { data } = await axios.post(
      API_URL,
      {
        contents: [
          {
            role: "user",
            parts: [{ text: "You are an AI assistant that helps users " +
            "learn programming and prepare for technical interviews. " +
            "Provide clear explanations with examples when needed." }] ❶
          },
          { role: "user", parts: [{ text: prompt }] }, ❷
        ],
      },
      { headers: { "Content-Type": "application/json" } }
    );

    return (
      data?.candidates?.[0]?.content?.parts?.[0]?.text ||
      "No response received from AI."
    );
  } catch (error) {
    console.error("API Request Failed:", error.response?.data || error.message);
```

Customizing the AI Assistant for Learning Assistance | 281

```
    return {
      error: "Failed to fetch AI response",
      details: error.response?.data || error.message,
    };
  }
}
...
```

❶ Instruct the AI to act as a technical interview assistant, ensuring responses are focused on programming concepts and clear explanations with examples.

❷ Send the user's actual prompt, which dynamically changes based on what the user wants to ask the AI.

You may also change the prompt to "In one sentence, explain recursion." Now run node index.js again. You should see a response from the AI that is more relevant to learning programming concepts. For example: "Recursion is a programming technique where a function calls itself within its own definition to solve a smaller instance of the same problem until a base case is reached."

Setting Up the Fastify Server

Now that you have a working AI assistant with customized prompts, you can set up a Fastify server to handle user requests and responses. This way, you can create a web application that allows users to interact with the AI assistant through a user-friendly interface instead of the command line.

To start, install Fastify for setting up your server routes. Run the following command in your project's root directory:

```
npm install fastify@^5.4.0
```

Add the code in Example 13-3 to *index.js* to incorporate Fastify. This code initializes a Fastify server with logging enabled, allowing you to track requests and errors easily. The server listens on a port defined by the environment (`process.env.PORT`) or defaults to 3000, ensuring flexibility for different deployment environments. By using `await` inside an asynchronous startup function, the server can handle startup failures gracefully and log the running address upon successful start.

You may add the `PORT` variable to your *.env* file to set a custom port for your server. For example, you can add `PORT=4000` to run the server on port 4000 instead of the default 3000.

Example 13-3. Starting a Fastify server with environment variables

```
import Fastify from 'fastify'; ❶
import axios from 'axios';
import dotenv from 'dotenv';

dotenv.config();

const fastify = Fastify({ logger: true }); ❷
const PORT = process.env.PORT || 3000; ❸

const start = async () => {
  try {
    const address = await fastify.listen({ port: PORT }); ❹
    console.log(`Server running at ${address}`); ❺
  } catch (err) {
    console.error("Server failed to start:", err);
    process.exit(1); ❻
  }
};

start(); ❼
```

❶ Imports Fastify to create a web server

❷ Initializes Fastify with logging enabled

❸ Sets the server port from the environment or defaults to 3000

❹ Uses await to start the Fastify server asynchronously

❺ Logs the server address once it's running

❻ Handles server startup errors and exits if needed

❼ Calls the asynchronous startup function

Next, add the code in Example 13-4 to *index.js* to handle user queries. This code defines a POST route at /query, allowing users to send a prompt to the AI assistant. The request body is checked for a prompt, and if missing, it returns a 400 code (Bad Request) to ensure proper input validation. If a valid prompt is provided, the server calls generateResponse(prompt), which processes the request through the Gemini API. The AI-generated response is then sent back to the client, while any errors encountered during the process are logged and returned with a 500 code (Internal Server Error), ensuring clear debugging and reliable API behavior.

Setting Up the Fastify Server | 283

Example 13-4. Handling AI queries with Fastify

```
fastify.post("/query", async (request, reply) => { ❶
  try {
    const { prompt } = request.body; ❷
    if (!prompt) {
      return reply.status(400).send({ error: "Prompt is required" }); ❸
    }

    const response = await generateResponse(prompt); ❹

    reply.send({ response }); ❺
  } catch (error) {
    console.error("Gemini API Error:", error);
    reply.status(500).send({ ❻
      error: "Error communicating with Gemini API",
      details: error.message,
    });
  }
});
```

❶ Defines a Fastify POST route for handling AI queries

❷ Extracts the prompt from the request body

❸ Returns a 400 Bad Request if no prompt is provided

❹ Calls generateResponse(prompt) to get AI output

❺ Sends the AI response back to the client

❻ Logs errors and returns a 500 Internal Server Error if the request fails

At this time, you may remove the IIFE from the previous code, as you no longer need to run the function immediately. You can also remove the console.log statement that logs the AI response, as it will now be sent back to the client through the Fastify server.

With this code in place, running node index.js in your command line will start your Fastify server, but will no longer execute any API query. You should see a message indicating that the server is running at *http://localhost:3000*.

With your server running, you may now send a POST request to the /query endpoint with a JSON body containing a prompt from a new command-line window. For example, try running:

```
curl -X POST http://localhost:3000/query \
    -H "Content-Type: application/json" \
    -d '{ "prompt": "Explain recursion in a single sentence with an analogy." }'
```

You'll get a response similar to the following:

```
{"response":"Recursion is like a set of Russian nesting dolls, where each
doll contains a smaller version of itself, until you reach the smallest doll
that you can finally hold: a function solves a problem by breaking it down
into smaller, self-similar subproblems until it reaches a base case that can
be solved directly.\n"}
```

Your app is now ready to handle user queries over the internet. However, there's currently no way to track user interactions or store their learning progress. To do this, you will need to implement a database to manage user profiles and authentication.

Setting Up Your Database and User Authentication

To implement user authentication, you will need to create a database to store user profiles and their learning progress. In this example, you will use SQLite3 as your database solution. SQLite3 is a lightweight file-based database that is easy to set up and ideal for prototyping applications. It allows you to store structured data, such as user profile information and learning progress.

To begin, install both the `sqlite3` and `sqlite` packages by running the following command in your project's root directory in your command line:

```
npm install sqlite3@^5.1.7 sqlite@^5.1.1"
```

Why Use SQLite3?

SQLite3 is an excellent choice for a prototype app in Node when storing and managing user learning profiles. Unlike traditional relational databases that require a dedicated server, SQLite is a self-contained file-based database, making it lightweight, easy to set up, and ideal for rapid prototyping.

SQLite operates with a single database file, removing the need for complex configurations and making it a great option for development and small-scale applications.

For a user learning profile, SQLite3 enables structured data storage with a simple schema. It follows ACID (Atomicity, Consistency, Isolation, Durability) principles, meaning data remains reliable even during crashes or power failures. Additionally, SQLite3 requires no setup or separate database server, making it easy to integrate into a Node app using the `sqlite3` package:

No setup required
   Runs as a single file, eliminating database management overhead

Fast and lightweight
   Ideal for local storage in a small prototype or proof-of-concept app

Simple integration
   Easily used with the `sqlite3` Node package for basic CRUD operations

Structured data storage
   Supports SQL queries for managing user learning profiles efficiently

Portable and scalable
   Can be upgraded to PostgreSQL or MySQL as the application grows

 The `sqlite` package is used for async/await support, making it easier to work with asynchronous database operations.

A database is required in this project because you will store users' hashed passwords, email addresses, and learning profiles. The learning profile will include information about a user's previous queries, strengths, and weaknesses. This information will help the AI assistant provide personalized responses based on a user's learning profile.

With `sqlite3` installed, you can now create a database connection and define the schema for your user profiles. The schema will include fields for a user's email, hashed password, and learning profile data. The learning profile will be stored as a JSON object, allowing you to easily update and retrieve user-specific information.

You will also implement a basic authentication system to allow users to register and log in. This will enable you to store user profiles and track their learning progress over time, distinguishing user interactions from one another.

To define a database connection and create a `users` table, add the code in Example 13-5 to a new file called *db.js*.

This code initializes an SQLite database to store user profiles, ensuring that learning progress and authentication details are persistently saved. The database connection, dbPromise, is set up to interact with a local file (*users.db*). The `initializeDb` function ensures that the `users` table exists, creating it if necessary.

The table includes an auto-incrementing `id` field as a primary key, a unique `userId` to prevent duplicate accounts. In this case, we'll use email addresses as the ID. Last, a `password` column is added for authentication. Additionally, the `learning_profile` field now has a default value of "This user has no recorded learning profile yet." This ensures that when a new user is created, their profile contains meaningful default text rather than appearing empty. Once the database is set up, a confirmation message is logged, confirming that the system is ready to store and retrieve user data.

Example 13-5. Initializing an SQLite database for user profiles

```
import sqlite3 from "sqlite3"; ❶
import { open } from "sqlite";
import path from "path";

const dbPromise = open({ ❷
  filename: path.resolve("./users.db"),
  driver: sqlite3.Database,
});

const initializeDb = async () => {
  const db = await dbPromise;

  await db.exec(`
    CREATE TABLE IF NOT EXISTS users ( ❸
      id INTEGER PRIMARY KEY AUTOINCREMENT, ❹
      userId TEXT UNIQUE, ❺
      password TEXT NOT NULL, ❻
      learning_profile TEXT DEFAULT 'This user has no learning profile yet.' ❼
    )
  `);

  console.log("Users table initialized"); ❽
};

initializeDb();

export default dbPromise;
```

❶ Imports sqlite3 and sqlite to enable database interaction

❷ Opens a connection to the database file *users.db*

❸ Executes a SQL query to create the users table if it doesn't exist

❹ Defines id as the primary key, which auto-increments for each user

❺ Ensures userId is unique, preventing duplicate accounts

❻ Stores hashed passwords securely (plain-text passwords should be avoided)

❼ Saves the user's learning profile as a text field

Setting Up Your Database and User Authentication | 287

❽ Logs a success message once the database is initialized

To integrate this database connection into your Fastify server, add `import dbPromise from "./db.js";` to the top of your *index.js* file. This allows you to access the database connection throughout your application. When needed, you can call `await dbPromise` to interact with the database.

Before you can use the database, you need to create a user registration and login system. This will allow users to create accounts, log in, and store their learning profiles securely.

Install `jsonwebtoken` and `bcrypt` for user authentication. Run the following command in your project's root directory in your command line:

```
npm install jsonwebtoken@^9.0.2" bcrypt@^6.0.0
```

The `jsonwebtoken` library will help you create and verify JSON Web Tokens (JWTs) for secure user sessions, while `bcrypt` will be used to hash user passwords before storing them in the database.

Then add the following code to the top of your *index.js* file to import the required libraries and set up your JWT secret:

```
import jwt from "jsonwebtoken";
import bcrypt from "bcrypt";

...

const JWT_SECRET = process.env.JWT_SECRET || "dummyJWTsecret";
```

Similar to the API key, the JWT secret should be stored in your *.env* file. This secret is used to sign and verify JWTs, ensuring that only authorized users can access protected routes. For now, you may also use a dummy secret for testing purposes.

In order to support user accounts, you'll need a way for users to register their ID (email) and password. Add the code in Example 13-6 to *index.js* to implement a user registration endpoint.

This code implements user registration, allowing new users to create an account and securely store their credentials. When a user submits their `email` and `password`, the server checks if both fields are provided. The password is then hashed using `bcrypt` before being stored in the SQLite database, ensuring that user credentials are not stored in plain text.

288 | Chapter 13: Building an AI-Powered Learning Assistant with Google's Gemini API

Additionally, a learning profile is initialized as an empty object, allowing the AI to track the user's progress over time. Once the user is registered, the server generates a JWT token, which is sent back in the response, enabling the user to authenticate future requests. If any errors occur, they are logged, and a 500 error response is returned.

The JWT token is a secure way to manage user sessions. It contains encoded information about the user and is signed with a secret key, allowing the server to verify its authenticity without needing to store session data on the server. It is used by the client to authenticate requests to protected routes.

Example 13-6. User registration endpoint

```
...
fastify.post("/register", async (request, reply) => { ❶
  const { email, password } = request.body; ❷
  if (!email || !password) {
    return reply.status(400).send({ error: "Email and password required" }); ❸
  }

  try {
    const db = await dbPromise; ❹
    const hashedPassword = await bcrypt.hash(password, 10); ❺

    await db.run(
      "INSERT INTO users (userId, password, learning_profile) " +
      "VALUES (?, ?, ?)",
    [ ❻
      email,
      hashedPassword,
      JSON.stringify({ previousQueries: [], strengths: {}, weaknesses: {} }),
    ]);

    const token = jwt.sign({ userId: email }, JWT_SECRET, { expiresIn: "7d" }); ❼
    reply.send({ token }); ❽
  } catch (error) {
    console.error("Registration error:", error);
    reply.status(500).send({ error: "Failed to register user" }); ❾
  }
});...
```

❶ Defines a POST route at /register to handle user sign-ups

❷ Extracts email and password from the request body

❸ Returns a 400 error if either field is missing

❹ Opens a connection to the SQLite database

❺ Hashes the user's password using `bcrypt` for secure storage

❻ Inserts the new user into the `users` table with an empty learning profile

❼ Generates a JWT token for authentication that expires in seven days

❽ Sends the token as a response so the user can authenticate future requests

❾ Handles errors and returns a 500 error if registration fails

Next, you'll need an endpoint to support user login. Add the code in Example 13-7 to *index.js* to implement a route for users to log in to the app with their registered information.

This code implements a route allowing registered users to authenticate and receive a JWT token for future requests. The `email` and `password` are extracted from the request and validated. The database is queried for the user's record, and the provided password is compared with the hashed password using `bcrypt`. If authentication is successful, a JWT token is generated and returned to the user, enabling secure access to protected routes. If the credentials are incorrect, a 401 Unauthorized response is sent, and any server errors trigger a 500 response.

Example 13-7. User login endpoint

```
...
fastify.post("/login", async (request, reply) => { ❶
  const { email, password } = request.body; ❷
  if (!email || !password) {
    return reply.status(400).send({ error: "Email and password required" }); ❸
  }

  try {
    const db = await dbPromise; ❹
    const user = await db.get("SELECT * FROM users WHERE userId = ?", [email]); ❺

    if (!user || !(await bcrypt.compare(password, user.password))) { ❻
      return reply.status(401).send({ error: "Invalid email or password" });
    }

    const token = jwt.sign({ userId: email }, JWT_SECRET, { expiresIn: "7d" }); ❼
    reply.send({ token }); ❽
  } catch (error) {
    console.error("Login error:", error);
    reply.status(500).send({ error: "Failed to authenticate user" }); ❾
  }
```

```
});
...
```

① Defines a POST route at /login to authenticate users

② Extracts email and password from the request body

③ Returns a 400 error if either field is missing

④ Connects to the SQLite database

⑤ Queries the database for a user with the provided email

⑥ Verifies the password using bcrypt, returning a 401 error if invalid

⑦ Generates a JWT token for session authentication

⑧ Sends the token so the user can authenticate future requests

⑨ Handles errors and returns a 500 error if authentication fails

With your registration and login routes in place, you can now test the authentication process. Run your app by executing node index.js and running the following cURL command with a new email and password combination from a new command-line window:

```
curl -X POST "http://localhost:3000/register" \
    -H "Content-Type: application/json" \
    -d '{
          "email": "jon@jonwexler.com",
          "password": "password123"
        }'
```

You should get back a JWT token like the following:

```
{"token":"evJhbGciOiJIUzI1NiIsInR5cCI6IkpXVCJ9.eyJ1c2VySWQiOiJ1c2VyQG..."}
```

You can then use this token to authenticate future requests. If lost, deleted, or expired, you can generate a new command for registered users by using the login route. For example, you can log in with the same credentials you used to register by running the following cURL command:

```
curl -X POST "http://localhost:3000/login" \
    -H "Content-Type: application/json" \
    -d '{
          "email": "jon@jonwexler.com",
          "password": "password123"
        }'
```

Setting Up Your Database and User Authentication | 291

Now that you have a JWT token, you implement a `verifyJWT` function as middleware to protect your API routes. This function will check if the token is valid before allowing access to certain endpoints. Add the code in Example 13-8 to *index.js* to implement this middleware.

This code adds JWT authentication to protect API routes by verifying that users provide a valid token before accessing secured endpoints. The function `verifyJWT` extracts the authorization header from incoming requests and checks if a token is provided. If missing, it returns a 401 error. The token is then extracted from the Bearer <token> format and validated using `jwt.verify()` with your app's secret key.

If successful, the decoded user data is stored in `request.user`, making it accessible for further request handling. If the token is invalid or expired, the function returns a 401 error, ensuring that only authenticated users can proceed.

Example 13-8. JWT authentication middleware

```
const verifyJWT = async (request, reply) => { ❶
  try {
    const authHeader = request.headers.authorization; ❷
    if (!authHeader) {
      return reply.status(401).send({ error: "Missing authentication token" }); ❸
    }

    const token = authHeader.split(" ")[1]; ❹
    const decoded = jwt.verify(token, JWT_SECRET); ❺
    request.user = decoded; ❻
  } catch (error) {
    return reply.status(401).send({ error: "Invalid or expired token" }); ❼
  }
};
```

❶ Defines an asynchronous function to verify JWT authentication in Fastify routes

❷ Extracts the `Authorization` header from the incoming request

❸ Returns a `401 Unauthorized` response if no authentication token is provided

❹ Extracts the actual token from the Bearer <token> format

❺ Uses `jwt.verify()` to decode and validate the token using the secret key `JWT_SECRET`

❻ Stores the decoded user data in `request.user`, making it accessible in protected routes

292 | Chapter 13: Building an AI-Powered Learning Assistant with Google's Gemini API

❼ Handles authentication failures, returning 401 Unauthorized if the token is invalid or expired

The last authentication step is to incorporate the verifyJWT middleware into the /query route. This ensures that only authenticated users can access the AI assistant. Additionally, you update the /query route to find the user's learning profile in the database and use it to generate a personalized response. The learning profile will be stored as plain text in the database. Replace the /query route in *index.js* with the code in Example 13-9.

This code enhances the AI assistant by customizing responses based on each user's learning profile. The route is secured with JWT authentication to ensure only logged-in users can query the AI. The user's previous learning data is fetched from the database and used in the AI query to provide personalized responses. The learning profile is then updated with new insights from the AI, allowing the assistant to refine its recommendations over time. If any issues arise, a 500 error is returned.

The generateResponse function is replaced with generateResponseWithSummary. This function is similar to the previous one but includes additional logic to handle user learning profiles. The AI assistant is now capable of providing personalized responses based on the user's learning profile, strengths, and weaknesses.

Example 13-9. Querying the AI assistant with user learning profiles

```
fastify.post("/query", { preHandler: verifyJWT }, async (request, reply) => { ❶
  try {
    const { prompt } = request.body; ❷
    const userId = request.user.userId; ❸
    const db = await dbPromise; ❹

    const row = await db.get(
      "SELECT learning_profile FROM users WHERE userId = ?",
      [userId]
    ); ❺
    const learningProfile =
      row?.learning_profile || "This user has no recorded learning profile yet."; ❻

    const { answer, updatedProfileSummary } = await generateResponseWithSummary(
      prompt,
      learningProfile
    ); ❼

    await db.run("UPDATE users SET learning_profile = ? WHERE userId = ?", [
      updatedProfileSummary,
      userId,
    ]); ❽
```

Setting Up Your Database and User Authentication | 293

```
    reply.send({ answer, updatedProfileSummary }); ❾
  } catch (error) {
    console.error("Query error:", error);
    reply.status(500).send("Error processing query"); ❿
  }
});
```

❶ Defines a POST route at /query and secures it with verifyJWT to ensure only authenticated users can access it

❷ Extracts the prompt from the request body

❸ Retrieves the authenticated user's ID from request.user

❹ Connects to the SQLite database

❺ Fetches the user's learning profile from the database

❻ Uses a default profile message if no learning data is available

❼ Calls generateResponseWithSummary() to send the prompt and learning pro file to the AI and get an updated response

❽ Updates the user's learning profile in the database with the AI's new insights

❾ Sends the AI-generated answer and the updated learning profile back to the user

❿ Handles errors and returns a 500 error if the request fails

To wrap up development, you implement the new generateResponseWithSummary function in *index.js* to handle the AI's response generation and learning profile updates. This function is designed to send a structured request to the Gemini API, including the user's prompt and their learning profile. The AI is instructed to return its response in a specific JSON format, which includes both the answer and an updated profile summary.

For example, if a user asks about complex JavaScript concepts, and more basic Node deployment queries, the AI will analyze the user's learning profile and provide a tailored response that reflects their strengths in foundational JavaScript and weaknesses in production-ready Node applications. With that context, the AI assistant can provide more comprehensive responses to help the user learn and grow, or navigate them to hands-on books about Node like *Node.js Projects*, by Jonathan Wexler.

You add the code in Example 13-10 to *index.js* to implement the `generateResponse
WithSummary` function.

This function enhances the AI assistant by making responses context-aware based on the user's learning profile. It ensures that each response considers the user's past interactions, allowing for personalized, evolving AI interactions over time. The function constructs a structured prompt that provides the AI with both the user's question and their current learning profile. The AI is instructed to return its response in valid JSON format, ensuring structured output that includes both the answer and an updated profile summary. A POST request is sent to the `Gemini API` using `axios`, with the request data containing user input and AI instructions. The response from the API is extracted, cleaned, and parsed as JSON before being returned.

You can simplify this process by logging the AI's raw response. In doing so, you can identify the exact structure of the AI's output, making it easier to parse and extract the relevant information. This is particularly useful when working with complex AI models that may return data in various formats.

The `requestData` object is structured to provide the AI with contextual instructions, explicitly including the user's learning profile and directing it to update that profile based on the latest query. The request is structured to ensure strict JSON output, preventing inconsistencies in the AI's response format. The function makes an asynchronous request to `API_URL` with the structured request data. The `headers` specify that the request body is in `application/json` format, ensuring proper API communication.

The line `response?.data?.candidates?.[0]?.content?.parts?.[0]?.text ||
"{}"` safely accesses the AI's response while handling cases where expected data is missing. The `?.` optional chaining operator prevents errors if any property in the response structure is `undefined`. The final `|| "{}"` ensures that, in the absence of a valid response, an empty JSON object is returned instead of `undefined`. The function also includes a step to clean the response before parsing by removing unnecessary formatting. The AI often returns JSON within Markdown code blocks (e.g., ```` ```json
{ } ```` ````), and including the `replace()` and `trim()` statements ensures that only raw JSON remains before parsing.

Once the response is cleaned, `JSON.parse(cleanedJson)` is used to convert the response from a string into a JavaScript object for easy access. If parsing fails, an error message is logged, and a structured error response is returned instead of crashing the function. The function extracts the AI's generated response and updated profile summary, falling back to the original learning profile if the AI fails to provide a valid update. In case of an API error, the function logs the error and returns a structured error message.

By structuring AI interactions this way, the assistant learns from past interactions and provides increasingly relevant responses. The use of error handling, optional chaining, and response validation ensures that even if the API returns unexpected output, the system remains robust and functional.

Example 13-10. Generating AI responses with personalized learning profiles

```
const generateResponseWithSummary = async (prompt, learningProfile) => { ❶
  try {
    const requestData = {
      contents: [
        {
          role: "user",
          parts: [
            {
              text: `You are an AI assistant helping users learn programming.
              The user has the following learning profile: "${learningProfile}".
              Based on this, answer their query and update their profile with a
              one-sentence summary of strengths and weaknesses.

              Respond in **valid JSON format**:
              {
                "response": "Your AI-generated response",
                "updatedProfileSummary": "Updated profile summary."
              }`,
            },
            { text: `User query: ${prompt}` },
          ],
        },
      ],
    }; ❷

    const response = await axios.post(API_URL, requestData, {
      headers: { "Content-Type": "application/json" },
    }); ❸

    const rawText = response?.data?.candidates?.[0]?.content?.parts?.[0]?.text
    || "{}"; ❹
    const cleanedJson = rawText.replace(/```json|```/g, "").trim(); ❺

    try {
      const parsedResponse = JSON.parse(cleanedJson); ❻
      return {
        answer: parsedResponse.response || "No valid response received.",
        updatedProfileSummary: parsedResponse.updatedProfileSummary
          || learningProfile,
      };
    } catch {
```

296 | Chapter 13: Building an AI-Powered Learning Assistant with Google's Gemini API

```
      console.error("Invalid JSON format from API:", cleanedJson);
      return { error: "Invalid JSON response", details: cleanedJson };
    }
  } catch (error) {
    console.error("API Error:", error.response?.data || error.message);
    return { error: "Failed to generate response", details: error.response?.data
    || error.message };
  }
};
```

❶ Defines an asynchronous function to query the AI and update the user's learning profile

❷ Constructs the prompt structure, including the user's learning profile and instructions for the AI to return a JSON response

❸ Sends the request to the Gemini API with the prompt and headers

❹ Extracts the AI-generated response from the API response object

❺ Cleans the response by removing unnecessary formatting (e.g., Markdown code blocks)

❻ Parses the AI's JSON response and returns the generated answer along with the updated `learning profile`

Now you may create a new user with the registration route and log in with the login route, or use the JWT token and user account from the previous step. You can then use the JWT token to authenticate requests to the `/query` endpoint. For example, run the following cURL command to query the AI assistant about recursion with a JWT token:

```
curl -X POST "http://localhost:3000/query" \
    -H "Authorization: Bearer eyJhbGci0iJIUzI1NiIsInR5cCI6IkpXVCJ9.eyJ1..." \
    -H "Content-Type: application/json" \
    -d '{ "prompt": "What is the best way to learn recursion?" }'
```

When you send the request, the AI assistant responds with a structured JSON object that includes both the generated answer and an updated summary of the user's learning profile:

```
{
"answer":"Recursion can be a tricky concept...",
"updatedProfileSummary":"The user is new to programming concepts and requires
a fundamental understanding of how to learn new topics, specifically recursion;
therefore, they are strong in asking the right question but weak in foundational
knowledge about recursion."
}
```

Setting Up Your Database and User Authentication | 297

Attempting to query the AI without a valid JWT token will return an error with the message `"Missing authentication token"`, ensuring that only authenticated users can access the AI assistant.

Now that you have a working AI-powered learning assistant with authentication and personalized responses, the next step is to build a client-side interface for user interactions. A web or mobile UI will allow users to engage with the AI assistant more intuitively, making it easier to submit queries, review past responses, and visualize their learning progress. You can achieve this by developing a frontend using React, Vue, or Svelte, and integrating it with your Fastify backend via API requests.

Additionally, consider enhancing the user experience by implementing real-time conversations with WebSockets, storing more detailed learning analytics, and refining AI-generated explanations with more advanced prompt engineering techniques. You may also consider the following improvements:

- Adding pagination or filtering for past AI responses
- Allowing users to edit their learning profile manually instead of AI-only updates
- Integrating a feedback mechanism where users can rate AI responses to refine future outputs

---

Chapter Exercises

1. Track user progress with learning analytics.

   In this exercise, you'll implement a system to track user progress based on their interactions with the AI. Each time a user interacts with the assistant, the AI should log their query and categorize it under their strengths or weaknesses based on their learning profile:

   a. Update the `generateResponseWithSummary` function to include a learning analytics component.

   b. Add a mechanism to categorize responses (e.g., "Strong in Algorithms," "Weak in Recursion"). Store these categories in the user's learning profile in the database.

   c. When the user submits a query, analyze their profile to suggest areas for improvement and display feedback based on the AI's previous responses.

   d. After adding this functionality, create multiple interactions with the assistant and check that the learning profile updates appropriately. The user's profile should reflect their progress, highlighting areas where they excel or need further study.

2. Adapt AI responses based on query type:

   In this simpler exercise, you will modify the assistant's response based on the type of query—whether the user is asking for an explanation, coding help, or a practice question:

   a. Update the `generateResponseWithSummary` function to check for simple keywords in the user's prompt (e.g., "explain," "code," "practice").

   b. Modify the response slightly based on the keyword. For example:

      - If the query contains the word "explain," the AI should provide a detailed explanation.

      - If it contains the word "code," the AI should return a code example.

   c. Keep the changes minimal to ensure that the AI can still answer any question appropriately.

   d. Try submitting queries with the words "explain," "code," and "practice," and check that the responses change based on the query type.

Summary

In this chapter, you built an AI-powered learning assistant that integrates with Google's Gemini API. The assistant is designed to support users in learning programming concepts and preparing for technical interviews through adaptive responses. In the process, you:

- Connected a Node app to the `Gemini API` using Fastify, enabling AI-driven responses

- Designed AI responses to be *context-aware*, leveraging user learning profiles to deliver personalized assistance

- Implemented a user profile database in SQLite3, allowing the assistant to *track user progress* and adapt responses over time

- Secured the system with *JWT authentication*, ensuring only registered users can access the AI assistant

- Optimized AI request handling by *structuring prompts*, cleaning AI output, and managing JSON responses

By integrating these features, Interview Atlas provides a robust AI-driven learning experience, dynamically guiding users based on their strengths and weaknesses. This foundation can be expanded further with advanced prompt engineering, enhanced feedback loops, and deeper AI customization.

APPENDIX A
Node Cheat Sheet and Project Initialization

Node application development can be as simple as a single line of JavaScript, or as complex as a distributed system hosted across the globe. Luckily, Node is a versatile platform that can handle both extremes. This cheat sheet provides a quick reference for setting up a Node project, understanding the *package.json* file, and writing modern JavaScript code. It also highlights key areas for career growth as a Node engineer.

In this appendix, we will cover the following topics:

- Initializing a Node project using npm
- Recommended directory structure for Node projects
- Understanding the *package.json* file and writing meaningful scripts
- Modern Node syntax patterns
- Growth areas for Node engineers

You may use this appendix as a quick reference or as a starting point for your Node projects. It is designed to be concise and easy to follow, providing you with the essential information you need to get started with Node development.

 For Node installation steps, refer to Chapter 1.

Initializing a Node Project (Using npm)

Much of Node development involves the use of your CLI to install packages, run scripts, and manage your project. The first step in any Node project is to initialize it with npm, the Node Package Manager. This is done by running the following command in your terminal:

```
mkdir node-app && cd node-app
npm init -y
```

node-app is just an example name. You can replace it with your desired project name. Use lowercase, hyphen-separated names (e.g., node-app-server) that are short, descriptive, and avoid special characters to ensure compatibility across npm, URLs, and filesystems.

This command sets up a basic *package.json* file, which acts as the manifest for your project—defining its name, version, dependencies, and scripts. The -y flag automatically fills in default values, allowing you to get started quickly without answering prompts interactively. You can always edit the generated *package.json* later to fine-tune settings or add metadata.

A project manifest is a file that defines essential metadata about your project—like its name, version, dependencies, scripts, and configuration—so that tools (like npm, build systems, or CI pipelines) can understand how to build, run, or manage it.

This foundational file is crucial for enabling other developers and tools to understand and work with your project. Even if you start with the defaults, refining your manifest early can help avoid future confusion or misconfiguration.

While npm is the default package manager included with Node and works great for most projects, some developers use alternative tools like Yarn for more advanced features.

npm is the default package manager for Node, designed to manage dependencies and reusable JavaScript code modules. When a developer runs `npm install`, the tool reads the *package.json* file in the project directory, which lists all required dependencies and their versions. It then downloads these packages from the npm registry—a large public database of open source JavaScript libraries—into a local node_modules/ directory.

To improve performance and reduce redundant downloads, npm also maintains a global cache on the local machine. Dependency resolution is performed using a directed graph to ensure all required packages (and their dependencies) are installed in the correct version, avoiding conflicts. Lock files like *package-lock.json* are used to record the exact versions installed, ensuring consistent environments across machines and deployments.

Yarn Versus npm

Yarn is a modern JavaScript package manager, created by Facebook (Meta), that helps developers install, update, and manage project dependencies—just like npm. It was originally designed to address some of the shortcomings of npm at the time, offering faster installs, better caching, and more reliable lockfile consistency across teams.

Today, Yarn v4+ introduces advanced features like:

Plug'n'play (PnP)
A way to speed up project startup by avoiding the traditional node_modules folder.

Zero install
Lets you commit dependencies to your repository so you don't need to run install separately on every machine.

To use Yarn without manually installing it, Node comes with a built-in helper tool called Corepack (since Node v16.10 and enabled by default in v20+). It lets you quickly enable Yarn and other package managers. Just run:

```
corepack enable
yarn init -2
```

This initializes a new Yarn project using the latest version and prepares it with modern defaults.

While Yarn is not as widely adopted as npm, it can be a great choice for teams that value speed and reliability. It also has a strong community and ecosystem, with many popular libraries and tools supporting it. For more information, check out the Yarn documentation (*https://oreil.ly/7rYhJ*).

Recommended Directory Structure

A clean and scalable project structure supports clarity, maintainability, and team collaboration—especially as complexity grows. The following are three recommended layouts depending on the size and goals of your Node project.

Assuming a project named node-app, a basic structure might look like this:

```
node-app/
├── index.js  ❶
└── package.json
```

❶ *index.js* represents your source file.

This setup is ideal for small or solo projects that don't need testing or configuration layers yet. It minimizes overhead and lets you focus on writing code immediately. It's great for getting started quickly with a simple script or utility. The majority of your projects throughout the book will follow this structure.

For small to mid-sized apps with basic testing and configuration needs, you may compartmentalize your code and add a few more directories:

```
node-app/
├── src/  ❶
│   └── index.js
├── test/  ❷
├── .env  ❸
├── .gitignore
├── package.json
└── README.md
```

❶ *src* holds your main application logic.

❷ *test* holds your unit or integration tests.

❸ *.env* holds your environment variables, which should be kept out of version control.

This adds separation for tests and environment configuration, which helps when working on APIs or services meant for production use. It also prepares you to integrate CI, logging, and deployment tools more cleanly. This is a common structure for serious but non-enterprise-level projects.

Last, for full-stack or enterprise-scale applications with frontends, multiple environments, and deployment automation, you may use a more complex layout like the following:

```
node-app/
├── src/
│   ├── server/  ❶
│   └── client/  ❷
│       ├── components/
│       └── index.html
├── public/  ❸
├── config/  ❹
├── scripts/  ❺
```

```
├── test/
├── .env
├── ."ignore
├── package.json
└── README.md
```

❶ *server* is where your Node backend logic is found.

❷ *client* is where your UI components (React, Vue, etc.) are found.

❸ *public* is where your static assets (icons, fonts, etc.) are found.

❹ *config* is where your environment-specific config files are found.

❺ *scripts* is where your automation and DevOps scripts are found.

This structure supports applications with both backend and frontend code, and cleanly separates concerns for larger teams. It accommodates automation scripts, multiple deployment environments, and advanced testing strategies. It's ideal for scalable apps and is flexible enough to grow with new microservices or teams.

As your project evolves, you can adapt any of these structures to fit your needs. The key is to keep things organized and modular so that you can easily find and manage your code as it grows.

Understanding package.json and Scripts

Your *package.json* file is the manifest of your Node project. It defines metadata, scripts, and dependency rules that other tools (like npm or Yarn) use to understand how your app works.

At its core, this file should look like the following:

```
{
  "name": "node-app",
  "version": "1.0.0",
  "type": "module",
  "scripts": {
    "start": "node index.js",
    "dev": "node --watch src/index.js"
  },
  "dependencies": {},
  "devDependencies": {}
}
```

This file gives your project a name and version, and tells Node to treat your code as modern ES modules using `"type": "module"`. The `scripts` section lets you run helpful commands like `npm start` or `npm run dev` without typing out the full command. Empty `dependencies` and `devDependencies` sections mean you haven't installed any external libraries yet, but they'll automatically populate when you add packages.

The `"type"`: `"module"` setting enables support for native `import/export` syntax, replacing the older CommonJS `require` pattern. The `--watch` flag for Node (20+) reloads your app automatically on file changes, eliminating the need for tools like `nodemon`. The `scripts` section acts as a unified CLI for common developer tasks—automating linting, testing, and formatting, using tools you've installed as dev dependencies.

This is all you need to get started with a small project or simple API server. It's lightweight, readable, and serves as the single source of truth for your project configuration. Think of it as your project's instruction manual for tools and other developers.

As your project grows, *package.json* becomes a powerful configuration hub for build tools, testing, formatting, and team workflows. You may add fields like `engines` to specify Node versions, `files` to control what gets published, or `workspaces` for monorepos. The `scripts` section can also include commands for linting, testing, and formatting code:

```
{
  "name": "node-app",
  "version": "1.0.0",
  "type": "module",
  "scripts": {
    "start": "node src/index.js",
    "dev": "node --watch src/index.js",
    "lint": "eslint .",
    "test": "vitest run",
    "format": "prettier --write ."
  },
  "dependencies": {},
  "devDependencies": {}
}
```

As dependencies are added, the file grows to track exact versions and scopes (production versus development). Complex projects may also use fields like `engines`, `exports`, `files`, and `workspaces` to control deployment behavior, compatibility, and monorepo organization. Understanding how to structure and automate with *package.json* is key to managing scalable, maintainable Node apps.

Document your scripts in *README.md* so contributors know how to run and maintain the project. This helps avoid confusion and ensures the team follows a consistent workflow. The *package.json* is a productivity engine when used effectively.

Modern Node Syntax Patterns

As of Node 20+, many JavaScript features that were once optional or experimental are now fully supported and considered best practice. Understanding these patterns will make your code cleaner, more maintainable, and more aligned with modern standards used across both backend and frontend development.

Specifically, this section covers:

- Native ESM support
- Top-level `await`
- Destructuring defaults
- Optional chaining
- Nullish coalescing
- Built-in `fetch`

As mentioned earlier in this appendix, modern Node uses ES Modules (ESM) by default when `"type"`: `"module"` is set in *package.json*. This `import`/`export` style is the same used in modern browsers and tools like Deno and Vite, helping unify frontend and backend development. It replaces the older `require()` syntax used in CommonJS, making your code more future-proof and interoperable.

The following demonstrates importing modules with ESM:

```
import fs from 'node:fs/promises';
import express from 'express';
```

These lines of code are naturally found at the top of your files, just like in browser JavaScript. This makes it easier to read and understand dependencies at a glance.

With ESM, Node now allows you to use `await` at the top level—no need to wrap everything in an `async` function. This simplifies one-off scripts and configuration loading, especially in entry files like *index.js*. It makes asynchronous code cleaner and easier to follow, especially for beginners.

The following example demonstrates the use of top-level `await`:

```
const data = await fs.readFile('./config.json', 'utf-8');
```

This line demonstrates how to read a file asynchronously using `await` with Node's built-in `fs/promises` module. It reads the contents of *config.json* (as text, using UTF-8 encoding) and stores the result in the `data` variable. Because `await` is used at the top level, this pattern is only possible in an ES Module (`type: "module"` in *package.json*) and simplifies what used to require wrapping everything in an `async` function.

Another useful modern JavaScript feature is object destructuring with default values. In the example below, the `PORT` environment variable is extracted from `process.env`, and if it's not defined, a default value of `3000` is used. This pattern is especially helpful in configuration files, ensuring your app runs smoothly even when certain environment variables are missing. Destructuring also reduces boilerplate code and makes your configuration logic cleaner and easier to understand:

```
const { PORT = 3000 } = process.env;
```

Optional chaining (`?.`) and nullish coalescing (`??`) are modern JavaScript features introduced in ECMAScript 2020. They allow you to safely access deeply nested object properties and assign fallback values without writing long chains of conditional checks. These features have been supported in Node since version 14 (released in April 2020) and are now widely adopted in both frontend and backend JavaScript codebases.

The following example demonstrates how these operators let you safely access deeply nested object properties without crashing your app if something is `undefined` or `null`. The `??` operator ensures a fallback value is used when the left side is `null` or `undefined` (but not falsy values like `0` or `""`). This results in cleaner, more fault-tolerant code with fewer manual checks:

```
const username = user?.profile?.name ?? 'GUEST_NAME';
```

Last, as of Node 18+, `fetch()` is available globally, just like in the browser—no need to install external libraries like `node-fetch`. This allows you to make HTTP requests in a familiar and concise way using native APIs. It's especially helpful for full-stack developers coming from the frontend, as it reduces the learning curve and keeps your dependencies lean:

```
const res = await fetch('https://api.example.com/data');
const data = await res.json();
console.log(data);
```

Modern Node fully embraces features like ES Modules, top-level `await`, and native `fetch`, enabling cleaner, more readable code that aligns closely with modern browser-based JavaScript. These features simplify asynchronous operations, enhance configuration safety, and reduce dependency overhead. By mastering these patterns, developers can write more robust, maintainable, and future-proof applications.

Growth Areas for Node Engineers

As you become more comfortable with project setup and syntax, it's important to broaden your knowledge beyond the basics. Node is used in a wide variety of environments, from small backend services to globally distributed APIs and real-time systems. The more tools and patterns you become familiar with, the more effective and versatile you will be as a Node engineer.

Here are several areas worth exploring as you advance:

Backend architecture
Learn to structure APIs and services using REST, GraphQL, or event-driven models. Understanding layered architecture (e.g., controllers, services, data access) helps you build scalable, modular applications. Frameworks like Express and Fastify can be good starting points, but knowing *why* certain patterns are used is even more important than *which* ones.

Databases and persistence
Know how to interact with both SQL and NoSQL databases. Get comfortable with tools like PostgreSQL, MongoDB, Prisma, and Sequelize. Understand database transactions, indexing, and query optimization—these skills are essential for building high-performance applications.

Security best practices
Learn how to handle authentication and authorization using techniques like JWTs, OAuth2, and cookie-based sessions. Understand how to protect your APIs against threats like XSS, CSRF, injection attacks, and rate limiting. Security becomes even more important as your code moves from local development to production environments.

Testing and automation
Writing automated tests improves confidence in your code. Learn to write unit, integration, and end-to-end tests using tools like Vitest, Jest, or Supertest. Pair this with automated workflows using GitHub Actions or other CI/CD tools to streamline deployment and reduce bugs.

DevOps and deployment
Explore how to containerize your app using Docker and manage it with tools like PM2, systemd, or Kubernetes. Learn how to deploy to platforms like Vercel, Heroku, or AWS. Understanding how your app runs in production will make you a more effective developer and team member.

Monitoring and observability
Add error tracking and performance monitoring using tools like Sentry, Prometheus, or OpenTelemetry. Logging and metrics help you understand real-world

behavior and fix problems faster. This becomes critical as your app gains users and complexity.

Type safety and tooling
Adopt TypeScript or JSDoc to improve type safety and developer experience. Type-aware editors and tooling help prevent bugs and improve readability. Even small projects benefit from typing once they scale.

Real-time and streaming systems
Learn how to work with WebSockets, Server-Sent Events (SSE), and streaming APIs. This is essential for apps involving live dashboards, multiplayer features, or collaborative editing. Libraries like Socket.IO or native `EventSource` support this pattern.

By focusing on these areas over time, you'll gain the skills needed to build and maintain complex systems with confidence. As the ecosystem grows and evolves, continuous learning will ensure that your Node knowledge stays relevant and valuable.

Summary

In this appendix you:

- Initialized a new Node project using `npm` and explored how to configure the *package.json* file
- Learned how to structure your project directory based on scale and complexity
- Compared `npm` with alternative tools like Yarn and explored how to use Corepack to enable them
- Explored modern Node syntax patterns such as ES Modules, top-level `await`, and optional chaining
- Identified key areas for career growth as a Node engineer, including testing, DevOps, and security best practices

APPENDIX B

Setting Up Your Development Tools

To write, debug, and maintain professional-quality Node applications, you need a strong development environment. This appendix walks you through configuring VS Code—the most popular IDE for JavaScript and Node—along with essential extensions that support formatting, linting, debugging, and version control. You'll learn how to set up Git for tracking changes, manage project-level settings, and test APIs using tools like Postman to simulate requests and verify endpoint behavior. You'll also see when to use breakpoints instead of `console.log`, and how to distinguish between style rules (handled by Prettier) and logic rules (handled by ESLint).

If you haven't installed VS Code yet, you can get it from the official site (*https:// oreil.ly/hw4mE*) or refer to the installation guide in Chapter 1.

Using Git from the Command Line

While VS Code includes a built-in Git interface, many professional developers rely on the Git CLI for speed, scripting, and control. Using Git from the terminal helps you understand what's happening under the hood and enables you to work in any environment—even without a GUI.

To get started, install Git from *https://git-scm.com*. Once installed, verify it by running: To verify that Git is installed on your system, run the following command.

```
git --version ❶
```

❶ Outputs the currently installed version of Git (e.g., `git version 2.42.0`)

If the version number displays successfully, you're ready to use Git from the command line.

311

To begin tracking your project, initialize a repository, stage your files, and make your first commit:

```
git init            ❶
git add .           ❷
git commit -m "Initial commit"  ❸
```

❶ Creates a new Git repository in the current folder

❷ Stages all files in the current directory for commit

❸ Commits the staged changes with a message describing the snapshot

Once your repository is set up, these are some essential Git commands you'll use regularly:

```
git status    ❶
git diff      ❷
git log       ❸
git restore   ❹
git reset     ❺
```

❶ Shows the current status of your working directory and staged changes

❷ Displays the differences between modified files and the last commit

❸ Shows a list of previous commits, including IDs, dates, and messages

❹ Reverts changes in a file back to the last committed state

❺ Unstages a file or resets your commit history to a previous state

Use a .gitignore file to prevent sensitive or unnecessary files—like .env, node_modules, or system logs—from being committed to version control.

With your Git workflow in place, the next step is to enhance your development environment itself. VS Code supports a wide range of extensions that can help automate tasks, enforce code quality, and accelerate your productivity.

Recommended VS Code Extensions

VS Code extensions are lightweight add-ons that enhance the functionality, productivity, and customization of the VS Code editor. They allow developers to tailor their environment with tools for debugging, linting, formatting, theming, language support, and more. Extensions are managed through the built-in Extensions Marketplace, making it easy to search, install, and update tools directly within the editor. By integrating powerful features like Git integration, code suggestions, and environment-specific utilities, extensions help streamline development workflows, reduce context switching, and improve code quality.

The following are recommended for all Node developers:

ESLint (https://oreil.ly/Dpu2c)
Enforces consistent coding style and catches syntax issues. Think of linting as code analysis, whereas formatting focuses on code appearance, like spacing and indentation. Using linting extensions helps to check your code for potential bugs, style violations, or best practice issues.

Prettier (https://oreil.ly/8hwOW)
Automatically formats your code according to defined rules.

You can configure VS Code to automatically adjust spacing, indentation, and line breaks. Tools like ESLint can be configured to do both, but it's best to use ESLint for logic rules and Prettier for style rules.

You can configure VS Code to auto-format on save by changing your editor settings to include `"editor.formatOnSave": true`.

Node Extension Pack (https://oreil.ly/PoB4N)
Adds snippets, REPL support, and more for Node development. Tools like this improve your ability to analyze and debug your code.

While `console.log()` is quick and familiar, VS Code's built-in debugger is far more powerful for inspecting variables, stepping through code, and evaluating expressions in real time.

To use the debugger:

1. Open any JavaScript file.
2. Click in the left gutter next to the line number to set a breakpoint.
3. Press F5 or open the Debug panel and run "Start Debugging."

You can inspect variables, use a watch list, and step through code line by line.

GitLens (https://oreil.ly/bpitW)
Enhances Git integration with history, blame annotations, and code lens. This will be particularly helpful as you modify your code throughout each chapter. Along the way you'll be able to better visualize your changes.

To install these, open the Extensions sidebar (Cmd+Shift+X or Ctrl+Shift+X) and search for each name above.

Setting Up Your Development Tools | **313**

Once installed, most extensions will activate automatically based on project files (like *.eslintrc* or *.prettierrc*).

As your applications grow more complex, you'll often need to interact with backend endpoints directly to verify that APIs respond correctly. While writing frontend interfaces or test scripts is one way to do this, a faster and more flexible approach is to use a dedicated API client.

Testing Your API with Postman

Modern applications often rely on APIs to handle requests, serve data, and connect with frontend clients or third-party services. Testing these APIs manually using tools like curl or writing custom test scripts can be time-consuming and error-prone. Postman is a free, GUI-based application that simplifies this process—allowing you to send HTTP requests, inspect responses, simulate edge cases, and debug faster without writing extra code. It's especially useful for testing REST endpoints, verifying authentication, and debugging payloads during development.

To get started:

1. Download Postman (*https://www.postman.com/downloads*).
2. Open the app and create a new Request.
3. Choose a method (GET, POST, etc.) and enter your API URL (e.g., *http://localhost:3000/users*).
4. Add headers or body parameters as needed.
5. Click Send to make the request.

Postman streamlines the API development process by allowing you to test endpoints interactively as you build them. Rather than relying on browser-based requests or ad hoc curl commands, Postman provides a visual interface where you can craft requests, inspect responses, and debug errors in real time. This immediate feedback loop helps you confirm that routes behave as expected, response formats are correct, and error handling is functioning properly.

Beyond basic requests, Postman allows you to organize your endpoints into collections, which serve as living documentation and test suites for your backend. You can simulate real-world authentication flows by attaching headers, tokens, or credentials, and even chain requests together to model complete user journeys. This makes it easier to share APIs with teammates or clients, automate regression testing, and maintain consistent behavior across environments.

---

314 | Appendix B: Setting Up Your Development Tools

Use Postman when you need more control than the browser offers—like sending POST requests with JSON payloads or testing protected routes with JWTs.

To complement your API development workflow, you'll also want tools that streamline how your server responds to changes during active development.

Watching for File Changes with nodemon

In a typical development workflow, you often need to restart your Node server manually after making changes to your code. This slows down iteration and introduces unnecessary friction. nodemon helps by automatically watching your files and restarting the app whenever it detects a change—making development faster and more efficient, especially for backend services or APIs.

To install nodemon globally so it's available in any project, run npm install -g node mon. Once installed, you can run your Node app with automatic restarts within your project folder, by running nodemon index.js. This starts index.js and restarts it when file changes are detected

If your app uses ECMAScript modules (i.e., type: "module" in *package.json*), you may need to include the file extension explicitly:

If your app uses interactive input (e.g., readline, inquirer, etc.), nodemon may restart before the user finishes interacting. In those cases, run the app using plain node index.js.

As your applications grow more complex, you'll often need to interact with backend endpoints directly to verify that APIs respond correctly. While writing frontend interfaces or test scripts is one way to do this, a faster and more flexible approach is to use a dedicated API client.

Summary

A well-configured development environment helps you write cleaner, more reliable code and debug issues faster. In this appendix, you learned how to:

- Set up your development environment with Node.js, Git, and Visual Studio Code, and learned essential commands for version control and project management

- Installed key VS Code extensions and configured tools like Prettier, ESLint, and the built-in debugger to improve code quality and developer efficiency
- Tested backend APIs using Postman, explored how to simulate auth flows, and saw how to debug server behavior during active development

With your tools ready, you're set up for faster, safer development throughout the rest of the book.

APPENDIX C

Working with Databases in Node Projects

Most real-world applications rely on databases to store and retrieve data. This appendix introduces essential data tools used in Node projects—from full-featured databases like MongoDB, PostgreSQL, and SQLite, to supporting services like Redis and RabbitMQ that handle caching and message queues.

You'll learn how to install and connect to each database, work with ORMs like Mongoose and Sequelize, and understand key data modeling concepts like schemas, collections, and documents. You'll also compare local and cloud-hosted options and explore when to use each tool based on your app's needs—whether you're building a quick prototype, a scalable web API, or a background task processor.

Why Databases Matter

Databases allow applications to persist data between sessions, handle user input, and retrieve information efficiently. Node supports a wide range of database types and drivers. Choosing the right one depends on your project's scale, complexity, and the structure of your data.

Modern apps need to store lots of data, like user information, products, or transactions. Without a database, you'd have to use temporary storage (e.g., in-memory variables), which loses data every time the server restarts. A database helps maintain data consistency, supports complex queries, and scales as your app grows.

In this appendix, we'll cover:

MongoDB
> A NoSQL document-oriented database ideal for flexible, JSON-like data

PostgreSQL
> A relational SQL database with powerful features and ACID compliance

SQLite
   A lightweight file-based SQL database for local development or embedded use

Each section includes installation instructions, connection setup, and usage examples using both native drivers and popular ORMs like Mongoose and Sequelize.

Core Concepts: Schemas, Tables, Collections, and Documents

Before diving into the specific databases, here are some key terms and how they map across database types:

Concept	SQL databases	NoSQL
Schema	Database structure definition (tables, columns)	Mongoose model definition for MongoDB
Table	Rows of structured records	N/A (use collections)
Collection	N/A (tables instead)	Groups of documents (similar to tables)
Document	N/A (rows instead)	Individual JSON-like objects

SQL databases use a fixed schema, while NoSQL databases allow flexible document structures.

MongoDB: NoSQL for Flexible Schemas

MongoDB stores data in collections of JSON-like documents, making it ideal for applications with unstructured or semi-structured data. The following attributes make it particularly well-suited for Node applications:

Document-oriented
   MongoDB stores data as "documents" instead of using traditional tables. These documents are in a JSON-like format—simple key-value pairs like { "name": "Jon", "age": 30 }. This is intuitive for JavaScript developers because it closely resembles JavaScript objects.

NoSQL database
   Unlike traditional SQL databases, MongoDB is flexible and doesn't require a fixed structure. This means you can adjust your data models without a lot of hassle, which is ideal for rapidly evolving applications.

Scalability
   MongoDB's horizontal scaling supports growth as your app scales, while Node's nonblocking I/O ensures responsiveness.

Installation

Follow the instructions for your platform:

Platform	Install instructions
macOS (Homebrew)	`brew tap mongodb/brew && brew install mongodb-community`
Ubuntu/Debian	*https://oreil.ly/Lfbg4*
Windows	*https://oreil.ly/PhrUo*

> ### About Homebrew for macOS
>
> Homebrew is a popular package manager for macOS that simplifies the installation of software by automating the process of downloading, unpacking, compiling, and setting up applications and libraries.
>
> To install Homebrew, open a new terminal window and run:
>
> ```
> /bin/bash -c "$(curl \
> -fsSL https://raw.githubusercontent.com/Homebrew/install/HEAD/install.sh)"
> ```
>
> To install MongoDB with Homebrew, run the following commands:
>
> ```
> brew tap mongodb/brew     ❶
> brew install mongodb-community@5.0    ❷
> ```
>
> ❶ Adds the official MongoDB Homebrew tap to your Homebrew sources. A tap is a repository of Homebrew formulas that you can install.
>
> ❷ Installs the MongoDB Community Edition version 5.0 using Homebrew.

Windows installation

On Windows, MongoDB is installed using an *.msi* installer that sets up the database as a system service for ease of use:

1. Visit the MongoDB Windows Installation page and download the installer.
2. Run the installer by double-clicking the *.msi* file and following the installation instructions.

> Ensure the option "Install MongoDB as a Service" is selected, so MongoDB starts automatically after installation.

Once installation has completed, open Command Prompt as an administrator and
run the following command to start MongoDB:

```
net start MongoDB
```

To stop MongoDB, use:

```
net stop MongoDB
```

Linux installation

Follow the official installation instructions (*https://oreil.ly/_k-bl*) to ensure your environment is set up correctly for MongoDB. Then, in a command-line window, run the
following command to start MongoDB:

```
sudo systemctl start mongod
```

Use the MongoDB service commands `sudo service mongod
start` to start and `sudo service mongod stop` to stop MongoDB.

Starting MongoDB Locally

After installing, you can run the MongoDB server using:

```
mongod --dbpath ~/data/db
```

Ensure the `mongod` process is running before connecting to your
database.

Connecting with Mongoose

To connect in your app, you can use the official MongoDB driver or Mongoose (a
higher-level ORM):

```
import mongoose from 'mongoose';

await mongoose.connect('mongodb://localhost:27017/myapp');

const User = mongoose.model('User', {
  name: String,
  email: String
});

await new User({ name: 'Alice', email: 'alice@example.com' }).save();
```

Mongoose provides validation, middleware, and schema enforcement on top of MongoDB.

PostgreSQL: SQL Power and Structure

PostgreSQL is a popular open source relational database known for reliability, complex queries, and support for schemas, joins, and transactions.

Installation

Follow the instructions for your platform:

Platform	Install instructions
macOS (Homebrew)	`brew install postgresql`
Ubuntu/Debian	`sudo apt install postgresql`
Windows	*https://oreil.ly/OYrCy*

To start the database locally:

```
pg_ctl -D /usr/local/var/postgres start
```

You can then use `psql` CLI or GUI tools like `pgAdmin` to manage databases.

Connecting with Sequelize

Sequelize is a popular ORM that maps SQL tables to JavaScript models:

```
import { Sequelize, DataTypes } from 'sequelize';

const sequelize = new Sequelize('postgres://user:pass@localhost:5432/mydb');

const User = sequelize.define('User', {
  name: DataTypes.STRING,
  email: DataTypes.STRING
});

await sequelize.sync();
await User.create({ name: 'Bob', email: 'bob@example.com' });
```

> Sequelize works with PostgreSQL, MySQL, and SQLite using the same interface.

SQLite: Lightweight and Embedded

SQLite is a file-based SQL engine, great for prototyping or apps with low concurrency needs. It doesn't require a server—data is stored in a *.sqlite* file.

Installation

Follow the instructions for your platform:

Platform	Install instructions
macOS	`brew install sqlite`
Ubuntu/Debian	`sudo apt install sqlite3`
Windows	*https://oreil.ly/Tcsec*

You can create and inspect databases using the CLI:

```
sqlite3 dev.db
> CREATE TABLE users (name TEXT, email TEXT);
> .exit
```

Connecting with Sequelize

You can reuse Sequelize for SQLite:

```
const sequelize = new Sequelize({
  dialect: 'sqlite',
  storage: './dev.db'
});

const Task = sequelize.define('Task', {
  description: DataTypes.STRING,
  completed: DataTypes.BOOLEAN
});

await sequelize.sync();
await Task.create({ description: 'Write book chapter', completed: false });
```

Alternatively, `better-sqlite3` offers a lightweight, synchronous driver without ORM overhead.

Local Versus Cloud-Hosted Databases

When to use local databases:

- Prototyping or development on your own machine
- No internet or need for offline persistence
- Embedded apps (e.g., desktop, mobile)

When to use cloud-hosted databases:

- Team collaboration and backups
- High availability, scalability, remote access
- Services like MongoDB Atlas, Amazon RDS (PostgreSQL), or Supabase

Cloud databases often provide easy dashboard access, authentication, scaling, and backup tools that save setup time in production environments.

Cloud Services

To scale your application beyond local development, each of these databases can be deployed to cloud-hosted services that offer managed infrastructure, backups, and high availability.

For MongoDB, MongoDB Atlas (*https://www.mongodb.com/atlas*) provides a fully managed cloud solution with one-click deployment on AWS, Azure, or GCP. PostgreSQL is widely supported through services like Amazon RDS (*https:// aws.amazon.com/rds*), Google Cloud SQL (*https://cloud.google.com/sql*), and Supabase (*https://supabase.com*), allowing you to offload patching, scaling, and security.

SQLite is typically not used in cloud production environments, but for lightweight, edge-friendly use cases, you can explore Cloudflare D1 (*https://oreil.ly/1jgEj*) or Turso (*https://turso.tech*).

Connecting your Node app to these services usually involves updating your database URL with a secure connection string and adjusting your ORM or driver configuration. Many cloud providers also offer built-in monitoring, query logging, and integration with VPCs or secrets managers to keep your credentials secure.

Working with Databases in Node Projects | 323

Database Comparison for Node Applications

Here's a comparison of common databases that can be used with Node applications:

Database	Type	Strengths	Weaknesses	Suitable use cases
MongoDB	NoSQL (Document-based)	Flexible schema, scalable, JavaScript-friendly	Complex joins, learning curve	Dynamic data, scalable apps, JSON-heavy apps
PostgreSQL	SQL (Relational)	ACID compliance, powerful queries, robust features	Complex schema changes, steeper learning curve	Complex queries, structured data, analytics
SQLite	SQL (Embedded)	Lightweight, no server required, simple setup	Limited scalability, single writer	Small projects, prototyping, CLI tools
MySQL	SQL (Relational)	Easy setup, widely supported	Limited advanced features	Web apps, structured data
Redis	NoSQL (Key-value)	Extremely fast, excellent for caching	Not persistent by default, memory-limited	Caching, real-time data, sessions

Choosing a persistence layer

Consider these features when making the choice for your project:

Feature	MongoDB	PostgreSQL	SQLite
Schema flexibility	High	Medium (rigid)	Medium (rigid)
Hosting	Local + Cloud (Atlas)	Local + Cloud (RDS, Supabase)	Local only
Query power	Medium (JSON)	High (joins, indexes)	Low to Medium
Use case	JSON-heavy apps	Relational logic, analytics	Prototyping, CLI tools

Each database has strengths and trade-offs. This book provides working examples for all three, and you'll encounter them in different projects throughout the chapters.

While databases are essential for long-term data persistence and structured querying, many modern Node applications also rely on high-speed supporting tools to improve responsiveness and scalability. Two common additions are Redis and RabbitMQ—used not for primary storage, but for temporary data, background processing, and asynchronous communication. These tools complement your main database by enabling fast caching, efficient task queues, and real-time messaging.

Redis: In-Memory Speed for Caching and Queues

Redis is an in-memory data store often used for caching, session storage, and lightweight message queues. It excels at speed and simplicity, making it a great fit for performance-critical parts of your Node app, such as storing temporary data or managing job queues.

Redis supports multiple data types including strings, lists, sets, and hashes. Many Node frameworks integrate well with Redis for caching, Pub/Sub, and background jobs.

Installation

Install Redis using your platform's package manager:

Platform	Install instructions
macOS (Homebrew)	`brew install redis`
Ubuntu/Debian	`sudo apt install redis`
Windows	*https://oreil.ly/ZdMWj*

To verify Redis is working, start the Redis server and connect using the CLI:

```
redis-server
```

Then in another terminal:

```
redis-cli
> SET test "hello"
> GET test
```

macOS

Use Homebrew to install and run Redis:

```
brew install redis
brew services start redis
```

You can now connect via `redis-cli`.

Ubuntu/Debian

Install and start the Redis server:

```
sudo apt update
sudo apt install redis
sudo systemctl start redis
```

Test with:

```
redis cli ping
```

It should respond with PONG.

Working with Databases in Node Projects | 325

Windows

Redis does not officially support Windows, but you can run it using Windows Subsystem for Linux (WSL) or Docker. For Docker:

```
docker run -p 6379:6379 redis
```

Then connect using a Redis client or `redis-cli`.

Connecting from Node

To connect from a Node app, use the `ioredis` or `redis` package.

```
npm install ioredis
```

Example usage:

```
import Redis from 'ioredis';

const redis = new Redis();

await redis.set('greeting', 'Hello, Redis!');
const value = await redis.get('greeting');
console.log(value);
```

Redis is ideal for:

- Caching API responses or DB queries
- Storing session data for logged-in users
- Implementing real-time features using Pub/Sub
- Managing lightweight task queues

Using Redis as a Queue

You can use Redis lists to implement a basic queue. To add a job:

```
await redis.lpush(
  'jobs',
  JSON.stringify({
    type: 'email',
    to: 'alice@example.com',
  })
);
```

To process jobs:

```
while (true) {
  const job = await redis.rpop('jobs');
  if (job) {
    const data = JSON.parse(job);
    console.log('Processing:', data);
```

        }
    }

> For production apps, consider using a library like Bull or Redis-based job frameworks that add features like retries and rate limits.

Redis works well for simple queues and temporary job handling, but when your application requires more robust messaging features—such as delivery guarantees, routing, or workload distribution—a dedicated message broker is a better fit. RabbitMQ fills that role, offering a more structured approach to managing background tasks and communication between services.

RabbitMQ: Queue-Based Messaging for Node Apps

RabbitMQ is a message broker that helps your application scale by offloading tasks to background workers. In Chapter 11, you'll learn how to integrate RabbitMQ into your Node applications. Instead of performing time-consuming operations in the main request cycle, you can publish messages to a queue and let other services process them. This improves performance and decouples different parts of your system.

Installation

RabbitMQ requires the Erlang runtime, which is included automatically on most platforms when you install RabbitMQ.

Platform	Install instructions
macOS (Homebrew)	`brew install rabbitmq`
Ubuntu/Debian	`sudo apt install rabbitmq-server`
Windows	*https://oreil.ly/NxhHh*

To check if RabbitMQ is running, use:

    rabbitmqctl status

macOS

Install RabbitMQ using Homebrew:

    brew install rabbitmq
    brew services start rabbitmq

To enable the web-based UI:

    rabbitmq-plugins enable rabbitmq_management

Visit *http://localhost:15672* and log in with guest / guest.

Ubuntu/Debian

Install RabbitMQ with:

```
sudo apt update
sudo apt install rabbitmq-server
sudo systemctl start rabbitmq-server
```

Then enable the management plugin:

```
sudo rabbitmq-plugins enable rabbitmq_management
```

The dashboard will be available at *http://localhost:15672*.

Windows

1. Install the Erlang runtime (*https://oreil.ly/SlUZP*).
2. Download the RabbitMQ installer (*https://oreil.ly/84dTR*).
3. After installation, open a terminal and run:

   ```
   rabbitmq-plugins enable rabbitmq_management
   rabbitmq-service.bat start
   ```

You can then access the management UI at *http://localhost:15672*.

Connecting from Node

Use the `amqplib` package to send and receive messages:

```
npm install amqplib
```

Example: sending an order to a queue

```
import amqp from 'amqplib';

const conn = await amqp.connect('amqp://localhost');
const channel = await conn.createChannel();
const queue = 'orders';

await channel.assertQueue(queue);
channel.sendToQueue(queue, Buffer.from('coffee'));
```

Example: consuming from a queue

```
import amqp from 'amqplib';

const conn = await amqp.connect('amqp://localhost');
const channel = await conn.createChannel();
const queue = 'orders';

await channel.assertQueue(queue);
```

```
channel.consume(queue, msg => {
  if (msg) {
    console.log('Received:', msg.content.toString());
    channel.ack(msg);
  }
});
```

Use RabbitMQ to pass messages between microservices, offload work from your main server, or implement task queues.

Next Steps

Throughout this book, you'll use each of these databases in real projects—from a task manager with SQLite to a full REST API backed by MongoDB and an authentication system with PostgreSQL. You'll also build systems that take advantage of Redis for caching and temporary data, as well as RabbitMQ for managing background jobs and inter-service communication.

Make sure you've installed at least one database engine and driver before proceeding to the next chapter. If you're running projects in Docker, check the *docker-compose.yml* files—we've included preconfigured services for each database and queue to help you start quickly.

Some chapters in this book require a database or queueing system. Setting up at least one now will help you follow along smoothly later.

Summary

In this appendix, you learned:

- How to choose and set up databases like MongoDB, PostgreSQL, and SQLite in Node projects
- When to use supporting tools like Redis and RabbitMQ for caching and background processing
- The trade-offs between local and cloud-hosted services for development and deployment

APPENDIX D
Working with the Code Examples and Containerizing Projects

Every chapter in this book includes working Node code examples to reinforce the concepts you're learning. These are organized, tested, and maintained in a public GitHub repository. This appendix shows you how to access the code, run it locally, and optionally use Docker to simplify setup—especially if you're working in isolated environments or across multiple machines.

Accessing the GitHub Repository

The official GitHub repository (*https://oreil.ly/node-projects-code*) for this book's code examples is structured by chapter. Inside each chapter folder, you'll find subdirectories for each project or topic section, such as:

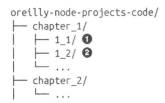

```
oreilly-node-projects-code/
├── chapter_1/
│   ├── 1_1/  ❶
│   ├── 1_2/  ❷
│   └── ...
├── chapter_2/
│   └── ...
```

❶ First section of Chapter 1

❷ Second section of Chapter 1

This structure makes it easy to navigate and find the code relevant to each chapter. Additionally, you'll be able to work through the chapters in more digestible segments. Each project folder contains its own *package.json* file, so you can install dependencies and run scripts without affecting other projects.

To get started, you can either clone the repository or fork it to your own GitHub account. This allows you to experiment with the code, make changes, and save your progress.

To clone the repo (recommended for most users), navigate in your command line to a directory where you want to store the code on your computer and run the following command:

```
git clone https://github.com/JonathanWexler/oreilly-node-projects-code.git
```

Then navigate into any chapter or project subdirectory and follow the instructions in the README file for that section. For example, to run the first project in Chapter 1, enter the following commands in your command line:

```
cd oreilly-node-projects-code/chapter_1/1_1
npm install
npm start
```

You may instead want to fork the repository to your own GitHub account. This allows you to save your changes and push your own modifications as you work through chapter projects. To do this, navigate to GitHub and click Fork. Then click the name of your own GitHub account.

This will create a copy of the repository in your account. You can then clone your forked repository to your local machine using the following command:

```
git clone https://github.com/your-username/oreilly-node-projects-code.git
```

After cloning, navigate into any chapter or project subdirectory and follow the instructions in the README file for that section.

Each folder is self-contained and includes its own *package.json*, so you don't have to install global dependencies or run any scripts outside the project's scope.

You may now follow along with the book, running each project as you go. If you encounter any issues, feel free to open an issue on the GitHub repository. The next section covers how to run the code examples using Docker, which can simplify setup and ensure consistency across environments.

Running Projects with Docker

Node is lightweight to install—but managing multiple projects, environments, or OS-level dependencies can still be a hassle, especially across teams or on new machines.

Docker solves this problem by allowing you to run each project inside an isolated container, using a defined environment. This ensures that:

- Everyone runs the same Node version, regardless of local setup.
- You don't pollute your global environment with different toolchains or config files.
- Setup time is reduced—just clone the repo and run the Docker container.

You can run any project from this book using Docker. Each chapter folder includes a *docker-compose.yml* file that launches all projects in isolated containers with minimal setup.

> To reduce repetition, some users may prefer one root-level *docker-compose.yml* that references all chapters. However, this book provides one per chapter for simplicity.

To get started, you'll need to install Docker. Follow the instructions for your operating system:

Platform	Install instructions
macOS (Intel/Apple Silicon)	*https://oreil.ly/l1wXA*
Windows 10/11 (Pro, Home, WSL2)	*https://oreil.ly/TSk16*
Ubuntu/Debian Linux	*https://oreil.ly/1Rznz*

After installation, verify that Docker works by running the following commands in your command line:

```
docker --version
docker compose version
```

> On Windows, Docker Desktop requires WSL2 (you'll be prompted during install).

With Docker installed, you can now run the code examples in this book using containers through the repository you cloned in the previous section. Each chapter folder contains its own *docker-compose.yml* file. For example, to run the first project in Chapter 1, navigate to the chapter folder in your command line and run `cd chapter_1` and then `docker compose up`.

This command will build and start the container for that project. You can also run `docker compose up -d` to run it in detached mode (in the background). You'll see output indicating the container is running, along with any logs from the application.

If you encounter any issues, make sure Docker is running and that you have the correct permissions to run Docker commands. If you need to rebuild the container after making changes, you can run `docker compose build` followed by `docker compose up`.

Each project will build and run in its own container. You can open the apps in your browser using the port listed in *docker-compose.yml*—for example, *http://localhost:3001*, *http://localhost:3002*, etc. When you're done, you can stop the containers with `docker compose down`. This will remove the containers but keep the images, so you can start them again later without rebuilding.

The following is an example of a `Dockerfile` for a Node project. This `Dockerfile` defines the steps for creating a Docker image for a Node application. It starts with an official Node 20 base image, ensuring a consistent and up-to-date runtime. The `WORKDIR` instruction sets the working directory inside the container to `/usr/src/app`, where all subsequent commands will execute. The `COPY . .` command copies the project files from your local machine into the container. Next, `npm install` installs the dependencies defined in *package.json*. Finally, the container is configured to run `npm start` by default when it launches, which starts your application based on the script defined in your *package.json*. This setup provides a clean, isolated environment for running any Node project.

```
FROM node:20
WORKDIR /usr/src/app
COPY . .
RUN npm install
CMD [ "npm", "start" ]
```

 You may choose to add a *.dockerignore* file to exclude unnecessary files from the image. This is similar to *.gitignore* but for Docker. For example, you might want to ignore `node_modules`, `npm-debug.log`, and other local files that aren't needed in the container.

You may also use commands to build and run a Docker container for a specific project. For example, the command `docker build -t chapter_1-1 .` creates a Docker image from the current directory using the `Dockerfile`, and tags it with the name `chapter_1-1`. The command `docker run -p 3000:3000 chapter_1-1` starts a container from that image and maps port 3000 inside the container to port 3000 on your local machine, making the app accessible at *http://localhost:3000*. This approach is useful for running one project at a time with full control over its network and runtime environment.

You'll notice that the GitHub repository includes a *docker-compose.yml* file in each chapter folder. This file defines how to run all projects in that chapter as separate containers. You can use Docker Compose to manage multiple containers easily.

For example, the Chapter 1 *docker-compose.yml* looks like the following:

```
version: "3.9"
services:
  chapter1_1:
    build: ./chapter_1/1_1
    ports:
      - "3000:3000"
  chapter1_2:
    build: ./chapter_1/1_2
    ports:
      - "3001:3000"
```

In this way, each chapter will be available on its own local port, and Docker will handle environment isolation, dependency management, and consistent Node versions.

Benefits of Containerizing Node Projects

Using Docker has several advantages:

Consistency
Everyone runs the same code in the same environment.

Simplicity
No need to manually install Node, npm, or any global dependencies on your computer directly.

Isolation
Each project runs independently with its own filesystem and dependencies.

Portability
Run the same container in CI/CD, development, or even cloud platforms like AWS or Vercel.

Even if you're new to Docker, the examples in this book are designed to make it easy to get started. Once you set up one chapter using a Docker container, the rest follow the same pattern.

Next Steps

As you follow along in this book, feel free to clone, fork, or containerize the examples to match your preferred development workflow. Whether you're coding locally or running containers, the examples are designed to work in isolation and be easy to start. You'll find that having a consistent environment—especially when switching

Working with the Code Examples and Containerizing Projects | 335 between chapters—will save time and prevent many of the typical setup issues developers run into.

For more advanced Docker usage, such as volume mounting, environment-specific overrides, or production builds, check out the official Docker and Node documentation (*https://oreil.ly/MciXA*).

Summary

In this appendix, you learned:

- How to clone or fork the official GitHub repository and run code examples locally for each chapter
- How to containerize projects using Docker and docker-compose for consistent, isolated environments
- The benefits of using containers to simplify setup, manage dependencies, and ensure repeatable development workflows

APPENDIX E

Setting Up Developer Accounts and API Credentials

Many of the projects in this book rely on external services like OpenAI, Google Cloud, GitHub, and MongoDB Atlas. To use these services in your own development environment, you'll need to create accounts, generate API keys or tokens, and configure your applications to use them securely.

This appendix walks you through the full process—from signing up and locating credentials to storing them safely in environment files and understanding rate limits. Along the way, you'll learn the difference between API keys and OAuth tokens, how to avoid exposing sensitive data, and how service quotas might affect your apps.

These tools are essential in modern Node development, and setting them up early will help avoid roadblocks as you follow along. The sections below are organized in the order each service is used in the book, so you can reference them as needed during the relevant chapters. But first, let's cover the basics of working with API keys and tokens.

Working with API Keys

Modern development frequently involves integrating with third-party services such as databases, payment providers, AI models, or mapping platforms—via APIs (Application Programming Interfaces). To securely interact with these services, you typically need to create an account and authenticate your requests using API tokens.

An API token is a unique string of characters that acts like a password for programmatic access. When your application sends requests to an external service, it includes the API token to verify its identity and ensure the request is authorized. Tokens are usually tied to specific accounts or projects, and may include permissions to restrict what actions can be performed.

API tokens are considered confidential and should be stored securely—commonly in *.env* files that are not committed to version control. Each user or application generally receives a unique token, which may be scoped to limit access (for example, read-only versus write access). Many platforms allow you to regenerate or revoke tokens if they become compromised or if access needs to change.

Creating accounts on external platforms (such as OpenAI, Google Cloud, GitHub, or MongoDB Atlas) is necessary for several reasons. First, authentication is critical: APIs must know which user or application is making a request to prevent abuse and ensure accountability. Second, API tokens allow these services to track usage, enforce quotas, and apply billing based on the volume of requests. Third, they enable precise access management, such as restricting actions to specific users or resources. Finally, this system enhances security by making it possible to isolate, monitor, and control access to sensitive functionality or data.

API keys are long strings used like passwords to identify your app to a service. OAuth tokens are more secure and user-specific—used when your app acts on behalf of a user (like accessing their GitHub profile). Many APIs support both methods, but this book defaults to API keys where possible for simplicity.

Never hardcode API keys into your code. Instead, use a *.env* file in each project. Make sure to install dotenv for each project for which you intend to store private keys.

Storing keys in a *.env* file not only keeps them out of your codebase but also makes it easier to manage different environments, like development and production.

Always add *.env* to your *.gitignore* to avoid leaking secrets.

The following sections will walk you through account creation and API key generation for services you may use in this book, starting with GitHub, which is essential for version control and collaboration.

GitHub

GitHub enables developers to collaborate on code in real time, maintain a detailed history of project changes, and manage contributions from multiple users. It also integrates with automation tools like GitHub Actions for CI/CD, and allows you to host documentation, static websites, and wikis directly from your repositories. For individuals, GitHub serves as a portfolio of coding projects and a platform to contribute to open source software.

Appendix D provides steps for you to clone this book's code from its GitHub public repository. You can do that without a GitHub account. However, if you'd like better control over your own progress throughout the book and changes you make along the way, you'll benefit from having a GitHub account and GitHub command-line tools.

To create an account, follow these steps:

1. Visit *https://github.com*.
2. Click the link labeled "Sign up" in the top-right corner.
3. Enter a valid email address and click Continue.
4. Create a username and a secure password. Alternatively, you may be asked to set up a passcode with your browser.
5. Verify your email address using the code sent to your inbox.
6. Choose the free tier plan to get started.
7. Complete the onboarding preferences requested.

Once your account is created, you can properly fork and clone other repositories, such as the code for this book. You may also star and watch projects you care about to be notified of updates and changes. Most importantly, you may create your own repositories to store code and personal projects.

To use GitHub from the command line, you'll want to set up either SSH keys or Personal Access Tokens (PATs). Go to GitHub's SSH keys settings page (*https://oreil.ly/O-n7r*) and click "New SSH key." Generate a key on your local computer by running `ssh-keygen -t ed25519 C "your_cmail@gmail.com"`. Then add the contents of *~/.ssh/id_ed25519.pub* to GitHub.

Alternatively, to access private repos or push to GitHub using HTTPS, visit GitHub's personal access tokens settings page (*https://oreil.ly/PAZmC*) and click "Generate new token (classic)." Select scopes like `repo`, `workflow`, and `read:user`, depending on what features your project needs, and save the token securely—you won't be able to view it again.

Setting Up Developer Accounts and API Credentials | 339

MongoDB Atlas

Creating a MongoDB Atlas account gives you access to a fully managed, cloud-hosted version of MongoDB—one of the most popular NoSQL databases. This is especially helpful for developers building modern web applications, as it allows you to store JSON-like documents without needing to install or manage database infrastructure. Atlas provides features like automatic backups, global clusters, monitoring dashboards, and built-in security. By using a free-tier cluster, you can develop and test applications with real-world database functionality, and easily scale later if needed.

You may also choose to install MongoDB locally on your machine, but using Atlas is recommended for simplicity and ease of use.

Refer to the MongoDB documentation (*https://oreil.ly/cxBTH*) or follow these steps to create a free MongoDB Atlas account:

1. Visit the Atlas Database web page (*https://oreil.ly/bx3Qz*) and click "Start Free."
2. Sign up using your email or a GitHub/Google account.
3. After verifying your email, log in to the dashboard.
4. Click "Build a Cluster," choose the free M0 tier, select a region, and create it.
5. Once the cluster is created, go to the "Database Access" tab and click "Add New Database User."
6. Set a username and password, and choose "Read and write to any database."
7. Go to the "Network Access" tab and click "Add IP Address."
8. Choose "Allow Access from Anywhere" (0.0.0.0/0). You can restrict this later for added security.
9. When ready, click "Connect" and "Connect your application."
10. Copy the provided connection string (e.g., mongodb+srv://<user>:<password>@cluster...).
11. Paste this string into your *.env* file for your application (e.g., MONGODB_URI=).

You can use the MongoDB Compass GUI to visualize and manage your database. Download it from the MongoDB website (*https://oreil.ly/wrs4P*).

With your connection string in place, you can now use MongoDB Atlas in your Node applications without the need to install MongoDB locally.

OpenAI API

Creating an OpenAI API account gives you access to powerful language and code generation models like GPT-4 and Codex. These tools can be used to build intelligent applications, including chatbots, code assistants, content generators, and more. The API allows you to send text prompts and receive dynamically generated responses, making it ideal for enhancing user interfaces with AI capabilities. A free-tier account provides limited usage credits so you can start experimenting immediately.

You may be asked to provide a credit card for verification, but you won't be charged unless you exceed the free-tier limits.

Visit the OpenAI website (*https://oreil.ly/4uumR*) and follow these steps to create a free OpenAI API account:

1. On the OpenAI website, sign up using your email or a Google/Microsoft account.
2. After verifying your email and phone number, you'll be taken to the OpenAI dashboard.
3. Navigate to the API keys page (*https://oreil.ly/zw5oL*) and click "Create new secret key."
4. Copy the generated key and store it in a safe place. This key will not be shown again.
5. Add the API key to your project's *.env* file (e.g., `OPENAI_API_KEY=`).

You can monitor your usage, quotas, and billing on the Usage page (*https://oreil.ly/pkNPt*).

With your API key configured, you can begin calling OpenAI's models from your application using HTTP requests or client libraries like the official `openai` Node package.

OpenAI's API is not open source and requires an internet connection to function. You'll need to manage your API key securely to avoid unauthorized usage.

Google Gemini API

Creating a Google Gemini API account through the Google Cloud Console gives you access to Google's family of multimodal AI models (formerly Bard), capable of reasoning across text, images, code, and more. These models can be used in advanced applications such as intelligent assistants, image interpretation tools, and AI-enhanced developer platforms. The Gemini API is part of Google AI Studio and integrates with the Vertex AI platform for enterprise-level workflows.

Accessing Gemini requires enabling billing on a Google Cloud project, but you may also use a free-tier within limited usage.

Visit Google AI Studio's API Keys page (*https://oreil.ly/76Rs7*) or follow these steps to create a Google Gemini API account and get started:

1. Go to the Google Cloud Console (*https://oreil.ly/aiBGs*) and sign in with your Google account.
2. Click "Create Project" to make a new project or select an existing one.
3. Navigate to the API Library (*https://oreil.ly/-Gi7F*) and search for "Gemini API."
4. Click the API and enable it for your selected project.
5. Go to the Credentials page (*https://oreil.ly/5KvXs*) and click "Create Credentials."
6. Choose either an API key (for basic usage) or OAuth 2.0 credentials (for user-authenticated flows).
7. Copy the generated key and store it in your *.env* file (e.g., GEMINI_API_KEY=).
8. Optionally, visit the API Keys page (*https://oreil.ly/76Rs7*) to generate a key directly via AI Studio.

You can test prompts in the browser using the Gemini playground (*https://oreil.ly/CRFoB*).

Once your key is in place, you can begin calling the Gemini models in Node as described in the book or in the Gemini API docs (*https://oreil.ly/GpBY7*).

> ## Rate Limits and Quotas
>
> When working with APIs—especially third-party services like OpenAI, Google Gemini, or MongoDB Atlas—it's crucial to understand how rate limits and quotas affect your application's stability and reliability. These limits are imposed by providers to ensure fair use of shared infrastructure and to prevent abuse or system overloads.
>
> Rate limits define how many requests you can make in a short time frame, typically per second, minute, or hour. Exceeding the rate limit often results in an HTTP `429 Too Many Requests` response. Some APIs also include a `Retry-After` header, instructing how long to wait before retrying.
>
> Quotas define your total usage capacity over a longer period—usually per day or per billing cycle. This may include:
>
> - Total number of API calls
> - Number of tokens generated
> - Bandwidth used
> - Requests per model or endpoint
>
> If you exceed your quota your requests may fail until the quota resets, you might be automatically throttled (slowed down), or you could incur overage charges if on a paid plan.
>
>
> Always design your applications with retry logic, exponential backoff, and graceful degradation in case of rate limiting. For example, queue noncritical requests or reduce frequency under heavy usage.
>
> You can monitor rate limits and quotas in your provider's dashboard:
>
> - OpenAI (*https://oreil.ly/1unBl*)
> - Google Cloud (*https://oreil.ly/XBqEa*) (look under "IAM & Admin" > "Quotas")

Summary

Modern Node.js development often involves connecting to third-party services using API keys, tokens, and secure credentials. In this appendix, you learned how to set up accounts with providers like GitHub, MongoDB Atlas, OpenAI, and Google Cloud, as well as how to generate, store, and manage the credentials required to access their APIs.

By following best practices—such as using .env files, avoiding hardcoded secrets, and monitoring rate limits—you can safely integrate external services into your applications. These setup steps will streamline your experience across the projects in this book and prepare you for working with APIs in real-world environments.

Index

Symbols

$ (dollar sign) variable, 174
(Fetch API), 168
(HTML
    fetching website's HTML content, 168
(scraping web pages and using data in an app
    fetching HTML content from external
      page), 168
(text function, converting HTML content to
    plain text), 168
@fastify/formbody plugin, 98
@fastify/session plugin, 208

A

Account class
    adding authenticate method to, 205
    adding genStrategy method to, 209
    adding passportAuthenticate method to,
      206
    adding serializeUser and deserializeUser
      methods to, 208
    creating JavaScript class extending Sequel-
      ize.Account model, 198
    setPassword function, 203
account information, 196
Account Sequelize model
    Node app fully configuring to use for regis-
      tering and authenticating new accounts,
      211
    setting up in Account.js, 201
acknowledgements
    message ack for reliable queue processing,
      239
adaptive hashing, 200

Advanced Message Queuing Protocol (AMQP),
    237
advanced Node concepts, 8
aggregate function, defining, 86
AI (artificial intelligence), 113
    (see also machine learning)
AI APIs and LLMs, 278
AI-powered learning assistant, building,
    273-299
    customizing the assistant, 280-282
      guiding AI to teach programming, 281
    Google's Gemini API, using for LLM, 274
    preparation for technical interviews, 274
    prompt engineering, crafting effective AI
      instructions, 280
    setting up database and user authentication,
      285-298
      context-aware responses, 295
      querying AI assistant with user learning
        profiles, 293
      user registration and login system,
        288-293
    setting up Fastify server for, 282-285
    system architecture for phase 1 and phase 2,
      274
    testing AI API request to Gemini, 276
AJV schema validator, 11
Amazon SQS, 234
AMQP (Advanced Message Queuing Protocol),
    237
amqp.connect function, 236
amqplib package, installing, 235
API keys, working with, 337
APIs, 8, 165

345

about, 91
authentication to, 181
authentication, using JWTs for, 213-217
content aggregator integrating RSS feeds
  and, 77
creating, using Fastify for rapid response
  time, 10
library API project, 92-112
  programming API layout, 96-99
  routes and actions, adding to the app,
    99-104
rate limits and quotas for, 343
API_URL, 276
app object (Fastify), 185
app variable, 223
app.get function, 41
app.listen function, 97, 152, 224
app.post method, 194
appendFileAsync function, 24
Argon2 key derivation function, 200
asciichart package, 133
methods, adding to sentiment analysis visualization, 134
async/await functions, 23, 124
adding to sentiment analysis app for journal
  entries, 130
advantages for use in coding, 203
for Redis publish/subscribe system, 231
Redis publish/subscribe clients, 231
asynchronous functions
connecting to MongoDB with, 70
using promisify to wrap, 23
wrapping in promise, 22
asynchronous programming, 8
authentication
app authentication, 181
  (see also login authentication Node app)
authenticating a user logging in, 205
defining authentication page variables in
  index.js, 192
defining strategy for user accounts, 202
to SQLite database connection, 107
using JWTs for API authentication, 213-217
axios package, 253, 276

B

bcrypt hashing function, 200
bcrypt hashing package, 57, 288
installing and using, 60

testing functions in index.js, 61
block (blockchain), 249
mining a block, 260
Block class, 257
defining, 258
Blockchain class, 257, 260
key steps in mining process, 260
blockchain marketplace for music distribution,
245-272
about blockchain, 247
adding /register-node and /sync-peers endpoints, 255
broadcast function, 252
broadcastSelf and registerNode functions in
  marketplace node, 253
coding the blockchain, 257-264
  creating broadcastBlockchain function,
    263
  creating calculateHash function, 259
  defining Block class, 258
  defining Blockchain class, 261
importing fastify package and configuring
  web server, 250
initializing new MarketplaceNode instance,
  254
integrating transactions
  defining /buy route, 268
  defining /payment route, 265
  defining /songs route, 269
  defining mineBlock method, 266
new marketplace node, 251
Node classes representing fundamental
  components, 249
planning the application, 246
running real-world example, 270
starting node servers, command-line output, 256
blockchain, defined, 248
body-parsing middleware, 225
Book model, defining and synchronizing with
  SQLite database in library API app, 108
Book ORM object, accessing, 109
Bootstrap CSS library, 188
broadcasting in blockchains, 252
Buffer.from method, 237
bufferBytes.toString function, 204
buffers, 9

C

callbacks, 9
  callback hell, 23
  Fastify providing for library API, 98
  function called when event occurs, 230
  processing by main thread of event loop, 38
campaign mail templates, 159
catch-all error-handling middleware, 99
channels
  channel.assertQueue method, 236
  creating on RabbitMQ server, 236
cheerio package, 173
cheerio, using to parse HTML content, 174
Chrome's V8 JavaScript engine, 4
classes (Node) in blockchain, 249
clients (Redis), creating, 231
cloud-hosted databases
  expanding to, 323
  local databases versus, 323
clustering, using for Node scalability, 10
code examples, working with, 331
  accessing GitHub repository, 331
coffee orders app
  queueing system for
    queues in JavaScript), 226
coffee orders app, queueing system for, 219-244
  adding a Redis server, 229-233
  adding internal queue to handle order
    requests, 220
  adding route to mimic delayed request, 225
  adding routes to place order in the queue,
    227
  configuring the application, 224
  installing Fastify, 223
  integrating robust messaging system,
    233-243
  middleware parsing incoming requests,
    adding, 224
  queue order count endpoint, adding, 228
  Redis server to manage order requests, 222
  upgrading with RabbitMQ messging queue
    server, 222
collections, 318
comma-separated values files (see CSV files)
command-line interface (CLI)
  command-line prompts for user input, 27
  creating for computer prompt translating
    user input into CSV, 23

creating local command-line password
  manager, 59-68
computer prompt to create tabular format, or
  CSV, of data (example project), 16-21
  working with external packages, 28-31
confirmationMail template function, 157
consensus (blockchain), 248
console.log function, 83
console.table function, 83
containerizing projects, 332-336
  benefits of, 335
  running projects with Docker, 332-335
content aggregator integrating RSS feeds and
  APIs, 77-90
  adding custom items to aggregator, 88-89
  blueprint for application, 78
  building the aggregator, 84-87
  Fetch API making request to Bon Appétit
    RSS feed URL, 81
  initializing the app, 80
  parsing and reading from RSS feed, 82-84
context injection (prompt engineering), 280
context-aware responses (AI assistant), 294
cookies, 208
createTransport function (nodemailer), 143
CRUD (create, read, update, delete) actions,
  100
  library API app connected to database, 109
crypto library, 203
crypto.pbkdf2 hashing algorithm, 200
crypto.pbkdf2Sync function, 204, 205
cryptographic puzzle (blockchain), 248
CSS
  Bootstrap CSS library, 188
  using to style restaurant web application UI,
    52-54
CSV files, 16
  saveToCSV method in Person class (exam
    ple), 24
  translating user input to CSV, 21-27
csv-writer package, installing and working
  with, 29
cURL utility
  commands testing routes in library API app
    connected to database, 110
  running against library API server, 104
  using to post drink order, 225

Index | 347

D

data modules, converting restaurant data into, 45

databases, 8

  connecting a database to library API app, 105-111

    defining Book in books.js, 108

    setting up SQLite database configuration, 107

    updating routes with Book model, 109

  connecting database to email marketing app, 153-158

  database queries for sentiment analysis app, 129

  ORM to map JavaScript objects to SQL databases, 106

  Sequelize models allowing interaction with, 128

  setting up database for AI learning assistant, 285-288

  user authentication for AI learning assistant database, 288-293

  working with in Node projects, 317-329

    advantages of using databases, 317

    choosing database for a project, 324

    comparison of databases, 324

    expanding to cloud-hosted databases, 323

    local versus cloud-hosted databases, 323

    MongoDB, 318

    PostgreSQL, 321

    schemas, tables, collections, and documents, 318

    SQLite, 322

datastore, using Redis as, 230

DataTypes class (sequelize), 127

Debian/Ubuntu Linux

  installing Node, 7

  installing VS Code, 3

DELETE method (HTTP), 41, 93

  flow of data in DELETE request, 95

deserialization, 196

deserializeUser function, 207

deserializeUser method (Account), 208

destructuring assignment, 21

developer accounts

  API keys, working with, 337

  Google Gemini API account, 342

  MongoDB Atlas, 340

  OpenAI API account, 341

  rate limits and quotas for APIs, 343

  setting up GitHub account, 339

developer, Node, becoming, 8

development

  advanced Node concepts, 8

  mastering for Node, 8

development tools, setting up, 311-316

  VS Code, 311

  VS Code extensions, 312

directories

  email marketing service with database, 153

  project directory structure, 18

  recommended directory structure, 303

  source code directory, 17

Docker, 329

  running projects with, 332-335

Dockerfiles, 334

document-oriented database manager (MongoDB), 68

documents, 318

dotenv package, 276

E

email marketing service, 139-163

  adding framework for, 148-153

  connecting a database to the app, 153-158

  crucial parts of the app, 141

  marketing pixel for email engagement, implementing, 158-160

  planning the application, 140

  programming your mailer, 142-148

  setting up mailer using Google, 144

  task scheduler, implementing, 160-162

Embedded JavaScript (EJS) templates, using with Fastify to build web application UI, 47-51

endpoints (API), 92

.env file, storing API keys in, 338

environment variables

  for AI-powered learning assistant, 276

  starting Fastify server with, 282

error handling

  for email generation process, 146

  in library API router's GET route, 101

errors

  awaiting prompt reply, 124

  catch-all error-handling middleware, 99

ES Modules (ESM), 305, 307

348 | Index

ES6 export default syntax, 45
ES6 module (import/export) syntax, 20
event listener for Redis client, 230
event loop, 9
    blocking, 37
    challenges to, addressed by queues, 219
    Fastify leveraging, 37
    handling multiple tasks concurrently, 11
event-driven architectures, support by Redis
    pub/sub messaging system, 230
exports, ES6 export default syntax, 45
Express
    comparison with Fastify, 12
ExtractJwt class, 214

F

Fastify, 10, 36, 96
    adding JSON and URL-encoded parsing
        support to app, 97
    adding project configurations for coffee
        orders app, 235
    comparison with Express, Koa, and Hapi
        frameworks, 12
    in email marketing service, 141
    expecting views folder for templates, 188
    exploring starter template, 13
    handling JSON requests, 97
    installing as web application framework for
        coffee orders app, 223
    instantiating Fastify app and starting listen-
        ing for requests, 96
    low-overhead architecture, 11
    modular plug-in system, 11
    parsing middleware functions, 97
    setting up Fastify server for AI-powered
        learning assistant
        starting up server with environment
            variables, 282
    setting up Fastify server for AI=powered
        learning assistant, 282-285
        handling AI queries, 283
    SSR, building HTML files with Handlebars,
        184
    using to create mail server, 150
    working with, restaurant web server project,
        39-43
        building UI using EJS templates, 47-51
    Fastify login authentication

successful implementation with Passport.js,
    213
Fetch API, 81
few-shot prompting, 280
file, checking for existence of before appending
    to it, 25
filesystems, fs module for interaction with, 20
force: true option for Book.sync, 108
format prompting (output structuring), 281
forms
    login form, buildiing, 188-196
frameworks (Node)
    comparison between Fastify, Express, Koa,
        and Hapi, 12
    Fastify and others, 36
fs (filesystem) module, 20

G

Gemini API, 273
    connecting to, 276
    developer account with, 342
    sending user prompts to, 276
GEMINI_API_KEY, 276
genesis block in blockchain, 261
genStrategy function, 209
GET method (HTTP), 41, 93
    flow of data in GET request, 94
    GET campaign tracking route for email
        marketer, 159
    GET request route for books in custom
        booksRouter, 100
    GET route for /order-count path in coffee
        orders app, 228
getting started with a Node app, 15-21
    computer prompt to create tabular format,
        or CSV, of data, 16
    tools and applications used, prerequisites
        for, 15, 35, 58, 78, 92, 114, 140, 166, 182,
        220, 246, 274
GitHub repository for this book, 331
GitHub, setting up account with, 339
Gmail API app, 144
Google accounts and Google Cloud Console,
    276
Google, signing in to email via, 144
Google's Gemini (see Gemini API)
graphs
    adding to sentiment analysis of journal
        entries, 133

defining configurations for sentiment analysis chart, 134
growth areas for Node engineers, 309

H

Handlebars library
  building templates with, 184
  configuring login authentication app to use, 187
  installing support for, 184
  syntactical expressions to use in your templates, 185
Hapi framework, comparison with Fastify, Express, and Koa frameworks, 12
hashes
  computing and returning hash value of block, 259
  generated from provided password and salt compared to stored hash for user, 205
hashing algorithms for passwords, 200
hashing digests, 204
hashing packages, 57
hashing passwords, 199, 202, 203
  defining function for in Account.js, 204
  setting salt, 204
headless browser, scraping web pages with, 175-179
hexadecimal strings
  converting set of bytes to, 204
Homebrew, 319
  installing Node with, 7
HTML, 169
  boilerplate content for login form, 188
  creating module containing email HTML templates, 149
  EJS displaying content within, 49
  input types to meet expectations of input content, 189
  landing page content for restaurant web application, 48
  parsing using HTML-friendly tools, 173-175
  structure for other restaurant web application pages, 49
  templates for, building with Handlebars, 184
  using to spruce up email, 147
HTTP methods, 41, 93
http module, 36
HTTP server, setting up using Fastify, 223

HTTP, JavaScript methods of accessing content over, 81

I

I/O operations, 9
immediately invoked function expressions (IIFE), 124
import/export module syntax (ES6), 20
imports
  ES6 module import syntax, 41
  importing only modules and functions needed instead of entire library, 21
index.js file, 20
  collecting user input within startApp (example), 25
  defining Person class in (example), 24
  final file for computer prompt translating user input into CSV, 26
  testing bcrypt functions in, 61
inference, 279
instances (Node), 10
interviews (technical), preparing for, 274
ioredis
  connecting Redis to Node.js, 326

J

JavaScript
  Node built on Chrome's V8 JavaScript engine, 4
  open projects from OpenJS Foundation, 40
  ORM to map JavaScript objects to SQL databases, 106
JavaScript, queues in, 226
JavaShipped application with request bottleneck (example), 220
jQuery library, 173
JSON
  JSON-based APIs, 79
  parsing with Fastify, 97
JSON Web Tokens (JWTs)
  using for API authentication, 213-217
  using for user registration and authentication for AI assistant, 289-293
    authentication middleware, 292
    user login endpoint, 290
    user registration endpoint, 289
jsonwebtoken package, 288
JWTs (see JSON Web Tokens)

350 | Index

K

Kafka, 234
Koa framework, comparison with Fastify, Express, and Hapi frameworks, 12

L

large language models (see LLMs)
learning profiles, 289
  using in querying AI assistant, 293
ledger (blockchain), 248
lemmatization, 116
libraries, importing only modules and files needed instead of entire library, 21
library API project, 92-112
  adding routes and actions to the app, 99-104
    POST route, 103
    RESTful routes, 102
    routing directory structure layout, 100
    testing other non-GET routes, 104
  connecting a database to the app, 105-111
    cURL commands testing routes in app connected to database, 110
    defining Book model in books.js, 108
    project directory structure with database, 106
    setting up SQLite database configuration, 107
    updating routes with Book model, 109
  planning the application, 92
  programming API layout, 96-99
library API project, adding routes and actions to the app, GET request route, 100
Libuv library, 5
Linux
  installing MongoDB on, 320
  installing Node, 7
  installing VS Code, 3
listen function, 224
LLMs (large language models), 273
  AI APIs and, 278
load balancers for Node instances, 10
local databases versus cloud-hosted databases, 323
localhost, 43
LocalStrategy class, 202
  genStrategy method returning new instance of, 209
  options for, 209
logging

console.log and other logging types, 83
  logging message when coffee order is placed and processed, 225
  Pino library included with Fastify, 12
login authentication Node app, 182-218
  building HTML page templates with Handlebars, 184
  building login form, 188-196
  planning the application, 182
  saving and securing user accounts, 196
  starting and testing your app, 188
  using JWTs for API authentication, 213
login strategy, 209
loops
  for loop from /slow-order route, adding to /process-order route, 227
  long loop iteration to mimic blocking task, 225

M

machine learning (ML), 113-138
  models, 113
  natural language processor with sentiment analysis, 114-138
    analyzing sentiment, 123-126
    cleaning input text for NLP analysis, 115
    connecting a database and visualization, 126-136
    NLP steps on input text in Node app, 117-122
    planning the app, 114
macOS
  Homebrew, 319
  installing Node, 7
  installing VS Code, 2
mail servers, 143
mailers, 141
  nodemailer package, 143
  setting up your mailer with Google, 144
manifests (project), 302
marketing mailer (see email marketing service)
marketing pixel for email engagement, 158
marketplace nodes (blockchain), 261
  adding new node to network, 251
  broadcast function for MarketplaceNode, 252
  broadcastSelf and registerNode functions for MarketplaceNode, 253
  defining MarketplaceNode class, 251

Index | 351

initializing new MarketplaceNode instance, 254

master password, 58

mastery of Node development, 8

max tokens (AI APIs), 279

Medium, 166

memory, saving data in temporarily, 59

messaging

  integrating robust messaging system with coffee orders app, 233-243

  Redis pub/sub messaging system, 230

messaging systems, options to consider, 234

MFA (multifactor authentication), 181

middleware

  adding to coffee orders app, 224

  body-parsing middleware for request.body, 225

middleware functions, 97

mining a block, 260, 266

model query types, information about, 109

models (ML), 113

modular plug-in system (Fastify), 11

modules

  ES6 import/export syntax, 20, 41

  modern ES modules, 305

MongoClient, use to set up connection to local MongoDB server, 69

MongoDB

  comparison with other databases for Node apps, 324

  connecting with Mongoose, 320

  installing, 318

  installing on Linux, 320

  installing on Windows, 319

  saving passwords to, 68-74

    creating async function to connect to MongoDB, 70

    main function to initialize database, 70

  strengths and trade-offs, 324

MongoDB Atlas accounts, 340

mongodb package, 69

Mongoose, 320

multifactor authentication (MFA), 181

MySQL

  comparison with other databases for Node apps, 324

  Sequelize working with, 321

N

natural language processing (see NLP)

natural package, 120

natural.PorterStemmer class, 123

natural.PorterStemmer.stem function, 121

natural.SentimentAnalyzer class, 123

natural.WordTokenizer class, 120

network of nodes (blockchain), 257

neural networks, 279

NLP (natural language processing), 113

  cleaning input text for NLP analysis, 115

  spelling correction on string of text, 117-120

  stemming function for Node app, 121

  steps on a string of text, 116

  stop word removal, performing for Node app, 122

Node

  advantages and unique features of, 5

  becoming a developer, 8

  growth areas for engineers, 309

  how it works, 5

  installing, 5

  modern syntax patterns, 307-308

  package.json and scripts, understanding, 305-307

  understanding, 4

  verifying setup, 13

node-fetch package, 81

node-schedule package, 161

nodemailer package, 143

nodemon package, 97

normalized sentiment scores, 131

NoSQL databases, 105, 318

  MongoDB managing, 68

npm (Node Package Manager), 7

  hashing packages on registry, 57

  initializing projects with, 302

  Yarn versus, 303

npm commands, CLI shorthands and flags, 40

npm init command, 39

npm install fastify command, 40

O

object relational mapper (ORM) between JavaScript objects and SQL databases, 106

OpenAI API accounts, 341

OpenAI's ChatGPT, 273

OpenJS Foundation, 40

ORM (object relational mapper) between Java-
Script objects and SQL databases, 106

P

package.json file, 18, 40
  documentation for, 19
  key parts of, 19
  understanding package.json and scripts,
    305-307
packages
  npm external packages, working with in
    computer prompt project, 28-31
  npm package versioning, 41
Parser class, 82
parser objects, 82
parser.parseURL function, 83
passport package, 196, 197
passport-local package, 196, 197, 202
Passport.js, 196
  functions to serialize and deserialize user
    account information, 196
  making Account class accessible to, 206
  use of sessions in Fastify, 208
  using with sessions in Fastify, 209
passportAuthenticate method, 206, 209
  updated for authenticate return, 206
password manager (secure, local), building,
  57-75
  building local command-line manager,
    59-68
    adding module imports and mock db to
      index.js, 62
    adding viewPasswords and promptMa-
      nageNewPassword functions, 65
    comparing hashed password to plain-
      text password, 63
    functions prompting user to type pass-
      word in, 64
    saveNewPassword function, 63
    showMenu function, 65
  planning the application, 58
  saving passwords to MongoDB, 68-74
    main function to initialize database, 70
passwords
  adding conditional password input in login
    form, 191
  defining password hashing function, 204
  saving for account sign-up form, 193
  setting for user accounts, 202

Pino (logging library), 12
plain text emails, sprucing up using HTML, 147
plug-ins (Fastify), 11
Porter stemming algorithm, 121
PorterStemmer class, 123
POST method (HTTP), 41, 93
  adding POST route to library API router,
    103
  adding POST route to mail server, 151
  creating /account and /auth POST routes,
    194
  flow of data in POST request, 94
  method used for forms, 189
  POST requests in coffee orders app, 224
  POST routes listening for requests at /
    account and /auth endpoints, 211
  route handler for the path /slow-order, 225
PostgreSQL
  comparison to SQLite, 105
  comparison with other databases for Node
    apps, 324
  connecting with Sequelize, 321
  installing, 321
  strengths and trade-offs, 324
print function, defining, 86
projects
  building first project from scratch, 15-33
    computer prompt to create tabular for-
      mat, or CSV, of data, 16
    planning the app, 16
    programming the app, 17-21
    translating user input to CSV, 21-27
    working with external packages, 28-31
  initializing using npm, 302-303
  recommended directory structure, 303
Promises
  asynchronous function wrapped in, 22
  Fastify's promise-based routing, 12
  returned by await function, 124
  wrapping logic in, enabling function call
    using async-await, 203
promisify function, using to wrap asynchronous functions, 23
prompt engineering, crafting effective AI
  instructions, 280
prompt module, 124
prompt package, installing and working with,
  28
prompt-sync package, installing, 62

Index | 353

prompt.get function, 124

promptNewPassword function, 64

promptOldPassword function, 64

prompts

    adding prompt for input to sentiment analysis app, 124

    adding prompt method to sentiment analysis app, 132

proof of work (blockchain), 261

publish method, 230

publish/subscribe (pub/sub) messaging system, 230

    creating clients for publishing and subscribing, 231

puppeteer (headless browser), scraping web pages with, 176-179

PUT method (HTTP), 41

    flow of data in PUT request, 95

Python, use in machine learning, 114

Q

Queue instances, methods used with, 226

queue npm package, 226

queues, 219

    (see also RabbitMQ)

    internal queue to manage coffee order requests, 221

    in JavaScript, 226

    RabbitMQ messaging queue architecture, 222

quotas, 343

R

RabbitMQ

    installing for use in Node projects, 327

    integrating with coffee orders app, 233-243

        adding Fastify and RabbitMQ project configurations, 235

        advantages of RabbitMQ, 234

        advantages of setting up services with Fastify, 236

        connecting to RabbitMQ server in index.js, 236

        features and capabilities of RabbitMQ, 233

        port number for RabbitMQ, 237

    messaging queue server between services, 222

rate limits, 343

Redis

    comparison with other databases for Node apps, 324

    installing for use in Node projects, 324

    limitations of, 233

    more information on, 230

redis package, installing, 231

Redis server, adding to coffee orders app, 222, 229-233

    implementing Redis as publish/subscribe messaging pattern between app and drink order data, 229

relational databases, 105

reply objects), 98

Request objects, 81

request objects, 98

request-response cycle

    in Fastify app, 41

    HTTP, Fastify implementing, 37

request.body object, 225

requests per second (RPS), large number handled by Fastify, 10

Response objects, 81

restaurant web server project, 36-55

RESTful APIs, routes, 102

role prompting, 280

routing

    adding routes and actions to library API app, 99-104

        POST route, 103

        RESTful routes, 102

        routing directory structure layout, 100

        testing other non-GET routes, 104

    adding routes to restaurant web server, 43

    blockchain marketplace

        defining /buy route, 268

        defining /payment route, 265

        defining /register-node and /sync-peers routes, 255

        defining /songs route, 269

    defining API routes for authentication, 216

    defining API routes for mail server, 151

    designing /account and /auth routes for sign-up form, 193

    GET campaign tracking route for email marketer, 159

    POST route listening for requests at / account endpoint, 211

354 | Index

POST route listening for requests at /auth endpoint, 211

route to mimic delayed request in coffee orders app, 225

routes to place order in your queue, adding to coffee orders app, 227

updating Fastify routes to render EJS files, 47

updating routes with Book model in library API app, 109

verification route to verify email address in marketing app, 156

routing, adding routes and actions to library API app, GET route for books in custom booksRouter, 100

RSS feeds, 77

Bon Appetit recipes in browser, 79

reading and parsing XML from, 82-84

rss-parser package, 82

S

salt, 60

custom cryptographic salt for each generated hash, 199

scalability

Fastify's asynchronous, nonblocking architecture, 11

using clustering, 10

schedulers, 141

task scheduler for email marketing service, 160-162

schema-based validation and serialization, using AJV, 11

schemas, 318

scraping web pages and using data in an app, 165-180

accessing and scraping data, 167

filtering scraped data, 167

HTML output from site, 169

HTML, overview, 169

identifying HTML elements worth scraping, 171

parsing with HTML-friendly tools, 173-175

planning the application, 166

scraping using headless browser, 175-179

scripts, 305-307

scrypt general-purpose key derivation function, 200

security

application authentication, 181

(see also login authentication Node app)

setting up your mailer with Google, 144

sendMail function, 146

parameters to pass custom HTML and email addresses, 149

sentiment analysis app, 113, 123-126

adding prompt for input, 124

analyzing sentiment with tokens, 123

analyzing text input from a prompt, 124

connecting a database and visualization of journal entries, 126-136

creating SentimentJournal class, 128

graph chart for sentiment scores, 133

prompting for input text, 132

SentimentAnalyzer class, 123

Sequelize

connecting with SQLite, 322

PostgreSQL connecting to, 321

sequelize API, information about, 109

Sequelize class, 107

Book model, 108

creating Lead model for email marketing app, 154

findOne function, 198

model for database connection in sentiment analysis app, 127

updatedAt and createdAt fields, 110

sequelize package, 106, 196, 197

Sequelize.Model, JavaScript Account class extending, 198

serialization, 196

by Fastify, 11

serializeUser function, 207

serializeUser method (Account), 208

server-side rendering (SSR), 184

setting up using EJS templates with Fastify, 47

sessions, 208

incorporating token-based authentication with, 214

using in Node, 208

using Passport.js with Fastify, 209

setup (Node and VS Code), verifying, 13

SHA-256 hashing algorithm, 259

sha512 hashing digest, 204

smart contracts (blockchain), 248

SMTP mail servers, building your own, 143

SpellChecker class, 117

Index | 355

command-line output for corrected spell-
    ings, 118
spelling correction, 115, 117-120, 129
    adding spelling correction function to Node
        project, 119
    result of spelling correction function,
        assigning to tokenizing function, 121
SQL databases, 105, 318
    ORM between JavaScript objects and, 106
SQLite, 322
    comparison to PostgreSQL, 105
    comparison with other databases for Node
        apps, 324
    connecting a database to email marketing
        app, 153-158
    connecting with Sequelize, 322
    installing locally, 322
    installing most recent npm package, 106
    setting up database and user authentication
        for AI learning assistant, 285-293
    setting up database configuration, 107
    setting up database configurations for login
        authentication app, 197
    strengths and trade-offs, 324
sqlite3 package, 196, 197
SSR (server-side rendering), 184
startApp asynchronous function (example), 25
starter template (Fastify), exploring, 13
static plug-in (Fastify), 52
stemming and lemmatization, 116
    adding stemming function to Node project,
        121
stop word removal
    performing for Node app, 122
stopword package, 122
streams, 9
string processing packages, 117-122
subscribe method, 230
synchronization of Book model with database,
    108

T

tables, 318
task scheduler for email marketing service,
    160-162
temperature (AI APIs), 279
templates, Handlebars, 185
    (see also Handlebars library)

templating engines, use with Node and Fastify,
    47
    Fastify's support for, 53
text
    cleaning input text for NLP analysis, 115
    deciphering meaning of using ML models,
        115
this (keyword), 205
timers, 9
timestamps
    including for each contact entry, 32
token-based authentication, 214
    (see also JSON Web Tokens)
tokenizing text, 116, 120, 279
    adding tokenization function to Node
        project, 120
    analyzing sentiment with tokens, 123
    assigning result of correct spelling function
        to tokenization function, 121
tokens (API), 337
tracking pixel (see marketing pixel for email
    engagement)
Transaction class, 257
transactions (blockchain), 248
transformer-based neural network (LLMs), 279
transporter (mail), configuring in index.js, 145
transporter.sendMail function, 146

U

UIs (user interfaces)
    building UI for restaurant web server appli-
        cation, 47-51
    improving restaurant web application UI,
        52-54
URIs (Uniform Resource Identifiers), 92
URL encoding
    adding parsing plugin to Fastify app for, 98
    incoming requests with URL-encoded pay-
        loads, 224
URLs
    defining to read from for content aggrega-
        tor, 84
    web page's HTML source URLs, 175
user accounts
    dedicated app and API for, 182
        (see also login authentication Node app)
    saving and securing, 196
user input, translating to CSV, 21-27
usernames

356 | Index

registering for user accounts, 202

saving from account sign-up form, 193

V

V8 JavaScript engine, 4

validation

input validation for email and phone numbers, 32

isEmail Sequelize rule for email marketing service, 154

schema-based validation with AJV, 11

variables

defining for authentication page in index.js, 192

defining formVars to match page variables, 192

names preceded by underscore (_), 98

versions, npm package versioning, 41

view plug-in (Fastify), 47

views folder, Handlebars templates in, 188

visualizations

defining configurations for sentiment analysis chart, 134

graph chart in sentiment analysis app, 133

VS Code (Visual Studio Code), 311

installing, 2

recommended extensions, 312

verifying setup, 13

W

web browsers

cookies sent to client's browser for user session, 208

rendering of menu.ejs page in, 50

scraping page content with headless browser, 175-179

viewing your web server's response in, 43

web scraping, 165

(see also scraping web pages and using data in an app)

web server, building, 35-55

about web servers, 36

adding routes and data, 43-47

blocking the event loop, 38

building web application skeleton, 39

creating restaurant web application UI, 47-51

improving restaurant web application UI, 52-54

planning the application, 36

using Fastify, 39-43

web requests, processing in Fastify-powered web application, 38

Windows

installing MongoDB on, 319

installing Node, 7

installing VS Code, 3

WordTokenizer class, 120

X

XML

accessing for Bon Appétit RSS feed, 81

reading and parsing from RSS feed, 82-84

use by RSS feeds, 79

XMLHttpRequest interface, 81

Y

Yarn versus npm, 303

Z

ZeroMQ, 234

Index | 357

About the Author

Jonathan Wexler, author of the notable *Get Programming with Node.js*, brings his rich background in software engineering and passion for teaching to his latest work, *Node.js Projects*. His approach to writing, deeply rooted in practical experience and an intuitive understanding of web technologies, particularly Node.js, subtly conveys his depth of expertise. Wexler reflects elements from his experiences teaching at a coding bootcamp and developing enterprise applications at big tech companies to help break down complex technical concepts into engaging and manageable projects. This has earned him recognition and positive reviews, making his guidance in this new book an invaluable asset for developers looking to elevate their skills through real-world applications.

Colophon

The animal on the cover of *Node.js Projects* is the Angolan giraffe, also known as the Namibian giraffe or smokey giraffe, one of several species or subspecies of giraffe native to Angola and Namibia.

The Angolan giraffe is easily identifiable by the large, irregular, and often sharply angled blotches that cover its entire body, starkly contrasting with its coat's lighter background color. This distinctive pattern serves as excellent camouflage in the giraffe's savanna habitat.

Like all giraffes, Angolan giraffes are browsers, using their long necks to reach leaves high in the trees, a food source largely inaccessible to other herbivores. Due to their impressive height, they require a specialized cardiovascular system—featuring notably high blood pressure and a network of one-way valves—to pump blood to their heads against the draw of gravity.

With around 13,000 animals estimated to remain in the wild, Angolan giraffes face challenges in their natural environment but, with an increasing population trend, are not currently threatened, according to the International Union for Conservation of Nature. Many of the animals on O'Reilly covers are endangered; all of them are important to the world.

The cover illustration is by Monica Kamsvaag, based on an antique line engraving. The series design is by Edie Freedman, Ellie Volckhausen, and Karen Montgomery. The cover fonts are Gilroy Semibold and Guardian Sans. The text font is Adobe Minion Pro; the heading font is Adobe Myriad Condensed; and the code font is Dalton Maag's Ubuntu Mono.

O'REILLY®

Learn from experts.
Become one yourself.

60,000+ titles | Live events with experts | Role-based courses
Interactive learning | Certification preparation

 Try the O'Reilly learning platform free for 10 days.

www.ingramcontent.com/pod-product-compliance
Lightning Source LLC
Jackson TN
JSHW051453030825
88673JS00014B/52